W9-ASW-515

PRACTICAL HORSEMAN'S

BOOK OF

Riding, Training, and Showing
HUNTERS AND JUMPERS

BOOKS BY M. A. STONERIDGE

A Horse of Your Own, revised edition

Great Horses of Our Time

Practical Horseman's Book of Horsekeeping, editor

PRACTICAL HORSEMAN'S

BOOK OF

Riding, Training, and Showing

HUNTERS AND JUMPERS

EDITED BY

M. A. Stoneridge

WITH A FOREWORD BY

George Morris

Doubleday

NEW YORK   LONDON   TORONTO   SYDNEY   AUCKLAND

PUBLISHED BY DOUBLEDAY
a division of Bantam Doubleday Dell
Publishing Group, Inc.,
666 Fifth Avenue, New York, New York 10103

DOUBLEDAY and the portrayal of an anchor with a dolphin are
trademarks of Doubleday, a division of Bantam Doubleday
Dell Publishing Group, Inc.

Library of Congress Cataloging-in-Publication Data

Practical horseman's book of riding, training, and showing hunters and
jumpers / edited by M. A. Stoneridge.—1st ed.
    p.   cm.
    1. Show jumpers (Horses)—Training.   2. Show jumpers (Horses)—
Showing.   3. Show hunters—Training.   4. Show hunters—Showing.
5. Horses—Training.   6. Hunter seat equitation.   I. Stoneridge, M. A.
II. Practical horseman.   III. Title: Book of riding, training, and
showing hunters and jumpers.
SF295.5.P72 1989   88-21706
798.2′5—dc19   CIP

ISBN 0-385-19691-1

Copyright © 1972, 1973, 1974, 1975, 1976, 1977, 1978, 1979, 1980,
1981, 1982, 1983, 1984, 1985, 1986, 1987 by *Practical Horseman*

Foreword Copyright © 1989 by Bantam Doubleday Dell Publishing
Group, Inc.

Book design by Tasha Hall

All Rights Reserved
Printed in the United States of America
April 1989

FIRST EDITION

BG

Foreword

As I write this Foreword, I feel honored and thankful. M. A. Stoneridge is an old friend of mine. Her brother, William Steinkraus, editorial consultant to the Equestrian Library, has been one of my greatest mentors. They have each, in their own way, done so much to promote, as well as preserve, good equitation over the years. Few people will really know how much: M. A. Stoneridge through the written word and William Steinkraus by setting his example as a rider and horseman of the highest class. We all tried to copy "Billy" back in the fifties, and that is certainly one of the reasons we are where we are today!

What we learned "by the seat of our pants" years ago—a slow process—we can now tackle through literature. In this effort, *Practical Horseman's Book of Riding, Training, and Showing Hunters and Jumpers* is a veritable gold mine. Rather than have to go back through stacks of *Practical Horseman* magazines, now one can simply pick up a book or, if necessary, carry this book as a reference work to a clinic or a horse show.

Years ago people were suspicious of riding lessons, clinics, and reading. Yes, believe it or not, of learning more about riding by reading. In fact, people were still suspicious of education in general when it came to equestrian matters. (Of course, that was in the dark ages—about twenty-five years ago!) Now one can learn a lot from books, and there are enough out there to read around the clock. I am *never* without a horse book of some kind at my bedside. In this way I am always learning something new or perhaps reviewing something I'd forgotten.

By browsing through this book, nonreaders who ride may discover not only how much they could learn by the printed word, but may also be stirred to pleasurable recollections of their own dimly remembered experiences. If it is not new, it is review. And for the technician, whether rider, teacher or trainer, both are equally important.

All things concerning horses and riders are basic and simple. The more one understands the classic fundamentals of horsemanship, the simpler and more successful his or her system of riding, training, or teaching will be. For a system to work, it must be consistent in approach and have at least one solution for every problem encountered. That is the beauty of this work. It can teach you how to bolster your system, making it stronger, and it can also provide a quick reference when in trouble.

We are all always in a bit of trouble. Every day there is something, big or small, that is perplexing. Whether you're a beginner on a lead line, trying to understand a shoulder-in, or jumping a Grand Prix course, doors sometimes get stuck. I promise you, reading in general, and especially reading a book such as this comprehensive work, will help unlock most of the doors.

We are all lucky and, I'm sure, most thankful that M. A. Stoneridge now again makes our horse life a whole lot easier—and more successful!

—George H. Morris
Pittstown, New Jersey

Contents

II
HUNTER SEAT EQUITATION

III
SELECTING, RIDING, AND TRAINING HUNTERS

IV
SHOWING A HUNTER

VI
SHOWING A JUMPER

I

Training Basics

1

First Lesson for a Young Horse: Longeing

George Morris

From the time he was the youngest rider on record (aged fourteen) to win both the American Society for the Prevention of Cruelty to Animals (ASPCA) and American Horse Shows Association (AHSA) equitation finals, George Morris has gone from one equestrian achievement to another to become a superstar of the horse-show world. Former member of the U.S. Equestrian Team (USET) and of the 1960 U.S. Olympic Team (individual fourth at Rome) and a leading grand prix rider, he has been phenomenally successful as a trainer of riders and horses. More than thirty AHSA Medal and Maclay champions and reserve champions were coached by him, as well as grand prix riders Buddy Brown, Jimmy Kohn, Katie Monahan, and Norman Dello Joio, and four of the five 1984 Olympic show-jumping gold medalists: Conrad Homfeld, Melanie Smith, Leslie Burr, and Anne Kursinski. He has even been asked to coach foreign teams. Where could he go from there? Back to competition!

Since 1983, George has divided his time between managing his show stable, Hunterdon, in Pittstown, New Jersey; giving riding and teaching clinics at home and abroad; and competing again with distinction on the international jumper circuit, including three grand prix victories during his first "comeback" year—with more to come—and a prize-laden European tour with the USET in 1985.

> The training he describes and demonstrates is concerned with a young, green horse. But his longeing technique is just as applicable to horses of all ages and stages of education.
>
> The practice of longeing was far more widespread in Europe than in America until Bertalan de Némethy, a former Hungarian cavalry officer, became the coach of the USET and demonstrated its value as a training tool. Today there is probably not a single top jumper in the country that is not worked with some regularity on the longe.

My number-one training consideration is my horse's physical apparatus. A horse that's badly schooled or badly ridden can continue to compete; a horse that's mentally bad can win classes; but a horse that is physically damaged stays in the stall. For this reason more than any other, my approach to training horses that compete over fences is largely a program of training on the flat. And the first lesson of my program is longeing.

The cardinal principles of all my training are *forward, straightness, relaxation*. The longe line, while not a substitute for a rider, is a valuable tool for teaching the beginnings of these habits. It lets a young horse become familiar with the aids you can apply without having to cope with the burden of a rider. For a horse of any age, longeing is a safety precaution: it relaxes a green horse, getting out the humps and playfulness before he's ridden; it warms up a "cold-backed" horse; it provides a lifelong means of taking the edge off an excitable horse before schooling or competition.

While your horse is learning the lessons of forward, straightness, and relaxation, you must work to master three habits that form the basic equipment of an effective trainer: repetition, consistency, and attention to detail.

Repetition. Horses learn by repetition, and repetition takes patience. To teach your horse a response to an aid, you'll have to repeat the aid over and over again.

Consistency. When you give an aid, you must give it in exactly the same way every time, and each time you must require the same response from your horse. If you are consistent from the beginning, the aids you apply from the ground during longeing will carry over into your riding and form a foundation on which your horse can build the rest of his education without having to unlearn or relearn.

Attention to detail. If it's part of a consistent system, anything you teach your horse now you can use later. However, your horse can also use anything you teach him as a defense against you. For example, if you teach him to do a shoulder-in to the left, you've taught him how to bulge his shoulder left off the track on a turn. But if you've been thorough and also taught him to do a right shoulder-in equally well, you'll be able to counter his evasion by moving his shoulder back to the track. Thoroughness is a matter of unfailing attention to detail.

In order for your horse to develop his body evenly, always work him for the same number of minutes in each direction. Limit each longeing session to ten or fifteen minutes and the number of sessions to no more than four a week.

Equipment

Work in an enclosed area that will help direct your horse around your longeing circle. A round pen is perfect, but one end of an indoor arena or the corner of a field is an acceptable alternative.

So that your horse becomes thoroughly comfortable with bridle and saddle, tack him up for each longeing session. Make sure his bridle fits correctly: you should be able to slip two fingers under the noseband and four fingers under the throat-latch. I use an ordinary full-cheek snaffle bit, but any straightforward snaffle is fine. You should see two wrinkles on either side where the bit meets the corners of the mouth. Use a standing martingale adjusted so that it can almost reach the throat-latch when your horse is standing still.

EQUIPMENT FOR LONGEING

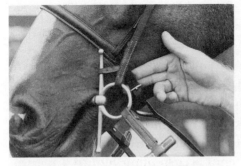

Tack up your horse in saddle and bridle. You should be able to fit two fingers under the noseband . . .

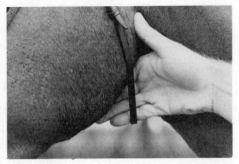

. . . and four fingers under the throat-latch.

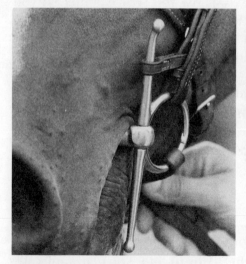

Adjust the bit so that it forms two wrinkles at the corners of your horse's mouth.

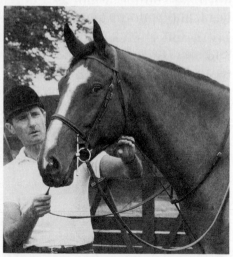

Your standing martingale should almost touch the throat-latch when your horse stands naturally.

Loop the reins under your stirrup leathers, run up the irons, and wrap the leathers securely around them.

Put on a halter over the bridle, resting its noseband just above the bridle noseband, and attach your longe line to the left side of the halter. Photos: *Practical Horseman*

Put a halter over the bridle, with the halter noseband resting just above the noseband of the bridle; attach your longe line to the left side of the halter. (Later, when your horse has caught onto the general idea of longeing and is responding to your aids, you can switch your line to the near bit ring of the bridle and begin accustoming him to a natural elastic contact with his mouth.) Use a longe line equipped with just a buckle or snap at the end to simulate the weight of a normal rein. Don't use a line with a chain: the extra weight will make your horse dip his head, and you won't be able to establish the natural feel of his mouth.

In order to keep the reins anchored safely out of the way while you're longeing, tuck them under the stirrup leathers, with the buckle resting on the pommel of the saddle. Run up the irons and wrap the leathers around them so that they can't come loose and bang against your horse's sides. Always protect your horse's front legs with galloping boots and bell boots when you longe him.

Getting Started

As you lead your horse from the stable to the work area, teach him his first lesson in going forward. Walk on his left side with your right hand on the longe line a foot or two from his head, holding the rest of the line coiled in your left hand. Carry your longeing whip in your left hand too, with the lash end pointing behind you. As you walk, encourage your horse to walk briskly at your side. If he lags, move your whip hand back a little, just behind your left hip, and flick your wrist inward and slightly upward so that the lash taps your horse lightly at the level of his buttock or gaskin. Keep the lash away from his lower legs; it might tempt him to kick. As you flick, make a clucking sound. Since he probably learned during breaking that a cluck means "forward," he'll transfer its meaning to the whip, which, during longeing, will be your primary forward aid.

As you flick your whip, glance frequently at your horse's expression: the look in his eye and the position of his ears are barometers of his attitude. Watch them carefully and you'll know when he's relaxed, when he's fearful, and when an explosion is just around the corner.

As you enter your work area, say "whoa" and stop. Turn to face your horse while you organize your equipment for longeing. Transfer the whole line into your left hand, making sure that the loops are stocked in your hand in the order in which they will unwind; this will allow you to let the line out smoothly, one loop at a time. Move the whip to your right hand, with the lash now turned toward your horse. Let out about 10 feet of line and move around to his left side, positioning yourself just behind his shoulder, which is where you'd be if you were riding.

Lift the whip to the height of his buttock, tap him very lightly, and cluck. At the same time, hold your left hand out in front of you so that the line acts like an opening rein, to lead your horse around the track. As he takes his first steps, walk with him to enlarge his circle. Even though you need the short line for now to show him what to do, aim to keep him on a circle about 60 feet in diameter at this stage of his training. Small circles are too difficult for young horses.

Later you'll work on keeping the circle round, but for the moment you have only two objectives: showing your horse the track and teaching him to go forward. In order to be consistent throughout your horse's training, the aids you use for longeing should work on the same principles as the aids you'll use later from the saddle. Think of the longe line as your reins: now it's attached to the halter, but later it will work directly on your horse's mouth via the ring of the bit. You'll use it just as you would use the reins: to steady your horse, to slow him, to stop him. Work to establish a consistent, elastic feel through the line.

The longeing whip reproduces the effect of your legs: like them, it works from back to front. When you close your legs on your horse, they not only press inward; they also squeeze slightly forward at the same time. You'll simulate this effect with your whip by working it in a circular motion, urging your horse forward with the upward and forward segment of the arc, then circling backward and downward to begin again. Supplement your whip with a cluck and, as you introduce new gaits, use the voice commands: "walk," "trot," "canter." Of course, in competition you won't be able to use your voice; but by the time you

GETTING STARTED

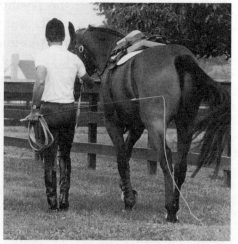

Lead your horse to the work area, with your right hand controlling his head and your whip in your left hand, pointing rearward.

Introduce him to the idea that the whip means forward. Move your left hand back a little and flick your wrist so that the lash taps him lightly at the level of buttock or gaskin. At the same time, cluck to him so that he learns to associate the encouraging sound with your whip.

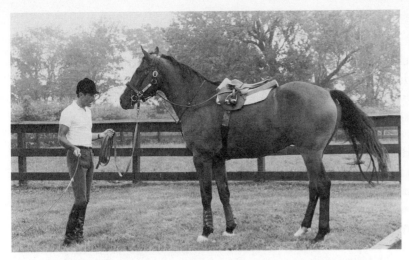

When you reach your work area, say "whoa," stop, and turn to face your horse. Move your whip to your right hand with the lash toward him, and arrange the coils of line in your left hand.

Stack the coils in the order in which they'll unwind, the first one on top, so that you can pay out the line smoothly.

Let out about 10 feet of line and move to your horse's left side. Tap him lightly on the buttock with the whip, and cluck.

Hold your left hand in front of you so that your line acts like an opening rein to lead him around the track.

Walk with him to enlarge the circle to about 60 feet.
Photos: *Practical Horseman*

9

begin working from the saddle, your horse will understand your aids well enough not to need it.

Most horses will move off at the first flick of the lash. But if your horse doesn't respond, repeat the aid, making it gradually stronger if necessary. Walk a circle with your horse and watch him carefully. Watch all parts of him—his shoulder, his hock—so that you become familiar with how he uses himself. Watch his eye to read his mood.

How is he reacting to your aids? If he's lazy or sluggish and resists moving forward energetically, repeat the light taps with your whip. If he still doesn't move forward energetically, strengthen the taps little by little until you get the response you're seeking.

Or is he the hot sort of horse whose nerves move him too much? You'll see it in his expression and you'll feel the pull in your hand as he hurries away from your forward aid.

At this point, don't worry about what might seem to be signs of a poor attitude. The consistent discipline of the training program you've begun will overcome most temperament problems. But do use your assessment of your horse's moods to choose the best method of overcoming his resistance. If your horse is the hot, nervous type, make a mental note to turn him out before you work him. To deal with his residual nervous energy, teach him the half-halt.

When you feel your horse pulling against your hand, simply close your fingers more tightly around the longe line, as if you were squeezing water out of a sponge. It's the same aid you'd use for a half-halt if you were riding. Whether or not your horse responds, squeeze briefly and release; if necessary, squeeze again. Continue repeating the squeeze until you feel him slowing down. However slight the response, reward your horse by returning to your usual elastic feel on the line. Maintain it until he hurries again; then reapply the aid.

If, after twenty or so repetitions, there's no sign that your horse even notices your squeeze, follow the same procedure you'd use with a forward aid: strengthen it gradually until you get a response. Replace the squeeze with a soft tug on the line and say "whoa." This will probably be sufficient to get your horse's attention and cause him to slow; if not, increase the force of your tugs by increments until your pressure matches his pressure. But don't pull against *his* pull. Follow each tug with a softening "give" to keep your horse from hanging on your hand. Be patient. Be consistent. Most young horses will slow to a soft tug within a couple of circles.

When your horse walks forward in response to your whip aid, neither pulling nor hanging back, so that the feel in your longe-line hand remains reasonably elastic, you can begin to increase the distance between you. Release one loop of your line and step back quietly to take up the slack. Continue to walk in a circle so that your horse's circle maintains its 60-foot diameter.

Observe your horse's reaction. If he lags, use your whip as I've described to restore his forwardness. If he pulls, use half-halts to steady him. Once he's stabilized, let out one loop and then another until he's 16 to 20 feet away from you. As he moves away, replace taps of the whip with the circular motion of the whip behind him to direct him forward.

Now test his brakes. Turn your whip so that the lash points away from him; say "whoa" and make repeated soft half-halts on the longe line. With each finger-squeeze, repeat the voice command until he halts. Your horse should stop on the circle and stand facing in the direction in which he was moving. But since you've turned your whip away to encourage him to halt, there is no aid operating to hold him on the circle: he'll probably turn in and start moving toward you.

Turn your whip so that the lash faces forward again and point it gently toward your horse's head. This should be enough to stop him; you don't need to wave the lash. Now slowly move around to your position at his side. Discourage him from continuing to turn toward you by holding the point of the whip toward his head until you've reached a position where you can once again use it at his quarters. Open your left hand to lead him forward, and tap his buttock while you cluck to send him forward on the track again.

As you practice walking and halting, experiment to find a combination of aids that produces a reasonably prompt halt while keeping your horse out on the track. If he's slow to halt, you'll have to minimize the presence of your whip and increase the force of your half-halts. If he halts readily and strolls toward you, put a little more "forward" into your halting aids. Keep your whip toward him, but lower it so that it points to the ground as you give half-halts. If he turns toward you, you can quickly raise the whip to discourage him.

Trotting

Walking in circles soon becomes boring for a young horse. Begin the trot as soon as your horse has a rudimentary halt and has grasped the general idea of walking around you at the end of twenty or so feet of line; if you do this, you won't have to run around a big circle at the faster gait.

To give the signal forward into a trot, use the circular whip motion

First, test your brakes. Turn the point of your whip away, say "whoa," and take repeated half-halts on the line. With no aid operating to hold your horse out on the circle, he will probably turn in and start toward you.

Turn the lash to him and point it smoothly toward his head. This will stop him from approaching you.

Hold the whip toward him as you move slowly around to his side.

Send him forward again.

Experiment until you find the right combination of half-halts and whip position to stop your horse on the track and keep him there, facing in the direction he was going.

When your horse has grasped the idea of walking around you on a circle, let out your line and send him forward into a trot, using a circular motion of your whip. Arc it away from him and down, and then . . .

. . . forward and up to urge him into the faster gait. You might have to step toward him to push him through his ignorance barrier.

Walk with him on a smaller circle of your own. Once he's trotting forward at a steady speed, strive for a consistent, elastic contact through the line while your whip follows without circling. Photos: *Practical Horseman*

accompanied by a cluck and the word "trot." You may have to take a step or two toward your horse to push him through his ignorance barrier at first. If he bounds forward into the new gait, move with him so that you don't give him a confusing tug with your line just as he's obeying your forward signal. Even if he's moving faster than you'd like, give him several strides to reorganize himself while you move with him on a small circle of your own; then ask him to slow down with half-halts. Use the same method that you may have needed to steady his walk, and repeat the aid patiently until he responds, gradually strengthening it into soft tugs if necessary. If he breaks into a canter when you ask him to trot, you'll have to be more forceful, bringing him back to the trot promptly so that he doesn't get the notion that he can run around on the line as he pleases. Move toward him, reeling in the line as you go; tug repeatedly and repeat the command "whoa."

When he's trotting, return to repeated half-halts in order to steady his gait. At any sign of slowing, reward him with a steady elastic contact on the line; when he speeds up again, resume your half-halts. Remember to keep moving with him on a circle of your own so that you don't ask him to turn more tightly than he can do with reasonable ease.

If he's sluggish, use your whip in circular movements to keep him trotting forward. After a few minutes of trotting, choose a moment when he has responded to your aid and reward him by signaling for a halt. When he has stopped, walk toward him, preventing him from turning toward you, and switch the line to the right side of the halter. Re-coil the line into your right hand, placing the loops in the order in which they will unwind, and transfer the whip to your left hand. Move to a position just behind your horse's right shoulder and repeat the same work to the right.

Dealing with Rebellion

Sooner or later, your horse is going to test you. And since many young horses are less comfortable moving to the right than to the left, this may be the moment.

If your horse balks, don't fly off the handle and escalate your aids. Use patient repetition to get him over the hurdle. With your right hand, open a leading rein; with your left hand, tap, tap, tap with the tip of

Bring your horse to a halt and walk toward him, coiling the line as you go. Don't let him come toward you.

Switch the line to the other side of his halter.

Re-coil the loops into your right hand, switch the whip to your left, and move into position on your horse's right.

If he feels uncomfortable traveling to the right, he may try to escape the effort by turning to face you. Open a leading rein with your right hand and try to regain your position opposite his shoulder, where you can use taps of your whip to send him forward again.

If he moves faster than you can keep up with him, it's better to lose position for a moment than to lunge forward with big hurried movements.

Smoothly regain your position. Keep tapping, clucking, and leading.

With consistent repetition, you will get your way.

But when balking doesn't work, he may try plunging forward to escape your whip. If he canters, reel in the line with repeated tugs while you say "whoa" so that he doesn't learn he can run around as he pleases. Photos: *Practical Horseman*

15

the whip. If your horse backs up or swings to the side away from you, follow him. Try to keep your body in position behind his shoulder. But if he moves faster than you can keep up with him, it's better to lose position for a moment than to lunge toward him with a frantic movement. Smoothly regain your position as soon as you can, and resume your aids. Keep tapping, clucking, and leading, and you will get your way.

Perhaps your horse will walk forward willingly enough but express resentment in the trot. At a faster gait, everything happens faster. As he wheels to face you, you'll have to move quickly to his side to send him forward again. But the aids should still be smooth, not violent. At the faster gait, he's more likely to plunge forward, away from your whip. If he canters, bring him back to a trot by reeling in the line with repeated tugs while saying "whoa." When he trots, reward him by relaxing the line. Steady his pace with half-halts if necessary. If, on the other hand, he lags, urge him forward with circular motions of the whip. Once he's trotting forward and relaxed, maintain a steady, elastic contact on the line while you follow his hindquarters with your whip without the circular motions.

If you've managed to achieve all this in one session, now would be a good moment to stop. Signal your horse to walk, and then bring him to a halt. Walk toward him—don't let him come to you—coiling the line as you approach. Pat him and lead him to the barn.

Teaching Straightness

When your horse is walking and trotting around you on the longe line, going forward with reasonable relaxation at least half of the time, you can begin to work on the third pillar of his education: straightness.

Straightness means moving the hind feet in the path of the front feet. On a circle, your horse is straight when he bends his body to conform to the curving path. There are two ways your horse can avoid straightness on the longe line: he can hang on the line, letting his quarters trail to the outside of the circle (you'll feel him pull against your hand), or he can reduce the size of the circle by turning his forehand inward (the line will go slack). Even though it may be difficult to judge slight deviations in the angle of his body as you view him from the side, you'll know he's straight when the feeling in your hand remains unchanged.

If your horse evades straightness by pulling out of the circle, give little nips and tugs on the line while you restore his forward motion with circular movements of your whip. Experiment until you find just the

If your horse hangs on the line, letting his quarters trail to the outside, you'll feel the pull in your hand. Give little nips and tugs on the line while you use circular movements of your whip to restore forward movement.

If he cuts in on the circle, the line will go slack. Bring your whip hand forward, opposite his shoulder.

Raise the whip so that the tip points at his withers. This will return him to the track. Photos: *Practical Horseman*

right combination of whip and hand; then simply repeat your aids. Repetition always succeeds.

If your horse cuts in on the circle, you'll need a new whip aid. Bring your whip hand forward until it's opposite your horse's shoulder and

17

raise it so that the tip of the whip is pointing at his withers. This will return him to the track. Do this every time until he doesn't cut in anymore.

Cantering

You must establish reasonably good control of your horse in the trot before you'll be able to control him in the canter. During the next few practice sessions—before you canter—continue to impress upon your horse the habits of staying forward, straight (in this case meaning conforming to the circle), and relaxed. But spend a little less time with your horse traveling around you and a little more time on transitions between gaits. Bring him from walk to trot, back to walk, to halt, again to walk, and then to trot, making sure to keep your aids consistent. Always start softly and work up. In the downward transitions, begin with finger-squeezes and progress through soft tugs to actual pulls. Ultimately your horse should respond every time to repeated soft half-halts. When you sense that you're approaching this stage—when he responds to finger-squeezes about half the time and to light tugs the other half—you can begin to canter.

Establish a relaxed forward trot, gradually moving away to the end of the line so that your horse will have the freedom to balance himself at

CANTERING

Establish a relaxed, forward trot, gradually moving to the end of the line. Point your whip at your horse's quarters and crack it softly while you say "canter" and cluck to him.

Keep repeating your aids, running him into the canter if necessary until he learns to prepare his balance for faster gaits.

If he bucks to the outside, give little half-halts to hold him on the track.

But don't try to correct him if he goes too fast; let him choose his own pace, and after a couple of circuits he'll probably slow himself. Photos: *Practical Horseman*

the faster gait. Raise your whip to point directly at his quarters; crack it softly at the same time that you say "canter" and cluck. Make sure there's enough slack in the line to permit him to obey without restriction. By making the canter aid distinctly different from the aid to trot, you'll allow your horse to learn to recognize what you want immediately, just as a schooled horse knows immediately that you want him to canter when you move your leg behind the girth.

Until your horse has learned the meaning of your aid, he won't know how to respond. Keep repeating all the components, running him into the canter if necessary. Later he'll learn to prepare his balance for the faster gait, but that's a long way in the future.

If he leaps forward into a gallop, don't discourage him. If he bucks, ignore it for now. Give him the full length of the line; correct him with little half-halts only if he tries to fly off the circle or bucks to the outside. Don't drag him back as punishment; you'll merely make it more difficult for him to balance and may even cause him to injure himself. If you're patient, he'll probably slow down of his own accord after two or three circuits, in order to recover his balance. Let him go around for one more circle at a comfortable speed. Then bring him back to a trot, then a walk, and halt. Switch sides and canter him in the other direction.

The purpose of the longeing phase of basic training is to teach your horse to respond to your hand and to your whip, to make him reasonably reliable but not to make him perfect; that would require more drilling than is good for a young horse. It might take anywhere from ten days to two months, depending not only on your horse's receptiveness but also on your skill as a trainer. If you're not experienced with a longe line, it may take several weeks just to establish the effectiveness and consistency of your aids. The average horse in the hands of an adept trainer needs about three weeks for this phase of the program.

During every training session, run through your mental checklist: Is he going forward? Is he traveling straight? Is he relaxed? When you can answer yes to all three most of the time, your young horse is ready to ride.

2

Training on the Flat in
Five Easy Lessons

Dana Douglass Jungherr

Formerly director of Cedar Lodge Farm in Connecticut, Dana Douglass now runs Starlite Farm in Salisbury, Massachusetts, with her husband, grand prix rider Mark Jungherr, and directs training at Hamilton Equestrian Center. She has developed a realistic attitude and method for training a horse to make the most of his ability, not necessarily to jump over the moon. The technique is as classic as can be, but her practical approach makes it accessible to every reasonably competent horse and rider.

These days, a well-broken hunter is apt to break your bank account too. But the main thing he has that your green horse lacks is education, and you can supply that yourself. I could never afford a fancy horse, so I learned to turn my imperfect hunter prospects into polished performers who could hold their own in A-circuit competition. And this is how I do it.

What is a made horse, after all, but one that is supple from nose to tail, responds to subtle aids, and jumps in good form? Your horse may not have the long, fluid stride of a top conformation hunter. But whatever his natural way of going, you can improve it to a marked degree. He may not round his back and snap his knees in perfect style over each fence; but if you teach him to maintain his balance around corners, lengthen and shorten his stride, and respond to your aids willingly, he'll be able to produce consistent, workmanlike rounds in hunter classes. A supple, well-schooled horse, no matter how humble his origins, is a pleasure to watch and a pleasure to ride.

I always start with a series of simple exercises on the flat that supple the horse's muscles and improve his balance, while correcting any problems he may have. When a green horse is unbalanced or unresponsive, the cause is usually *stiffness*. You probably know what this problem feels like. Your horse is heavy in your hands, and his stride may be short. When he reaches a corner, he points his nose to the rail and leads with his inside shoulder. You feel as if you're sitting crooked; you have trouble keeping your own balance. When you ask him to lengthen his stride before a fence, he hurries instead. When you ask him to jump several fences in a row, he loses his balance and leans even harder on the reins. By the third fence, neither you nor the horse is in control. You're likely to be headed for disaster if you don't do something about his way of going.

To make your horse more supple, you have to work on all of his muscles at once. As you persuade him to reach further under his body with his hind legs, he'll be inclined to swing his shoulders further forward, round his back, and move closer to the ground. His conformation may prevent him from pointing his toes; he may still break a little at the knee. But his stride will be longer and flatter than it was, closer to the "daisy-cutter" movement that hunter judges like to see.

I use *five basic exercises* to supple a green horse. They are so simple that I can perform them all in various combinations during each schooling session: (1) I start by walking and trotting a circle about 60 feet in diameter. (2) I then connect two large circles to make a figure eight. (3) Next I work on a shoulder-in. (4) I then combine the shoulder-in on the straightaway with small circles in the corners of the ring. (5) The final exercise is a serpentine, which asks the horse to keep his balance both around turns and on straight lines. I intersperse these five lateral exercises with lengthening work to increase the horse's adjustability.

You don't have to produce shoulder-ins and serpentines of grand prix dressage quality in order to obtain the full suppling and balancing benefits of these exercises. Your horse may find one or two movements particularly difficult, or he may have more trouble bending in one direction than the other. When you hit a snag, don't drill until he becomes bored and resistant. Go on to the other exercises and return to your problem later, perhaps not until the next schooling session. As your horse becomes more supple, he'll find it easier to do what you ask.

Be sure to vary the order of the exercises and vary their location too, if possible. If you can incorporate some of this flat work into a cross-country ride, you'll find it easier to hold your horse's attention, particularly if he's young and easily bored.

Your horse won't become supple overnight, but he'll be better at the end of each schooling session than he was at the beginning. If you work on these exercises four or five days a week, he should show lasting improvement in about two months.

Your horse has to be comfortable before he can relax and become supple, so before you even start to work, check to make sure that his tack isn't pinching him anywhere. Pay particular attention to the bit. I like to use either a loose-ring snaffle or a plain snaffle with a fixed ring for all my flat work. An aluminum loose-ring snaffle is light but thick; it encourages the horse to relax his jaw and seek the mouthpiece. Egg-butt snaffles are usually thicker and heavier and thus don't permit as much movement in the horse's mouth.

You, too, need to be relaxed and comfortable. Any stiffness in your body will be communicated by the reins from your hands down to your horse's mouth. Before you start, make sure that all your joints are soft and supple. If possible, use a sitting trot for most of the exercises so that your weight will be continually available to influence your horse's balance.

The Large Circle

Make your circle at least 60 feet in diameter (about twice the diameter of the circle your horse would make at the end of a longe line). Since the generous arc doesn't require much bend, it's easier for him to relax and take long, free strides. His muscles will need a chance to loosen up, especially if he's just come out of his stall, so start the exercise in a walk. As a matter of fact, it's a good idea to begin each exercise in a walk, to make sure that he's relaxed and listening to your aids.

Since it's easier for you and your horse to maintain your balance at the walk, this is a good time to check your position. Your inside shoulder should be slightly back; about 60 percent of your weight should be over your outside seatbone to help keep the horse from leaning toward the center of the circle. Later, when you canter around a hunter course, this weighting will remind your horse to balance himself on the turns without your having to use more obvious aids. Alternate squeezes of your calves will encourage the horse to lengthen his stride. As you feel his inside hind leg move forward, squeeze with your inside calf; squeeze with your outside calf as his outside leg comes forward. Keep a light, even contact through the reins to prevent him from hurrying.

Here the mare isn't really going forward. She's just come out of the barn and she's not warmed up. But . . .

. . . she's much more relaxed and ready to go on to something a little harder. Photos: *Practical Horseman*

Now change rein and circle in the opposite direction.

When your horse feels relaxed and comfortable at the walk, go into a rising trot and repeat the exercise. If his back remains relaxed, you can begin the sitting trot. If you then feel his back get tense, if his head and neck rise and his stride shortens in an attempt to escape from your weight, he isn't ready for it yet. Return to the rising trot, make sure he's relaxed, and then try again for no more than two or three strides at a time. A very stiff horse may need several weeks of work in the rising trot before he's ready for the sitting trot.

The momentum of the trot thrusts more weight toward the horse's forehand, so you have to work harder to keep him balanced. Each time you feel his inside hip drop, squeeze your inside leg against him to encourage a deeper stride of his inside hind leg. In the intervals between your leg squeezes, use a quick squeeze-and-release of the outside rein to keep him from speeding up. These two combined aids will induce him to carry more weight on his hindquarters and toward the outside of the circle.

Your horse doesn't need to circle perfectly before moving on to the next exercise, but he should begin to conform to the arc without throwing his quarters to the outside and his shoulder to the inside. As he shifts more of his weight onto his hindquarters, he'll lighten the burden in your hands. His jaw will be a little more supple at the end of the exercise than it was at the start. You'll have a more elastic feeling in the reins, and when you put pressure on the bit, his jaw will give a little rather than clamp down. As his balance and suppleness continue to improve week by week, so will his responsiveness.

Figure Eight

The figure eight asks your horse to keep his balance as he changes from one bend to the other. The ability to change direction smoothly in a balanced frame is essential in a hunter, which is rarely asked to jump more than two fences in a straight line in the show ring.

Combine two large circles to make your figure eight. If you use small circles, your horse will tend to shorten his stride in order to accommodate the tighter arcs. If your horse has trouble changing his bend, you may have to make the circles even larger a couple of times. Then, when he can handle the larger circles, try the 60-foot-diameter ones again.

Prepare early for the new bend. Lighten your inside rein when you are several strides ahead of the spot where you plan to change direction.

We're finishing the first circle of the figure eight.

Still bending right, but now I'm focusing on the point where we'll bend in the other direction.

This photo shows the straight stride at the juncture of the two circles.

Bending left.

The mare is slightly overbent, but her hindquarters are well underneath her and she's staying soft and supple.

She's still bent nicely, reaching well across the midline with her inside hind leg. I'm using my outside leg to maintain the rhythm of the stride. Photos: *Practical Horseman*

Using equal pressure on the reins, straighten the horse for at least one stride at the point where the two circles meet. During the straight stride, change your weight distribution in favor of the new outside seatbone, and move your new outside leg back a couple of inches to prevent your horse from throwing his quarters off the track. Then take a little more rein with your new inside hand to bend him around your leg.

First, walk through the exercise. Then, do it two or three times in a trot before moving on to something else. In order to bend correctly in the figure eight, the horse must pay attention more closely to your legs and hands than he did on a single circle. After several figure eights, he should be relaxing his jaw and bending a little more around your leg. Once he's relaxed and responding to your leg, he's ready to try the shoulder-in.

Shoulder-in

It isn't difficult to teach your horse to do a shoulder-in. The exercise will loosen his muscles and help him learn to bend. After you've practiced the shoulder-in, he should feel more supple the next time you ask him

This is the indirect rein cue you'd use for a shoulder-in to the right.

This is a nicely balanced preparation for the shoulder-in, but then . . .

. . . the mare's head goes up as I ask her to move her inside hind leg farther underneath herself.

Typical evasion. Just by adding my inside leg to my outside rein in the wrong balance, I've produced this resistance. I'll need to relax my hand and ride a quiet circle before trying again.

In our next attempt at shoulder-in, the mare throws her quarters to the outside. She's actually leaning toward the rail. I'll have to use my outside leg to push her quarters back to the track and bend her more forcefully with my inside leg.

This time the mare is a little better balanced, but she hasn't actually moved her shoulder in off the track; she's bending her neck but not her body. I'm using a slight opening rein to the outside to control the bend of her neck while I squeeze hard with my inside leg to encourage a bend in the body. My outside leg rests behind the girth, holding her quarters on the track.

On this attempt, the mare gives me a nice shoulder-in. Her back is round; she's soft, supple, and free of resistance; and her whole body conforms to the bend.

Here you can see that her inside hind leg is tracking directly behind her outside foreleg, just as it should. Photos: *Practical Horseman*

to bend around a corner. As his muscles relax and stretch, you may also find that he uses his back better when he jumps.

Walk across the short side of your ring and around the corner. As you come out of the corner, keep your horse's head turned as if you planned to ride across the diagonal. To prevent his head and neck from becoming rigid, use a low indirect rein, dropping your inside hand below the top of his withers and guiding his head around until you can see his profile. Keep squeezing and releasing your hand on the rein to remind him to bend.

Now your horse's shoulder is positioned inside the track. In order to prevent his body from following, you must push his inside hind leg back to the track each time he makes a stride. Squeeze with your inside calf each time his inside hind leg moves forward; the pressure tells him to move the leg across his outside hind leg. Remember to place 60 percent of your weight over your outside seatbone to encourage your horse to move under you and maintain his balance.

Since you want to encourage him to bend without restricting the forward reach of his hind legs, leave his mouth alone as much as possible. Keep your low indirect rein with your inside hand, and use a light squeeze-release of the outside rein immediately following each inside leg aid to signal him to stay on the path you've chosen.

Ask your horse to remain bent for three or four strides; then straighten him for three or four strides before he loses too much impulsion. Repeat

LENGTHENING STRIDES

I've asked for lengthening in the trot. The mare is reaching out in front, but her hindquarters aren't working as well.

I ask for more . . .

... and she resists by raising her head and hollowing her back.

We try again, and this time she responds, lengthening her stride from behind, stretching her whole frame.
Photos: *Practical Horseman*

the shoulder-in on the long side of the ring if there's enough room left for it. If not, go around the corner and do a shoulder-in on the short side. When you reach the next corner, change direction across the diagonal.

As you change direction, ask your horse for a lengthened walk. The shoulder-in is a fairly collected exercise, so he may need a chance to stretch out a bit while you rebuild lost impulsion. Besides, your goal is to teach your horse to maintain his balance and respond to your aids whenever you ask him to lengthen or shorten his stride, in order to be able to adjust his stride before a fence. The best way to achieve this is to alternate the more confining bending exercises with lengthening work.

As each hind leg comes forward, squeeze with your calf on that side. When you feel the energy you've generated pass through your horse, lighten your contact just enough to allow him to lengthen his stride. You may feel as if you had two pounds of weight in each hand when you begin to use your legs; that weight may drop to a pound and a half as you allow him to lengthen. Never simply throw him the reins. You'll lose the balanced frame you're striving for.

Shoulder-in and Circle

Large circles and figure eights have taught your horse to follow a generous arc; shoulder-ins have placed his body in a tighter bend for a few strides at a time. Now you'll ask him to combine the two efforts: making a pronounced bend in his body and moving in a circle.

As we do a small circle to the left, the mare is bending well. She's using her hind end effectively and she's light in front, but she needs to relax her head and neck just a little more and come into my hand.

Now she's leaning into my inside hand. I'll try to lighten her in front by squeezing with my inside leg and controlling the energy I generate with my outside rein.

Here the mare is beginning to relax her head and neck; she's on the verge of dropping into my hand and softening her jaw around the bit. She's listening to my leg aids, moving forward with deep strides, and bending well around my inside leg. Photos: *Practical Horseman*

Ask for several strides of shoulder-in on the long side of the ring. Let your horse relax with several straight strides and then do shoulder-in again for three or four strides before you reach the corner. As you approach the turn, lighten your shoulder-in aids, still keeping the majority of your weight on your outside seatbone. Guide your horse around a circle 20 feet in diameter, and continue along the short side to the next corner. Without using a shoulder-in to set him up, guide him around another small circle, using only your weight and inside-leg-to-outside-hand aids to help him conform to the arc.

Don't expect perfection right away. Your horse may hold the bend for half the circle and then throw his quarters out and his shoulder in, as he used to do. Return to the track, lengthen down the long side, and repeat the shoulder-in–circle exercise in the corner, followed by a small circle in the next corner. Then lengthen the walk across the diagonal and try the same exercise on the other rein.

Take a break with some large circles to let your horse stretch his muscles and to let you check his progress. He won't be perfect yet, but he should be lighter in your hands and easier to keep balanced on the track. He should be more sensitive to your bending aids, more relaxed and reaching forward into the bit. If your horse seems balanced and responsive, try trotting: first just a few strides of shoulder-in, then shoulder-in and one circle, and finally the entire exercise.

Don't hesitate to return to a walk if you've gone too fast and your horse has lost his balance. You might do half the exercise in a walk and the other half in a trot. Let your horse's ability determine your rate of progress. In other words, as he masters the simpler exercises, proceed to more difficult ones, but return to the easier movements whenever it is necessary to boost his confidence.

Serpentine

You've asked your horse to bend in both directions and to lengthen his stride. Now you'll combine these two efforts in a serpentine.

Start with generous loops, about forty feet across at the widest point. Try to keep the loops the same size so that you can demand an equal effort from each side of the horse's body.

The secret of success is to prepare for each new bend early enough. Allow about three strides as you cross the center of the ring for straightening your horse and changing your aids for the new bend.

When you finish the first serpentine at a walk, pick up a trot and come back the other way. The faster gait will give you less time to reorganize for each new bend, but you'll keep the loops wide and undemanding. If all goes well the first time you trot the serpentine—that is, if your horse maintains his balance and bends around your leg—try again, this time narrowing your loops to a width of thirty feet. If the narrower loops upset his balance, return to wider ones. Keep practicing until he stays even and light in your hands.

We've come out of a loop to the right, and I'm about to bend the mare left. The muscles in her neck tense a little, threatening resistance. I'll quickly lighten my new outside rein, increase the pressure from my inside leg, and carefully take with my inside hand.

She responds well, giving me a nice, balanced bend around the loop to the left. My weight is helping her balance to the outside, and I'm using my outside leg to hold her quarters on the track.

Still nice and round, giving to my inside leg. Her quarters are staying on the track where they belong.

This time, as we come out of the loop and prepare to change the bend, she's balanced and relaxed, and there's no sign of resistance.

Photos: *Practical Horseman*

I don't usually start cantering any of the exercises until I'm sure of my horse's balance in the trot. With a very green horse, it may take several weeks before he's ready to bend at the canter. I introduce the canter on large, undemanding circles and then trot for the rest of the session. Let your horse be your guide. If he's stiff, he won't be able to manage tight circles at the canter for at least a month.

When you're teaching your horse these movements, it's best to start with the easiest ones and work up to the more difficult. But once he has mastered them, you should vary your pattern in order to keep him interested.

The five simple exercises outlined here will make a dramatic difference in your horse's performance. They will improve his balance, flexibility, and responsiveness—essential ingredients of a good hunter round. And when he's ready for open jumping, you'll find that he can turn smoothly, lengthen or shorten his stride before a fence, and round his back as he jumps.

Cynthia Hankins demonstrates the outside rein while working with a Gladstone trainee.
Photo: Karl Leck

3

Schooling on the Flat at Gladstone: Why and How

Cynthia Hankins

An outstanding junior rider and winner of the Medal finals in 1975, Cynthia Hankins was selected by Bert de Némethy to assist him as coach of the USET Jumping Team at Gladstone, New Jersey, schooling the team horses daily and riding some of them at preliminary training shows.

Since this article was written, Bert has retired as coach and Cynthia has moved to the state of Washington. The Gladstone scene has also changed. While a few prospective team horses are still developed there and USET director Chrystine Jones organizes jumping clinics throughout the year, most team riders today own and school their horses at home. But all of them have been influenced and guided by the Gladstone training methods.

Here, Cynthia describes an awkward situation during a jumping competition and then prescribes the antidote, so to speak, in the form of a training exercise on the flat that might have saved the day.

Suppose you're on a course, rounding a corner to the left. You see your distance to the next fence, but your horse is stiff on the left. He leans on the inside shoulder as he starts to drift out with his hind end. You try to correct it, gathering and bending him around the corner, strongly influencing with an outside leg. But while you're concerned with the problem underneath you, you miss your distance to the fence.

Whether in a hunter class or in an international jumping competition, a well-behaved horse that accepts the rider will always outperform a stiff, resisting horse. And the foundation is proper flat work.

The U.S. Jumping Team has several young horses that are being brought along slowly on the flat. Some have already been successful at lower levels of hunter and jumper competition. But many have developed defenses, such as evading the bit by hollowing the back and raising the head above the bit. Many don't fully understand the rider's aids. This is why our first objective at Gladstone is to encourage the horses to relax and drop whatever defenses they may have developed.

We introduce flat work right away, supplementing work over fences with one day a week devoted entirely to work on the flat, and a warm-up period of suppling before each jumping session. A typical week consists of about forty-five minutes on the flat once a week, two cross-country days of an hour each, and three forty-five-minute sessions of flat work combined with jumping. The horses rest on Sundays.

The five-year-old gelding I'm riding in the first photos tended to drop his head behind the vertical and to stiffen behind and drop his head back of the bit as soon as I put a leg on him. So our first sessions consisted of a lot of walking forward, stopping, backing a few steps, and walking forward again, in order to encourage forward movement every time he felt a leg against him. If you're quiet with your leg, even a very hot horse will accept it in time.

When this horse drops his head behind the bit, I apply a driving aid to encourage his body and hindquarters to move forward. I use both legs and seat to push him forward into the bit. This results in a slightly longer stride. In order to balance the increased movement, the horse has to reach out with his head. All the time, I try to keep my hands as quiet as possible, with the reins resting lightly on either side of the neck, forming a "chute" for the head. I don't like to see the horse's head and neck seesawed into a set position.

After many walk-halt transitions, I begin to work at the trot, urging the horse forward and changing directions frequently, which loosens up his back and loin and encourages him to be supple in both directions, softly accepting the bit.

I trot across the diagonal, gradually asking for a stronger trot and then coming back to an ordinary trot again as we approach the corner. The changes of direction and the transitions keep him from getting bored, and it's good practice in leg response.

I don't ask a green horse for anything difficult at first. I keep my inside leg against the girth to encourage him to bend his ribs around the curve at the ends of the ring. My outside leg remains steady, just behind the girth, to keep his hind end from swinging out. It doesn't always work out this way at first! But if I continue to use the proper leg aids for each turn, the horse eventually becomes smooth and supple, and bends properly in both directions.

Since the horse must learn to accept his rider's seat as well as the hands and legs, I use my seat to encourage him forward. I influence him very slightly at each step of the walk, not obviously pumping, but sitting up on my seatbones and allowing my pelvis to sway slightly in rhythm with him, keeping my back firm at all times, but not overarched. At the posting trot, I let the thrust of the hind legs push me out of the saddle, forward and down. Posting enables the horse to maintain a steady rhythmic trot, from which I can ask him to go forward or back again to an ordinary trot by using my legs and hands.

When the horse is accepting my seat and leg and is turning fairly willingly, I introduce some easy serpentine turns, starting with only two changes of direction: one to the right, one to the left. I do them at a walk at first and then at an ordinary trot, concentrating on keeping the horse bent in the direction of each loop. My outside leg is at the girth, asking him to bend. After coming out of the turn, I straighten him to balance him and then encourage him to bend in the opposite direction for the next turn. This simple bending is a preliminary for work on the circle.

I guard against overbending. The horse's body should curve around the natural track of the ring without exaggerating the degree of bending of his head and neck. As the horse turns a corner of the ring or executes half turns on a serpentine, I want to see his inside eye, but no more.

Exercises on Circles

You're on a course in a hunter class and have just jumped an in-and-out down the side of the ring. Now you're turning around the end wall into a brush box with a three-foot spread. Halfway around the end, you feel your horse drifting to the outside. You try to keep him bent around your inside leg and increase the pressure of the outside rein and leg. You end up bulging out past the brush and the direct line to the next fence, spoiling your round.

Work on *voltes* (small circles) can correct this habit in many horses, making them equally supple on both sides, teaching them proper bending. A horse that can bend properly without stiffening is easier to steer around a course. He's able to maintain his own balance, doesn't poke his nose to the outside or fall to the inside around turns, but bends his body in the proper direction, according to the degree of the curve.

With young horses, I begin work on the volte at the walk. This is done slowly at first, because a green horse may walk a couple of steps, stop, and walk on again, reluctant to bend and not quite sure of himself as I stay on the circle, which is about 6 meters, or 20 feet, in diameter.

I start by encouraging him forward at a walk in a straight line. Then I ask for bending with the inside rein, my inside leg pressing against the girth. My outside leg is slightly behind the girth to keep his quarters from swinging out. The outside rein maintains a steady contact with the outside corner of his mouth to prevent overbending of the neck. It rests against the neck and, with the inside rein, confines the horse in a chute that directs his movements.

After circling at the walk and making several transitions to the halt, I ride forward at an ordinary trot around the ring, crossing the diagonal at a strong trot, urging the horse forward and lengthening his stride. Horses get impatient after a lot of slow work, so it's good to vary the routine with a strong trot.

At first, the horse may swing his hindquarters to the outside of the circle or simply bend his neck without bending the ribs. But with practice in these exercises, he'll learn to carry himself in balance and in even rhythm, and to relax.

I don't encourage exaggerated bending. I just want to see the corner of the horse's inside eye as we go around the volte. I try to feel with my seat and legs where his hind legs are under me, whether they are drifting out or following his forehand around the circle, as they should.

It's not unusual for a young green horse to stiffen when you first begin work at the canter. I'm careful to bend around turns when I'm cantering a green horse, and I try to canter an equal amount of time in each direction, to make the horse equally supple on both sides.

The circle is a valuable tool for teaching relaxation and effective use of the hindquarters at the canter. Starting with a large circle of about 20 meters, I gradually make it smaller and smaller, with my outside leg behind the girth and the outside rein maintaining steady contact. The inside rein guides, while my inside leg on the girth encourages bending in the ribs and forward movement. The horse has to bring his hind-quarters under himself to avoid losing his balance. When I get down to an 8-meter circle, I gradually increase the size again.

I teach an advanced horse to use its hind end more effectively by *cantering a square*. It's hard at first. I canter in a straight line and pick a point in the distance for a turn. When we've reached it, I wait for the horse to have his weight on his hindquarters and then signal for a 90-degree turn. I canter straight forward for several strides more and signal for another 90-degree turn. The turns encourage the horse to use his hind legs to support his body in balance. When a horse is doing this properly, he is accepting the steady contact of my outside hand and remains light on the inside, not drifting into the center of the square.

Certain exercises are easy for the horse one day and difficult on others. When a horse performs an exercise beautifully and the next day resists, it's best to be patient and, above all, not force things. I start all over again with the most elementary exercises and hope to work up again to the same good performance.

Leg-Yielding

While riding a course of fences, you misjudge a turn and find that you're aiming for a wing instead of the center of the fence. If you haul on the rein, hoping to arrive at the center of the fence, you'll probably end up jumping at an angle. But if your horse has learned to yield to your leg, you can ask him to move his entire body left or right. He'll make the adjustment smoothly, almost imperceptibly, and he'll meet the fence straight.

When the horse has mastered the previous exercises, it's time to introduce lateral work.

Leg-yielding is the simplest form of lateral work, as well as the basis for more difficult movements that are part of dressage: the shoulder-in, two-track, revers and travers. Until now, we've only asked the horse to bend his rib cage around our inside leg at the corners and on circles and serpentines. Now we're going to teach him to move away from the pressure of our leg.

In leg-yielding, the horse moves forward and to the side simultaneously. He departs from his forward track at a 45-degree angle, but his body remains oriented in the direction of forward movement, while his head and neck are bent slightly away from the direction of sideways movement. It is a movement on four tracks, with each leg moving in its own path. They should meet the rail at a 45-degree angle, no more. At the conclusion of the leg-yielding exercise, the horse resumes forward movement along the rail.

Let's say, for example, that you're riding a straight line down the center of the arena, with the wall several feet away to your left. You decide to do the leg-yielding exercise toward the rail. You turn your horse's head slightly away from the rail, toward the center of the arena.

Schooling over jumps is, of course, an important part of the Gladstone training program. But far more time is spent on developing a sound foundation by schooling on the flat. Photo: Karl Leck

His body remains positioned parallel to the rail, but he moves on a diagonal track toward the left, crossing front and hind feet as he goes. When you reach the rail, his body is already parallel to it. You straighten his head and neck and he resumes forward movement along the rail. It is these four separate but parallel tracks formed by the horse's footfalls that depart from his original course at a 45-degree angle.

The easiest way to teach leg-yielding is to bring the horse in off the rail and take advantage of his natural tendency to return to it. Begin at one end of the long side and proceed forward at a walk parallel to the rail but a yard or two in toward the center of the arena. When the horse is moving forward and relaxed, press your inside leg against his side at the girth, keeping your outside leg quietly behind the girth. At the same time, turn his head slightly toward the inside of the ring, giving an equal amount with the outside rein, so that you can just see the corner of his eye. He should move away from your inside leg by crossing his inside front and hind legs over the outside legs.

He may cross only one set of legs at first. Be patient. After you've relaxed him with other work, come back to the leg-yield and try again. You want him to respond to your leg equally with his front and hind legs. Be satisfied with a single step at first. Increase your demands gradually.

Be sure to practice leg-yielding in both directions of the ring so that the horse learns to move equally well in response to pressure from both legs.

He may resist your leg. He may move into it instead of away from it. Straighten him and ask again, reinforcing your leg with a cluck or a light tap of the stick behind the girth.

On the other hand, he may escape your leg by swinging his hind end away from the pressure. His quarters will be closer to the rail than his forehand and he'll move without crossing his hind legs. Apply pressure behind the girth with your outside leg.

When your horse accepts your leg and yields to it at a walk, include the exercise in your trotting work. Practice leg-yielding down the long side of the arena at a slow sitting trot. Start several feet out from the rail and gradually work toward it. Your horse may lean onto his forehand, allowing his hindquarters to trail behind him. His forehand will be closer to the rail than his quarters. Straighten him and ride forward with determination before asking again for leg-yielding.

Once your horse has mastered leg-yielding at the walk and trot, you're ready to try shoulder-in.

Shoulder-in

As in leg-yielding, you use your inside leg at the girth, but at the same time your outside leg behind the girth prevents your horse from moving sideways. Instead, he bends his body around your inside leg but continues forward, whereas in leg-yielding he holds his body straight but moves to the side.

Shoulder-in is a movement on three tracks. When the horse bends correctly around your inside leg, his inside hind leg follows exactly in the path of the outside front leg.

Begin the shoulder-in at a walk. Make a 20-meter circle in one corner of the arena. Establish contact with the horse's mouth, move him forward vigorously with your legs, maintaining the correct bend with your inside leg on the girth and your outside leg slightly behind. You should just see the corner of his inside eye, and his hind feet should follow in the

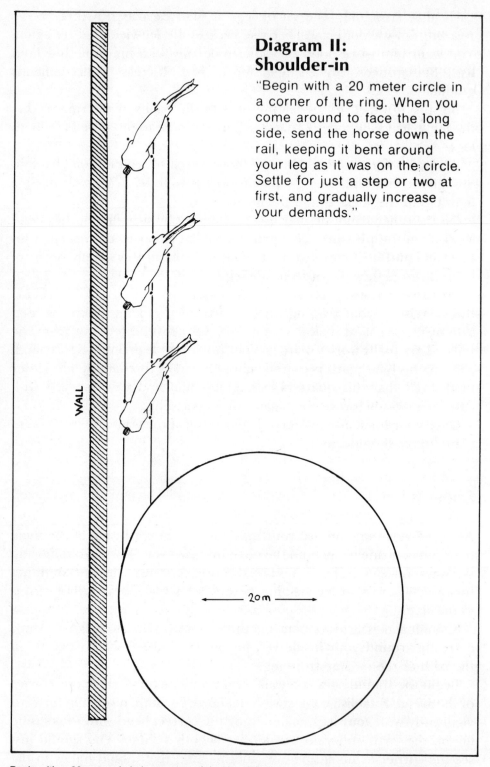

Diagram II:
Shoulder-in

"Begin with a 20 meter circle in a corner of the ring. When you come around to face the long side, send the horse down the rail, keeping it bent around your leg as it was on the circle. Settle for just a step or two at first, and gradually increase your demands."

WALL

20m

Begin with a 20-meter circle in a corner of the ring. When you come around to face the long side, send the horse down the rail, keeping it bent around your leg as it was on the circle. Settle for just a step or two at first, and gradually increase your demands.

tracks of his front feet. Now, as you come around to face the long side of the arena, maintain the bend as if you were planning to continue on the circle, but instead ask the horse to move forward parallel to the rail.

Keep your outside rein and leg steady, as they were on the circle. Maintain the bend of head and neck with your inside rein. But now increase the pressure of your inside leg at the girth. The horse can't move sideways because your steady outside rein and leg form a barrier. (The rail helps too, of course.) He can't swing his quarters out because your outside leg prevents it. At the same time, your strong inside leg is telling him to move away, so he moves forward off the circle and down the long side of the arena.

Reverse directions and repeat. Settle for just a few steps at first but then gradually ask for more.

Later on, introduce shoulder-in from the corner of the arena. Instead of relying on the circle to establish the proper bend, use the corner. Maintain shoulder-in the full length of the arena, and your horse will be nicely bent to enter the corner at the far end.

When you feel ready to advance to shoulder-in in the sitting trot, you should again first establish the proper bend on the circle. Follow the horse's movement with your seat resting on the outside seatbone. You should feel the inside hind leg coming up well underneath, following the path of the outside front leg.

Your horse may overbend with head and neck, which can make him pop his shoulder to the outside or swing his quarters out from the track. Either way, he avoids having to bend his body properly. Correct him by maintaining contact with your outside rein so that he will be unable to overbend his neck. Use your outside leg firmly behind the girth to prevent the quarters from swinging out.

Your horse may resist by not moving forward. If he cramps his stride, so that his gait seems stiff and forced, straighten him and reestablish free forward movement. If he doesn't respond to your leg, add a little reinforcement with your stick. Don't resume shoulder-in until he's moving forward correctly in a straight line.

Break up all this slow work by combining and varying the exercises. For example, when you've obtained a few satisfactory steps of shoulder-in, ask for a lengthened trot across the diagonal to give your horse a mental break and the opportunity to use some different muscles. Practice a serpentine at a trot and a couple of decreasing circles at a canter, and then try a little leg-yielding. Variety is important if you want to hold your horse's attention. Overdo a single exercise and he'll become tense, rigid, and irritated by the pressure of your leg.

Two-Tracking

If your hunter has a tendency to lean on your hands, the two-tracking exercise will help him learn to carry his own weight. And if your jumper has to perform a sudden pivot in a speed class, you'll be glad you taught him to balance over his hocks.

Two-tracking improves the horse's ability to bring his hocks under his body, where they will support a greater share of his weight and so lighten his forehand. Despite the name of this exercise, the horse's footfalls form not two but four distinct and parallel tracks. It is sometimes called "half pass," while the term "two-tracking" may be used in a general sense to describe any lateral movement.

In leg-yielding, the horse moves on an oblique path with his body straight; only his head and neck are bent, and they bend away from the direction in which he is moving. In the shoulder-in, the horse moves on a straight path with his body bent. The two-track now combines some of both previous exercises: in two-tracking, the horse moves on an oblique path, as in leg-yielding, but his body is bent as if he were performing the shoulder-in.

To introduce two-tracking, proceed around the arena at a walk, choosing the direction in which your horse performs shoulder-in best. Let's say it's to the right. When you near the end of the short wall, ask for a shoulder-in off the corner and continue down the long side of the arena on the rail, bending the horse slightly around your inside (right) leg.

Remember the specific job of each aid. The outside rein rests close against the neck and remains steady as it guides the horse down the line. The outside leg rests behind the girth, preventing the hindquarters from swinging. The inside rein maintains the bend of head and neck. The inside leg at the girth is active, pressing slightly more than the outside leg. It is this leg that keeps the horse lively and moving forward.

The horse is angled no more than 45 degrees off the rail. His front end is just one step closer to the center of the ring than his hind end. He is bent in the rib cage in response to light steady pressure from your inside leg. He moves forward energetically. His inside hind leg reaches well under his body, accepting his weight, lightening his front end. This is the balance he needs to begin two-tracking.

Continue shoulder-in all the way down the long wall and around the corner. Halfway along the short wall, turn right and proceed, still in

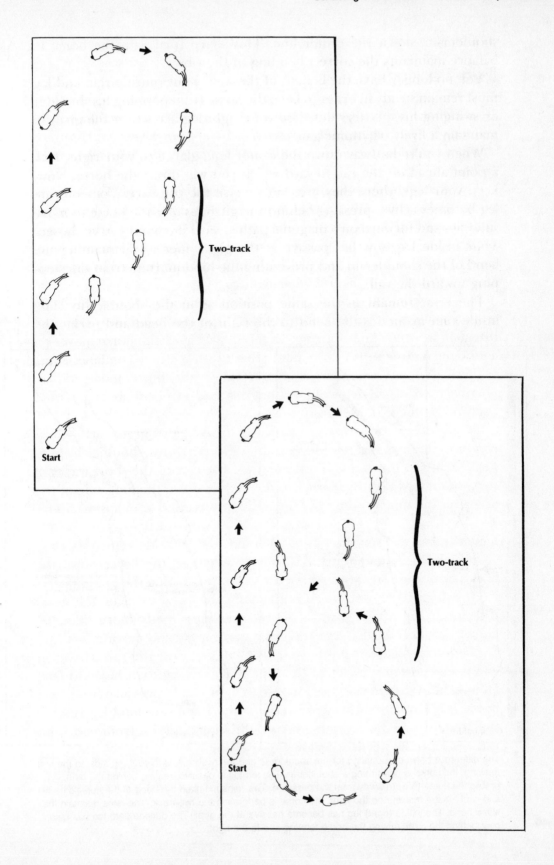

Two-track

Start

Two-track

Start

shoulder-in, down the center line. This sharp turn with the horse in balance maintains the correct bending of the ribs.

You no longer have the benefit of the wall. Your outside rein and leg must remain steady in order to keep the horse from popping his shoulder or swinging his quarters out. Use your right leg actively at the girth to maintain a lively, rhythmic gait.

When you're halfway down the center line, glance to your right. Pick a point ahead on the rail toward which you will direct the horse. Now, keep your legs where they are, but reverse the pressure. Your outside leg becomes active, pressing behind the girth, asking the horse to move sideways and forward on a diagonal path toward the point you've chosen. Your inside leg now lies passive at the girth, merely maintaining the bend of the shoulder-in and preventing the hindquarters from sidestepping toward the rail.

The reins remain in the same position as in the shoulder-in. The inside rein maintains the bend to the right of the head and neck. The

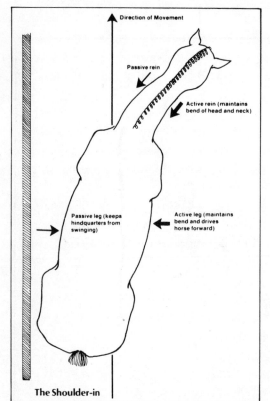
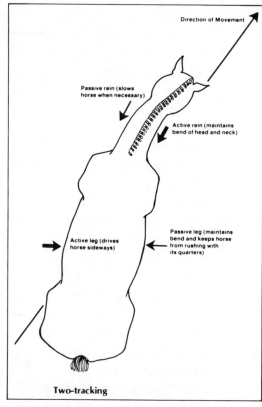

The difference between signaling for the shoulder-in and the two-track is in your leg aids. In the first drawing, the horse is performing a shoulder-in. The left leg is passive, resting behind the girth, driving the horse forward away from the pressure. The reins maintain the bend of the horse's head and neck. In the drawing on the right, the horse is performing the two-track. The reins maintain the same bend. The inside (right) leg has become passive at the girth. The outside (left) leg has taken over behind the girth, driving the horse forward and to the right.

outside rein rests gently against the side of the horse's neck, maintaining his balance while preventing him from rushing to the rail.

Your body and seat remain straight in the saddle. Don't twist toward the rail. Aim to arrive at your spot on the rail not with the horse's nose but with your right hip.

The horse should step toward the rail with his front end a little closer to the rail than his quarters. He should cross his outside legs in front of his inside legs one step at a time, without hurrying.

Some horses will try to hurry the two-track at first, in order to escape the rider's leg. If your horse is inclined to rush, then two-track only a couple of steps, straighten, and walk a couple of steps forward. Bend him again and encourage a few more steps on the diagonal toward the rail.

Later, when you progress to the trot, everything will happen much faster and you will have to guard against rushing with a more active inside (right) leg, keeping the hindquarters following behind the horse. If rushing is a problem, go back to two-tracking at the walk until the horse's balance improves.

If your horse's hindquarters advance toward the rail faster than his forehand, ease the pressure of your outside leg slightly and intensify the pressure of your inside leg until you find the right combination of aids.

If your horse pops his inside shoulder, make sure you have him bent in the right direction. A rider beginning two-tracking often inadvertently bends his horse away from the movement instead of toward it. The horse is then unable to bring his hindquarters up under himself, and the entire purpose of the exercise is defeated.

When you reach the rail, give the horse a chance to relax and use some different muscles with a little strong trot and a few exercises that are easy for him. Then repeat the two-tracking routine to the left.

When your horse is more proficient, you can combine two-tracking in both directions in a single exercise. When you reach the rail after two-tracking one way, instead of straightening, continue down the long wall in shoulder-in to the left, turn down the center line, and two-track to the left back to the rail. When your horse is two-tracking well at the walk, perform the same routine at the trot.

Incidentally, now that these advanced exercises have taken us off the rail and down the center line, we've lost our trusty reference points. Until now, "inside" or "outside" meant the side that was closest to the inside of the ring, or closest to the rail. However, these terms used to describe the rider's aids actually have no relationship to the riding ring.

They relate to the bend of the horse, and they'd be just the same if you were performing your exercises along a highway. So remember, the aids to the inside of the bend are the "inside" aids, and those to the outside of the bend, the "outside" aids.

Turn on the Haunches

Suppose you're in a jump-off making a turn to a big oxer combination with a long distance in between. You'll save time, of course, if you cut the turn. But do you dare? If your horse is uneducated, he'll land from the last fence of the previous line in a long, strung-out frame and will drag you around the turn, his hind end swinging wide. He'll sprawl over the first oxer, struggle for the second, and land in the middle of it.

But if your horse has been given the slow, methodical training as described, your efforts (and his) will be rewarded. Your horse will land from the last fence of the previous line and quickly regain his balance with his weight on his hocks, his front end light. You'll cut seconds off the turn without losing balance. His hindquarters will be under him, thrusting him over the big fences and carrying him through the long strides.

In the turn on the haunches, the forehand describes an arc of 180 degrees or less around the hindquarters, while the hind feet take springy steps to describe their own small arc.

Your horse is ready for turns on the haunches as soon as he can balance himself in the shoulder-in and two-track without trying to escape your leg, leaning on your hands, or drifting out with his quarters.

You can double-check your horse's balance by making a couple of tests at the canter. Ask for a canter down the long side of the arena. Take both reins in your outside hand. The horse should continue to move straight ahead without falling to the inside. Now, with one rein in each hand, leave the rail and canter a 20-meter circle. Still cantering, gradually decrease the size of the circle. If your horse can manage a 10-meter circle without falling to the inside or losing his balance, he is carrying himself correctly.

Begin the turn on the haunches by walking your horse along the rail. Make sure that you have an energetic walk. Take a stronger feel of his mouth and shorten his frame, at the same time increasing the pressure of your legs to ensure that his walk remains active and lively. You're striving for steps that are shorter but not slower. His head should rise slightly to balance the shorter frame.

Pick a point ahead, and when you reach it, use both reins to lead the

The Aids

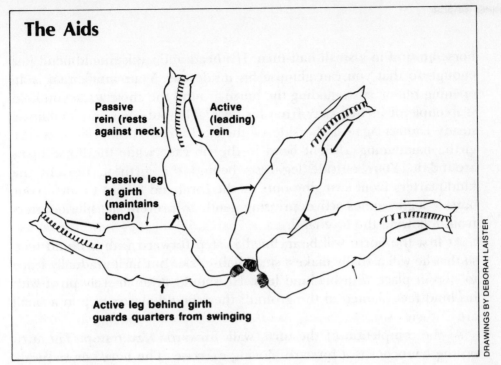

Passive rein (rests against neck)

Active (leading) rein

Passive leg at girth (maintains bend)

Active leg behind girth guards quarters from swinging

DRAWINGS BY DEBORAH LAISTER

Turn on the haunches.

Photos 18A, B

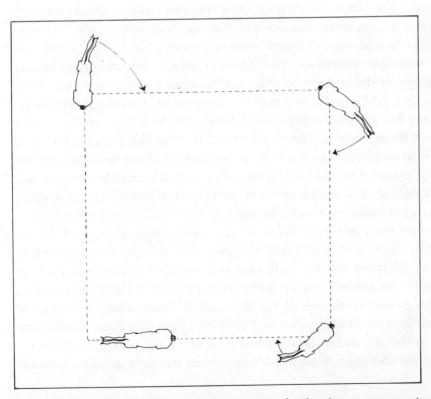

Practice 90-degree turns on the haunches at the corners of an imaginary square or rectangle.

horse around in a small half-turn. His head and neck should bend just enough so that you can glimpse his inside eye. Your inside rein is an opening rein at first, guiding the horse around the circle while you hold it a couple of inches away from his neck. The outside rein maintains a steady contact against the side of the neck. Your inside leg is at the girth, maintaining a slight bend in the rib cage while the horse turns around it. Your outside leg rests behind the girth to prevent the hindquarters from swinging out. As the forehand begins to turn, your outside leg becomes active, pressing gently to prevent the hindquarters from following the forehand.

At first the horse will be inclined to step forward with his hind feet, so that he will actually make a small half-circle. But he'll gradually learn to step in place with his hind legs. He should never merely pivot with his hind feet planted in the ground: they should always step in a small arc of their own.

At the completion of the turn, walk forward. Never stop. The turn on the haunches is a forward-moving exercise. The horse should walk into it and out of it without altering the rhythm of his gait.

Don't let your horse rush through the turn. He should respond to your aids one step at a time, always ready to stop turning and walk forward at the very next step. To prevent anticipation of the turn, vary the degree. Ask for a 180-degree turn one time and a 45-degree or a 90-degree turn the next. Practice the exercise in different places around the ring so that he doesn't know what to expect.

I like to practice turns on the haunches around an imaginary square or rectangle in the middle of the ring, making 90-degree turns at the corners. By changing the size and the location of the imaginary figure, I make my horse wait for my instructions at every step.

If your horse tries to creep backward during the turn, brace your back and strengthen your leg aids. If he tries to swing his hindquarters out, use a stronger outside leg. If he falls on his inside shoulder, causing his hind end to slip out of position, walk forward a few steps and try again, using a slightly stronger inside leg.

Don't drill your horse in this or in any other single exercise. Once he responds calmly and obediently to your aids for the turn, gradually polish his performance by including the exercise in a varied routine. For example, after warming up at the walk and trot, do some leg-yielding to the long rail. Continue along the rail in shoulder-in, turning the corner at the end of the arena and turning again down the center line. Return to the rail in the two-track. Perform a turn on the haunches, a few steps of shoulder-in with the horse bent in the opposite direction,

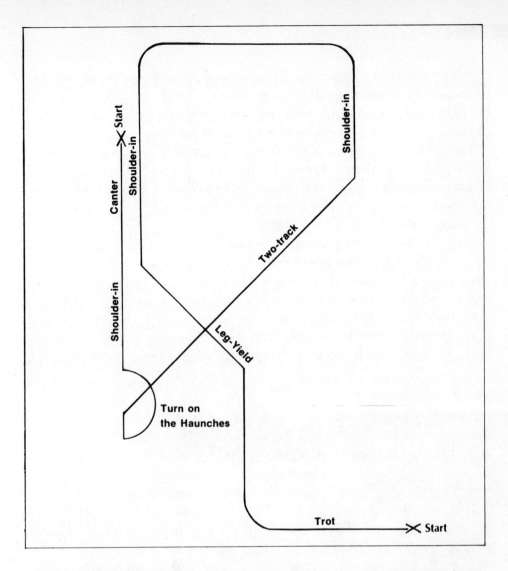

Here's an example of how you can combine the turn on the haunches with your other exercises to make a varied routine for your horse.

straighten him, and strike off in a canter. Later, repeat the sequence in the other direction.

Flying Change of Lead

The ability to do a flying change of lead increases the horse's maneuverability in the show ring. In classes against the clock, it's much easier to turn back to a large square oxer if the horse automatically changes his lead and maintains his impulsion and balance. When your horse has reached this level of suppleness and obedience, you're free to concentrate on lines and distances.

Before you start to teach the flying change, your horse should be able to break into a canter on the lead you desire from the walk. He should be light and sensitive to your leg aids, responding to the slightest pressure. He should accept your leg without pushing against it.

The easiest way to teach the flying change is if you first have your horse perform a collected canter. In the collected canter, the engagement of his hindquarters increases, the angles in his hocks close, and his head and neck rise slightly. His front end lightens, while the hocks carry proportionately more of his weight.

Start out by cantering around the outside of the ring in an ordinary canter to the right. Your upper body angles slightly forward. Your horse moves along in a natural rhythm with a long stride. His nose is slightly in front of the vertical and his neck is stretched out in front of him.

Partway up the long side, bring your upper body back to the vertical to increase the influence of your seat: it should gently follow the horse's back in a steady down and forward feeling. When a horse is not accepting

The outdoor ring at the USET headquarters in Gladstone, New Jersey. Photo: Courtesy of USET

the seat and leg and canters with a hollow back, the rider's tendency is to "save himself" by compromising his position. You often see a rider with his hips back, collapsing his stomach, following the motion of the horse in the only way that he can tolerate such an uncomfortable gait.

Take a little stronger feel of your horse's mouth and slightly increase the pressure of your legs. You want the horse to shorten his stride without any loss of the forward energy he had at the ordinary canter. Your inside leg is active at the girth, maintaining impulsion. Your outside leg is passive, resting slightly behind the girth and keeping the hindquarters straight. Your outside rein is steady and dominant, preventing the horse from falling to the inside. Your inside rein is light and passive, or should be, unless the horse is on his forehand and pulling. When he raises his head, raise your hands slightly to follow his mouth. To maintain the rhythm and keep him from breaking stride, push slightly toward the rail with your inside seatbone at each stride.

Canter around the corner and continue turning in a smooth arc away from the rail and back toward the same side of the arena you just left.

Cantering toward the wall, your horse is still on his right lead. You want him to change to his left lead as he reaches the wall and then proceed around the arena to the left. This is the moment to apply the lateral training you practiced earlier. In order to make it easy for the horse to switch to his left lead, you must lighten his left side. By shifting his weight from his left legs to his right legs, you make it easy for him to swing his left front leg forward to establish the new lead. The way you lighten a lateral pair of legs is to bend the horse slightly to the side you want to lighten. So now, as you approach the wall on the right lead, you bend your horse slightly around your left leg. Since you are about to join the wall to the left, this action seems perfectly natural to the horse and it's easy for him to comply.

Bring your left leg, which has been passive, forward to the girth, pressing it slightly against his side for the bend. At the same time, guide the horse to the left with your left rein, which has been active all along. Rest your right leg quietly for a moment against his side at the girth. Just before you ask for the new lead, your horse's hind legs will strike the ground: first the left hind and then the right hind. Wait just until the left hind strikes. His weight will then be mostly on the quarters, with his front legs preparing to swing forward. Ask for the change by moving your right leg behind the girth and pressing. If the horse has learned to pick up a lead, he'll associate your right-leg pressure with the canter signal for a left lead and, with his weight still on his hind legs, he'll swing forward with his left foreleg, striking off in the new lead.

The next time the hind feet meet the ground, they will have reversed their order, completing the change. Switch your rein aids. The left (inside) rein becomes passive. It's very important not to pull on the horse's mouth with your inside hand during the change. This can result in a conflict of aids, which will confuse and punish the horse. The right rein is active, keeping the horse to the outside of the ring.

If your horse has been brought along slowly, he'll probably perform the flying change the first time you ask him to. Later, he'll do it spontaneously as he reaches the turn on a hunter or jumper course. If his canter is balanced and collected, if he bends properly to the side of the change but then does not change, you can assume that he doesn't yet understand your aids and needs more practice at the basic canter departure from all gaits. Leave the flying change alone for the time being.

If your horse reacts by switching leads in front but not behind, he is not fully obeying the signal from your outside leg. Circle him at the end of the arena to bring his hind legs under his body and collect him. Come out of the circle and approach the wall as you did from the half-circle. Reinforce your outside leg aid by pressing harder this time when you ask for the change of lead at the wall. If this still doesn't work, try a cluck or a tap of the crop behind the girth when you ask with your leg. Work harder at lightening his inside by bending him more before you ask for the change, making it easier for him to switch. If this doesn't produce results either, then your horse simply isn't ready for the exercise.

When your horse is performing the flying change in both directions in response to your aids, you can incorporate the exercise in a varied routine. Because you don't want him to anticipate, don't ask for a flying change every time you change direction. Instead, alternate *counter-cantering* with changes of lead.

Start out at the ordinary canter and then collect your horse. Canter up the long side of the arena. When you reach the end, turn down the center and return to the rail in the opposite direction, but maintain the same lead. Counter-canter the short side. This time, come across the diagonal, which will put you back on the correct lead.

Continue around the short side and do several wide serpentine turns back and forth across the arena to the far end. Vary your routine, counter-cantering some loops, sometimes changing leads. When you reach the other end, proceed around the corner and turn down the center. Return to the long side and change leads. Then let your horse come back to an ordinary canter and rest.

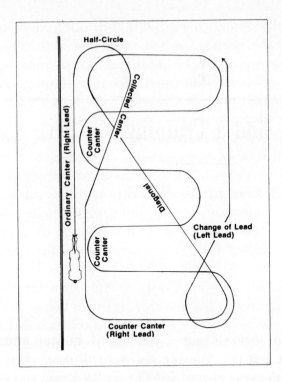

A varied routine.

The Aids

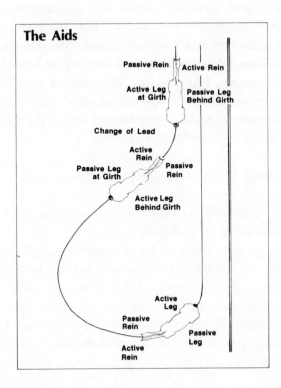

Flying change of lead.

4

When to End a Training Session

Denny Emerson

Like Thoroughbred jockeys, some successful hunter and jumper riders have left the training and schooling of their mounts to others. But every successful Three-Day Event rider has to be a good trainer as well. Denny Emerson is therefore admirably qualified to give advice on when to end a training session, when "more" would be "too much." He was one of the most successful international Eventers during the 1970s, a member of the gold-medal-winning U.S. team at the World Championship in Burghley, England, in 1974 and the 1976 Olympics. A former president of the U.S. Combined Training Association, he continues to train Event horses and riders at his Tamarack Hill Farm in Strafford, Vermont.

I've always felt that the time to end a training session is when you're ahead.

Assuming that the basic principle in training a horse or a rider is to increase ability and confidence gradually, the way to accomplish this is by a systematic series of steps. You must master the basics before moving on to more difficult tasks. So in each day's training session you should try to have certain objectives, set according to the ability, temperament, and training level of the horse concerned. Of course, your long-range objective is to develop a finished performer; but this might be a year away or even longer, whereas your immediate goal in any daily session is to work on the specific problems confronting the horse, the rider, or

Denny Emerson and York jump a cross-country obstacle. Photo: Courtesy of USET

both. When you feel some progress has been made, then I think it's time to quit for the day.

It's so easy to hammer or drill on a horse and, for example, do "just one more fence" and then "just one more" again and again. But you have to force yourself to say, "Okay, he's done it well, so now let's quit. We'll come back to it another time." If you keep on doing "just one more," your horse is going to get tired and uptight, and you'll have a negative school. You'd have been better off if you'd left the horse in the barn that day.

Obviously, you should try to avoid a long, drawn-out fight with a horse. It's always easier to start with baby horses, green horses, three- and four-year-olds, who have not acquired well-established vices. If you're careful, you can usually prevent vices from developing simply by proceeding slowly and methodically during training. However, if you get a horse that simply doesn't want to do something specific, such as jump a certain kind of fence, then I think you have no choice but to fight it out. But once the horse has complied a couple of times and I feel I've broken through his resistance, I'm always quick to reward him and go on to something else.

Of course, you must never ask for too much too soon. Always start with the easiest obstacles and work up slowly to more difficult versions of the same problem. You have to remember that the horse is a rather timid animal who learns through repetition, through practice without mishap. If there's nothing frightening or hurtful about the repetition, the horse will repeat a performance more willingly than if he complied under duress. But if, for no apparent reason, the horse refuses stubbornly to do something, then you've got to stick with it until he does it. When you've forced him to do it once, given him a chance to relax, and then asked for it again and received a willing response, it's time to quit.

When I'm working on the flat, I figure that twenty-five to thirty-five minutes is ample time. I warm up for about five minutes at the walk and a relaxed trot, put the horse to business for a while, walk and unwind a little, put him to business again, walk and unwind a second time, resume work again, and then at a certain point the horse begins to tire. This is the time to stop.

I always start a schooling session with something the horse can do with ease and confidence, introducing anything new toward the end. If the horse gets it even a little bit, I quit. It's often amazing how much better it will be when you go back to it in a day or so. You can't go out and say to yourself, "Today I'm going to teach my horse the shoulder-in," because that's not the way it works with horses. They learn a little bit each day until they're finally able to put it all together, thanks to uneventful repetition. You have to be careful and not let the repetition degenerate into drilling. Some horses can't take that at all. It makes them too fit and wound up.

Nobody can accomplish miracles in a day with any horse, so it's important to end each session on a positive, hopeful note—as important for the horse as for the rider. If you're having trouble with something difficult, by all means end up with something easier that's well done. I think horses don't like to go back to the barn with a feeling of defeat any more than you do.

5

How to Get Your Horse to Accept the Bit

——

Ian Millar

Longtime member of the Canadian Equestrian Team, Ian Millar is one of the perennial leaders in international equestrian ratings and one of the most respected by his peers. Canada's leading jumper rider today, he and his huge yet handy Big Ben won the individual and team gold medals at the 1987 Pan American Games as well as the 1988 World Cup finals at Gothenburg, Sweden. Millar has competed in almost fifty Nations Cups for Canada and has won almost fifty grand prix (including those in New York and Toronto in 1987), eloquent testimony for the soundness of his ideas on riding matters.

When a horse evades my signals by leaning on my hands, opening his mouth, or raising his head, I begin by longeing him to institute a different discipline approach and to encourage suppleness.

Longeing doesn't mean letting the horse careen around at the end of a rope. I work my horses in a longeing cavesson or bridle, side reins, and a saddle. I also use a set of voice commands. I want the horse to function from back to front, so I start with the side reins fairly loose, to encourage him to round his back, reach forward, and seek contact with the bit.

I prefer to use either a thin D-ring snaffle or a plain full-cheek. Fat snaffles and rubber bits are not generally my choice: they tend to encourage the horse to lean a little more than I like—but there are

Ian Millar rides Springer in the 1976 American Gold Cup. Photo: Karl Leck

always exceptions. When I'm approaching a jump, I don't want 1,200 pounds of horse leaning on my hands. A frank contact, yes. Leaning, no!

My object is to get the horse longeing quietly and steadily at the walk and trot, obeying voice commands and keeping contact with the bit through the side reins. For the problem at hand, teaching the horse to canter on the longe isn't necessary and might even be inadvisable in some cases.

When the horse is longeing properly, he's ready for work with a rider. I start with basic transition to sharpen his response to my legs: halt to walk, walk to trot. Forcing the horse into a frame with your hands only makes the resistance worse. The horse's motor is his hindquarters. Control the hindquarters and you control the horse.

I've found that a horse will seek contact on his own very quickly as long as the hands remain quiet and sympathetic. But if the hands try to take over the work of the legs or if they are unsteady or unfeeling, the horse usually resists in one way or another.

As I work on moving the horse forward from my leg and seat and smoothing his transitions, I incorporate a turn-on-the-forehand exercise. I halt him squarely and keep his head and neck straight; then I use my left leg just behind the girth to move his hindquarters to the right. I practice the exercise until he moves away from my leg readily in either direction. At this point, I'm using the turn on the forehand as a leg-yielding exercise to get him working more from my seat and leg and less from my hands.

When the horse is responding to my leg aids, I urge him forward in a steady, active posting trot, take a light feel of his mouth, and attempt to put him in the beginning of a frame. The object here is to establish a light but frank contact with his mouth, encouraging him to seek his own balance. If he hurries, stiffens, or leans on my hands, I go to a sitting trot on a circle.

The circle is my favorite training aid for a horse that resists my hands. On a straight line, a stubborn horse can set his jaw and plough forward; but the circle limits his speed and forces him to bend. It's an excellent remedy for stiffness because it loosens the horse's back and strengthens his hindquarters. As the horse becomes more supple, he'll start to accept a soft contact with my hands and wait for my signals.

When the horse is working in the desired frame of legs, seat, and hands, I increase the size of the circle, eventually moving to a straight line. If he stiffens or resists, I go back to the circle as a discipline and a means of reestablishing suppleness and yielding more through a response to my legs and seat, and less through my hands. Once I control the hind end, I'll be able to control the front.

6

Putting a Horse in a Frame:
What Does It Mean and How Do You Do It?

Rodney Jenkins and Bernie Traurig

When this question was put to Bertalan de Némethy, then coach of the USET, his immediate reaction was one of elegant irritation: "The phrase 'putting a horse in a frame' is not a proper horseman's expression," he said. "What people really mean is probably 'putting the horse on the bit.' This is the proper expression. Calling it a 'frame' just makes it complicated and confusing, when there are perfectly clear expressions for riding situations and feelings that have been in use for hundreds of years. To invent new ones is merely pretentious."

Basically, Bert is certainly right—as usual. But the fact remains that the expression has become a part of the serious horseman's vocabulary today and therefore merits explanation. Here are the interpretations of two of the outstanding jumper and hunter riders of our time, Rodney Jenkins and Bernie Traurig.

Rodney Jenkins

When we talk about putting a horse in a frame, I think we mean getting the horse to carry himself in a good balance, getting him to carry himself with his hind end, off his hocks, rather than on his forehand. Frame is how a horse gets to the fence. It's what makes him jump well. Basically,

Rodney Jenkins and the legendary Idle Dice. Photo: Karl Leck

we do it by holding the horse together with the hands and driving forward with the legs, pressing the horse's hind legs under him.

The picture I have in my own mind of a horse "in a frame" is a horse that carries his head with his chin a wee bit flexed, his hocks well up under him carrying his body, his front legs moving from the shoulder, his back relaxed and up under the rider on a smooth, flowing stride.

My idea of a frame might differ from other people's in that they might use more mouth contact than I do. I use lower leg and seat contact to get the frame, rather than using the reins and pulling on the mouth.

You teach a horse to go in a frame by doing a lot of flat work, bending the horse, getting him well broken in the bridle so that the aids mean something to him. A horse that is well broken in the bridle has a nice soft responsive mouth, gets balanced right away when you take hold of his mouth, instead of just lugging. With an unbalanced horse, you put him into the bridle and all he does is get on his forehand by pulling you.

Flat work is very good for building a horse's muscle tone and for his general state of mind. But when you get into jumping, it's a different ball game. No horse works on the flat like he jumps fences. The horse tenses up and the rider tenses up.

For a horse that is reluctant to come together, I'd try longeing in a bitting rig for an hour or so a day rather than risk losing your temper by riding him. Let him work it out for himself rather than have the rider do it for him. For a horse that is basically strong and strung out, I think cavalletti are good. They keep his mind on the ground and make him pull himself together. He's too busy with this to think of getting nervous and strong.

The various types of equipment people use on horses are only as good as the rider using them. Equipment can't help somebody who can't ride and won't hurt somebody who can. Draw reins, gag bits, various martingales—all of these can work if they're in the right hands. But I've seen a lot of people using draw reins, for example, thinking they're collecting the horse when they're really putting him on his forehand.

The most useful things to start off with are the bitting rig, cavalletti, and, of course, work on the basic leg aids. But different horses need different things. I wouldn't suggest a training method for a particular horse without riding him first.

Bernie Traurig

First of all, I don't like the word "frame." I picture a very rigid, stiff horse, forced into an uncomfortable position by a demanding and forceful rider. I think there must be a combination of words to describe frame better, such as balance, head carriage, and suppleness, all of which lead to getting the horse into the frame specifics.

The key word is "balance." It's something you're born with. We can improve it a bit, but it's certainly a natural talent I look for in a young horse. We've all had two- or three-year-olds that could canter around a teacup, and six-year-olds that couldn't canter around a football field. Balance is at the top of my list.

I'd prefer to buy a horse that carries his head and neck in a natural position or fairly close to it. But if necessary, head carriage can be developed a lot more successfully than balance in a basically unbalanced horse. The elevation of the neck varies with different horses and certainly differs between hunters and jumpers. Usually a bad head-and-neck carriage is the result of some kind of stiffness in the horse's mouth. This leads us to suppleness.

Suppleness, in my opinion, is the most important goal of flat training and the final touch required for achieving a frame. I try to develop a very soft mouth with a relaxed jaw that yields to the slightest pressure

Bernie Traurig schools on the flat. Photo: *Practical Horseman*

on the reins, either direct or indirect. I try to make the horse extremely supple laterally so that he will bend correctly through corners with the slightest indirect rein. I like to be able to regulate the angle of the nose and elevate the neck, sometimes to extremes, and then be able to drop the reins and have everything fall back into a normal position.

I favor a thin D-ring snaffle for most horses. I like to use draw reins for showing the way to a green horse or refreshing a made horse. However, as soon as the horse gets the idea, I loosen the draw reins and ride off on the snaffle rein. This is very important, because too often when you've been riding on the draw reins and not the snaffle reins, you're back where you started from when the draw reins come off.

To sum up, the frame I strive for is a well-trained, supple, balanced horse, carrying his head and neck in a natural, comfortable position.

7

How to Teach Your Horse to Halt

Judy Richter

Since "how-to" is virtually synonymous with "practical," it is only natural that a how-to article, presenting a reader's horse problem to a panel of experts, should be a regular feature of *Practical Horseman*. In this case, the expert is Judy Richter, who has been involved with horses all her life. Her father, Philip Hofmann, was a prominent jumper owner, a racing and coaching enthusiast. Her sister, Carol Hofmann Thompson, is a former member of the USET. Judy herself, AHSA Horsewoman of the Year in 1974, runs Coker Farm in Bedford, New York, a training facility that turns out Medal and Maclay qualifiers and accounts for major show championships in the Hunter, Equitation, and Jumper divisions every year. Here is her advice to the young owner of a six-year-old Thoroughbred bought off the track for local hunter shows who was a willing jumper but a nonstopper once he got rolling.

You're right not to tug back at your horse when he pulls, and your method of aiming for the wall (which, as you say, will never win ribbons) is still better than letting him run away with you. But if you teach your horse to respond correctly to your slowing aids, he won't get away from you in the first place.

Begin by teaching him to halt properly from the walk. Merely pulling on the reins won't work. You have to push the horse forward onto the bit or he won't respond to the pressure in his mouth. When you ask for a halt, plant your seatbones firmly in the saddle and brace your back so you don't get pulled forward. Then close your fingers on the reins and your legs on his sides. When he halts, reward him by relaxing your fingers. Don't let your horse move until you signal him forward with a slight increase in leg pressure.

Always use exactly the same aids for halt, no matter which gait you're making the transition from: close fingers and legs together, sit deep in the saddle, and brace your back. When your horse responds willingly at the walk, move into a slow sitting trot and ask for a halt. Next, stop from a normal-speed posting trot. If you do your preparatory work, practicing halting from walk and trot, canter-to-halt transitions shouldn't be any more difficult. To keep your horse balanced and submissive, you'll have to continue practicing downward transitions no matter where your horse is in his schooling.

If your horse still runs away with you, go ahead and use the wall to stop him, but remember to apply your slowing aids as well. He'll learn to respond to the aids only if you're consistent in using them every time you stop him, by whatever means.

If you're out in the open and cannot stop, a pulley rein should help. Take a short hold on one rein and brace that hand on the horse's neck by planting your thumb on one side of the crest and your fingers on the other. Pull straight back firmly with your other hand, rocking your upper body back behind the vertical to give you extra leverage. Use your seat and leg aids in conjunction with the pulley rein. Even in an emergency, your signals should be consistent.

8

Retraining a Retired Racehorse

Betty Oare

An expert rider, trainer, judge, and long a leading competitor in the Hunter Division, Betty Oare is the daughter of eminent horseman J. Arthur Reynolds (who contributed the fruits of his vast experience to this article); the wife of Ernie Oare (proprietor of E.M.O. Stables in Middleburg, Virginia, where he works with point-to-point, flat, and steeplechase horses as well as two-year-olds in training for the Thoroughbred sales); and the mother of two small sons who joined her on the horse-show circuit showing in lead-line and Pony Division classes. Betty and her Thoroughbred Spirit of Song won the Amateur-Owner Division championship at Madison Square Garden in 1983, when she also judged the Maclay finals and where she has ridden or judged every year since 1955.

Not all of the many Thoroughbreds that are put into racing training every year are successful. Some retire early because they lack sufficient speed, and some because they suffer aches and pains. Some never even race. Many of these horses can go on to a second career as useful pleasure horses: show horses, field hunters, or simply nice horses to hack across country with friends. Through years of trial and error, I've learned that it doesn't have to be a difficult transition, as long as the rider gives his horse the time needed to make the gradual progression from one world to the other. Many of the horses I've worked with and shown have been former racehorses that have made the transition successfully.

These are the principles that govern the way in which I take a horse through that transition until he is ready to take me on relaxing cross-country hacks or to compete in local shows.

If a horse is fresh off the track when you get him, you'll have to "let him down" before he'll be safe to ride. He'll need a month or two to come down from his high level of fitness and to take the edge off his excitability. You'll have to reorganize his surroundings, his routine, even his diet. In order to do so successfully, I always follow the method

Betty Oare is an expert in converting ex-racehorses, like this one, into good hunters. Photo: *Practical Horseman*

developed by my father, J. Arthur Reynolds, who has been buying horses from the racetrack and letting them down since before I was born. This can be summarized in the following points:

1. Stable your new horse where he can watch what's going on and preferably between two fairly quiet neighbors that follow the same schedule he does. He's used to track routine: a high level of activity up and down the shedrows from very early morning until about 10 A.M. and then quiet until the midafternoon feeding. It may take him a while to get used to the all-day activity of a hunter or pleasure barn.

2. Put him on a diet that will fill out his streamlined body to the well-rounded contours suited to slower, more sustained exertions. Start him on no more than 8 quarts of grain a day, half sweet feed and half crimped oats (which are digested easily and are better for his health than rolled oats)—2 quarts in the morning, 2 at noon, and 4 at night—plus all the hay he can eat. Hay will replace the rest of the grain ration he's been used to getting and help him put on weight without fueling his energy production.

He may go off his feed at first. Remove any uneaten portion of grain and cut back his ration for the next meal to an amount you estimate he'll eat. When he cleans up that amount, you can increase his ration half a quart at a time until you reach the amounts suggested. If he hardly touches his feed at all, try dividing the grain between two buckets and placing them in different parts of the stall.

Over the first couple of weeks, the extra hay your horse is eating will expand his intake capacity, which in turn will create more appetite. Encourage this with nutritious, tasty, high-protein alfalfa and clover hay, and keep fresh water in front of him at all times.

3. Within the first week, have your veterinarian check your horse's general health, including his teeth, and begin a regular six-week worming schedule. If the horse has some lumps and bumps you'd like to erase, ask the vet if these will respond to a light blister that you can paint on and leave uncovered for ten days, leave off for ten days, and apply again for a further ten days.

4. Have your farrier remove the horse's racing plates, trim and balance his feet, and fit him with normal lightweight hunter shoes.

5. When you groom him, remember that crossties are probably a new experience for him. Most racehorses are tied with a single shank to a ring in the stall wall for grooming. The first time you put him in crossties, make sure there's a wall behind him to keep him from backing away far enough to break the ties—and thereby discover that he *can* break them!

6. Turn the horse out as soon as you feel he's reasonably settled. But

take precautions. Put boots on him, front and back, so that he won't hurt himself if he plays hard. Hand-walk him for fifteen to twenty minutes to be sure he's really quiet. Then put him in a small paddock or round ring that doesn't give him much room to run, but leave his halter on when you unsnap the lead shank, to make it easier to catch him.

7. When you start riding your horse, perhaps one or two months after his arrival, you can begin to increase his grain, half a quart at a time, until you reach a total ration of 4 quarts in the morning and 6 at night. Let his personality be your guide in timing this increase. If he's basically quiet, you can work up to this amount over the next two or three months; if he's the anxious type, you'll have to make the increase more slowly.

8. Give your horse time and attention to help him settle. If he turns his quarters toward you when you enter his stall, he's probably showing apprehension rather than bad temper. Talk quietly to him as you stretch out your arm and give his quarters a gentle push to the side, keeping your body out of range of his legs. When he turns enough for you to reach his halter, do so quietly; don't lunge at him. If you spend a few minutes every day just handling him and talking quietly, he'll quickly come to trust you.

9. While you're letting your horse down according to my father's routine, use the time to study his behavior. Later, when you ride him, you'll be able to react much more appropriately to his actions if you have an understanding of his basic personality. Observe him in his stall and note whether noises and activity disturb him unduly. If he's easily upset in the barn, make a mental note to go very slowly and quietly with him in his training. Remember to be sympathetic to behavior that might ordinarily seem like stubborn resistance. Watch how he reacts when you enter his stall, put on his halter, lead him through the barn, and stand him in crossties. If new events unsettle him, try introducing them in more gradual stages. If this approach works in the barn, it will probably work later on when you ride him.

10. Take this opportunity to study his conformation—especially with regard to the way it might limit his performance—so that when you ride, you won't expect more of him than he's physically capable of doing. If his shoulder is upright, it may prevent his having a really long stride. If his pasterns are upright, his gait may always be a little rough and choppy. If his neck is set on "upside down" (that is, with a downward curve at the crest), he'll be harder to flex than a horse whose topline rounds upward from withers to poll.

Betty Oare and her father, the eminent trainer J. Arthur Reynolds, practice what they preach: "As soon as you feel you have enough control, start going for short rides outside the ring in the company of a more experienced horse. Let your horse follow, unless following makes him anxious. If so, let him get his head in front, but don't move so far ahead that you lose the calming influence the other horse provides." Photo: *Practical Horseman*

11. Observe him in the paddock. The way he goes when he's loose gives you an indication of the ability he has to start with and the development he needs. Watch how he stops from a fast trot or canter. If he's naturally well balanced, his stride will remain rhythmic and he'll keep his hind legs under his body as he comes smoothly to a stop. If he travels with a long, fluid stride, you'll know that his basic movement is good, even though it may be months before he's able to go smoothly under a rider.

The ground rules that govern my reeducation program after this preliminary adaptation period can be summarized in the following basic points:

1. When you begin riding, turn out your horse before each ride so that he will be relaxed and listen to you. If you ride him straight out of the barn, you'll have to spend the first half hour just taking the edge off

him. The extra riding time will make him feel fitter than he needs to be and harder to ride.

2. Let your horse's ability tell you how fast to progress. You might need two months or even more merely to complete the first lesson of stabilizing the walk and trot. On the other hand, if your horse adapts easily, you might progress through this work in less than a week. But even if he's a quick learner, give him plenty of practice time to make the lessons stick.

3. Each day be a little firmer about everything you do. If your horse walks off while you are mounting on the second day, let him go for two or three strides. Then bring him back to a halt and make him stand for a moment before asking him to walk off again.

4. Plan each day's ride, making it a point to include plenty of variety in your work. Riding different patterns, going over poles, and taking short hacks outside the ring will help keep your horse's mind fresh. But don't be a slave to a plan, and don't try to force your horse to follow a timetable. Be observant of him and receptive to what he's telling you about his progress and his problems. Give him a chance to show you how *he* wants to go.

5. Limit your schooling sessions to about thirty minutes. Not only do you want to prevent your horse from getting too fit, but you also want to avoid boring him. Don't drill on any one exercise for more than ten minutes. Break up demanding work with quiet walks on a relaxed rein.

6. Use ordinary hunter aids. Even though your horse was schooled to a different set of signals at the track, he was probably broken to the same aids you use. If you reintroduce the aids gradually, you'll find his early lessons coming back to him.

7. Make relaxation your main goal, and be content with modest progress. If you don't force your horse to slow to a hunter pace all at once, he'll slow himself down as he accepts his new life.

8. Finesse problems, especially in the early stages, rather than tackling them head-on. Often, if you ignore a problem and just "ride through it," you'll find that it disappears of its own accord. There'll be problems that you will eventually have to confront and correct. But give your horse a chance to correct them himself first.

9. Your horse will learn by repetition. At first, when you give an aid, he may not know exactly what response you seek. Don't demand a response by escalating to a harsher aid; just try again. You may have to repeat the aid again and again over many days or weeks until your horse gradually comes to understand what you want.

10. Appreciate your horse's point of view. He has already received

one education: he learned how to be a racehorse. Behavior that would seem unusual in the horses you're used to may be perfectly acceptable under the rules he has been taught. You'll have a much more positive, constructive attitude toward your horse and his progress if you realize that you're simply replacing a specialized education with a more generalized one.

11. Finally, after each session, think back over your ride and use what you have seen and felt to form the plan for the next day's work.

II

Hunter Seat Equitation

1

The Best Seat for Hunter Equitation

Paul Valliere

A highly successful trainer of riders as well as of hunters and jumpers at his Acres Wild Farm in North Smithfield, Rhode Island, Paul Valliere seldom sees his students or his horses leave a show without an impressive collection of ribbons.

Paul's show barn is one of the largest in the country as well as one of the most diverse, with students ranging from novices to advanced riders, horses from the green hunter division to grand prix level. Noted for his knack for matching horse and rider, he has trained numerous Maclay winners.

Between shows, Paul judges and gives clinics. When he's at home, he finds time to work on a breeding plan to produce homegrown top jumper prospects and on a book about teaching riding.

To win in hunter seat equitation, you must sit tightly in the saddle, with your inner seat bones just touching the seat near the pommel. You'll open your hip angle so that you will not get out in front of the motion, but you'll keep your seat clear of the back of the saddle. Your horse should look as if he's traveling forward freely, not as if you're driving him forward with your seatbones and back. A full driving seat would put you slightly behind the motion—fine for schooling greenies but not the free-flowing effect you want to achieve with your made equitation horse.

Even if you don't have the long, lean, leggy conformation to make a classic rider, you can learn to sit correctly, with a straight line connecting your shoulders, hips, and heels. Adjust your stirrups so they hang ½ to 1 inch below your ankle bones. This will give your leg a long, elegant look but still let you put your weight in your heels. Let your lower leg hang naturally just behind the girth and your toes rotate outward slightly at a natural angle. With your calf in position and the right amount of weight in your heels, your soles will be just visible from the side.

Apply steady leg pressure—it's a matter of pounds, but how many pounds depends on your horse—throughout the length of your calf. This will give your leg a firm appearance. Don't grip or pinch with your knee: you'll shorten the look of your leg and undermine your security.

Keep your back flat but natural, and hold your shoulders parallel to your horse's shoulders, turning when he turns, so that your inside shoulder travels a little behind the other one. Feel your collar with the back of your neck to remind yourself to keep your eyes up. If you look at the ground, your whole body will pitch forward and spoil the picture.

Your horse should accept full contact—no slack in the reins—and raise his poll above his withers by rounding the muscles that run from his shoulder up his neck. If your horse is a little strong, you'll have to carry

Paul Valliere advises his students on strategy and warns them of pitfalls before an important Equitation class. Photo: James Leslie Parker

extra weight in the reins; but you can camouflage the effect by bringing your elbows back slightly while you give half-halts with both hands.

To find the correct position for your hands, place your knuckles on the withers and then raise your hands to bit level. They should be about 4 inches apart, with a straight line from bit to elbow and your thumbs angled in a little.

It's easy to see from this informal picture why Hollywood studios once tried to lure George Morris into a film career. But he preferred riding to acting and has become a superstar of the horse-show world. Photo: Courtesy of George Morris

2

Jumping Clinic

George Morris

Ever since the inaugural issue of *Practical Horseman* in January 1973, George Morris's "Jumping Clinic" has been one of its most popular features. Hundreds of riders have sent in photos to be judged by his critical eye; countless more have been influenced by the riding principles he advocates. Many of the leading riders in the show ring today are his former pupils or pupils of his former pupils.

George is a perfectionist in every phase of the equestrian art: not only riding and training, but also turnout, tack, stable management, horse care, personal behavior, and style. Some of his students are terrified by the effort he demands, most are in awe of him, and many are subjugated by his charisma. All of them will tell you that it wasn't easy to be a Morris pupil. But results speak for themselves: four of the five members of the gold-medal–winning U.S. Olympic jumping team in 1984 had studied with Morris; and the four riders on the all-woman Nations Cup team at the 1986 Washington, D.C., International (Anne Kursinski, Katharine Burdsall, Lisa Tarnopol, and Katie Monahan, with George the *chef d'équipe*) were all former students of his. (They won.)

In the photographs sent to *Practical Horseman* every month for his appraisal, George usually finds something to criticize. Perhaps some riders and readers have wondered if a jumping photograph exists that could "stump the expert." Why not

one of the Horse Master himself? True to form, George still finds something to criticize!

I am criticizing a picture of myself. In this particular case, the style is not textbook perfect, but from a realistic point of view, the riding is good.

Starting from the leg position, which is what I usually do, the position is exemplary. The stirrup iron is perfectly placed on the ball of the foot, with the little toe touching the outside branch of the stirrup. There is a consistent contact down through the thigh, the inner knee bone, and the calf of the leg. All in all, it is a leg that demonstrates security as well as softness.

Now on up to the base of support—the thighs and seat. In this picture, the buttocks are too far out of the saddle. This is often the case when

Turning the tables on himself, George Morris submitted this photo for criticism. Photo: Rose

Rose/81

jumping bigger fences with shortened stirrups. However, to be absolutely correct, the hip angle should close and the seat be only slightly out of the tack.

My upper body is also slightly at fault. There is a slight "roach" (rounded back) in my lower back. This is also a common practice when jumping bigger fences with a shorter stirrup. Nonetheless, while it is a soft and supple form fault, it must be pointed out.

In this photo, I particularly like my hands and arms. This is an example of a short release, maintaining a soft contact through the arms (an automatic release would be a step further, maintaining a perfectly straight arm from elbow to the horse's mouth).

The horse is jumping well, although he tends to be a bit of a "splinter-bellied" jumper—that is, he doesn't bring his body up high enough. He almost rubs the rails with his belly! The stretch of his head and neck is beautiful, and he uses his legs magnificently.

While this is a casual picture of an open jumper at a summer show, nonetheless everything is spit-and-polish and clean. That is what counts. One does not have to be artifically "too perfect" to be well turned out. In fact, in the show ring of today, some of the casual elegance of yesteryear is missing.

3

Training Winning Riders

Bill Cooney and Frank Madden

Bill Cooney and Frank Madden were directing the equitation, junior, and amateur hunter activities at George Morris's Hunterdon when, at the beginning of 1984, George decided to devote his efforts (and his premises) to his first love, show jumping. Whereupon Bill and Frank struck out on their own, establishing a training stable, Beacon Hill, now located in Colts Neck, New Jersey.

Success was immediate and stunning: at the end of the first year, Beacon Hill riders won the Equitation Triple Crown (the USET Medal, the AHSA Medal, and the Maclay) thanks to Jenno Topping and to Francesca Mazella's "double"; and the feat was repeated in 1986 by Neil Ashe, Mia Wood, and Scott Hofstetter. This is their own account written in 1984 of how the Cooney–Madden system functions at home and at the shows.

People may be attracted to our barn by our track record for turning out winning horses and riders, but soon after new clients arrive, they learn that to be a good rider, like a good dancer or any other kind of athlete, takes a lot of time and a lot of effort. The key to the program is commitment. There's the financial commitment, of course, but what really counts is the personal commitment of the people who come here to learn and, on our end, discipline, dedication, care for horses, and attention to detail. These are the things, we think, that turn out winning riders.

Frank Madden and Bill Cooney (in the background) brief a group of students in the equitation finals. Photo: James Leslie Parker

The Riders

The best time for us to take on a new rider is right after the Garden, when we have the winter to get started. Before we take on someone new, we meet with them to get a basic feeling for what their interests are and what their direction is. To run our kind of program well, we have to limit the number of our clients. During 1983, for example, we had about eight in-barn clients with twenty horses altogether and a group of people who stabled outside our barn but followed our schedule and met us at the shows.

The most important consideration—more than innate talent—is the prospective client's desire to learn. Gifted riders aren't always the hardest workers, because things come so easily for them. We've had many extremely talented riders who continued to reach and grow, but we've taken on some rather ordinary riders who turned out to be very successful competitors because they were superb students. We feel that we can take the average rider and, as long as he or she is disciplined and extremely committed, we can supply the technical background necessary to compete against anyone.

We accept junior riders as young as twelve, and we've taken people in their last year of showing in the juniors; but the best time to arrive here is between the ages of fourteen and seventeen. We wouldn't take a beginner, but we'd take a novice or intermediate rider with some mileage at the shows. Of course, there's good mileage and there's bad mileage; we look favorably on the young rider who's been given good basics by their present trainer and now is interested in building on that.

Many of the people who come to us already know us from the show circuit, others by reputation. Either way, the initial meeting gives us a chance to make clear at the outset what kind of operation we run. It's pretty strict here, and it's not for everyone. At the first meeting, we tell new clients what we expect. We expect discipline, we expect attendance, and we expect them to follow directions.

We're geared to people who are very serious about learning. And there's the financial side too. An average month with training, lessons,

Cooney-Madden student Stacia Klein from Indiana was winner of the ASPCA Maclay finals in 1987.
Photo: James Leslie Parker

board, shoeing, and care, including maintenance vet work, costs $2,000 to $2,500 and a little less for the second horse. That doesn't include vanning and entry fees. Some people save on expense by keeping their horses at home; they meet us at the shows, and we help them there for $50 a day—the price of a lesson—but naturally we can't prepare them in the same way we prepare our in-house clients.

The Horses

We want to go to shows with top horses, and we want horses that can play a part in our riders' development. But we don't tell every client to buy a new horse. The horse the client has may serve a purpose; it may be a reliable old campaigner the rider can have lessons on and go to shows with more often than with a top horse. So we keep the horse and work with it.

After the rider has been with us for a while, we can get a more objective feeling for what would be the ideal horse for him. We're always wanting to upgrade, but it's a bit like buying a teenager a first car: you want something dependable, something he can make mistakes with, because mistakes are part of growth. Later you might buy something a bit nicer, but it may be a few years before you buy a Jaguar.

Because so many horses are specialists, a lot of our riders keep two or three. Many of the best hunters aren't used for equitation classes. If you can only afford one horse, you want one that's versatile, that can do the equitation and win a good ribbon in the hunters on his day. But if you have to make a choice between divisions, we'll steer you toward equitation, because it teaches you all three disciplines: hunter, equitation, and jumper. And if you really have the desire, we'll give you lessons on school horses to extend your riding time.

Just as commitment is the most important quality in the rider, personality is the most important quality in the horse. When we're looking for a horse for a client, we take into consideration the rider's conformation but also whether the personalities of the two will complement each other, depending on whether the rider tends to be soft or strong. And, of course, we have to take into account the financial commitment the parents want to make.

Horses are exorbitantly priced because there are so very few special ones. To buy a horse that will take you to the Garden, you'll have to spend between $50,000 and $150,000. For a horse like Dillon or Charge a Count, you have to be talking well over $100,000, and you're still not guaranteed to win because *you* could blow it. But up in this price range, at least you're guaranteed that the horse isn't going to let you down.

Sometimes you come across a horse that isn't outrageously priced. Playing Games was one of these. When we bought him for one of our best junior riders, Lisa Tarnapol, we gambled. He was a relative unknown, but Lisa had the style and presence it takes to get a green horse across at the major shows, and she was willing to put in the work. Now Playing Games's price has soared over the $150,000 mark.

Getting Started

We follow a yearly plan that's developed for each rider, and it's thought out down to the day. We begin by dividing the year into quarters. The first quarter is Florida: we close up shop here on January 1 and don't come back north until April 1. The second quarter takes us through the Children's Services and Devon shows. The third quarter is probably the most spur-of-the-moment of the four: horses that are already qualified for the indoor shows get a month or six weeks of rest. Meanwhile, we try to tie up loose ends and get everyone else qualified. The indoor shows make up the fourth quarter.

The Maclay finals are on a Sunday, the last day of the National Horse Show in New York. So our "new year" begins on Monday morning with a list of the horses and riders that now face changes. Horses whose riders have finished their last junior year must be sold, and new partnerships put together.

We sit down with each client and map out a schedule for the coming year. We have goals for every horse and rider; one of our goals is to have all our junior riders qualify for the equitation finals. Now we plan the adjustments we think will be necessary to make our goals realistic. This includes not only the shows we expect to go to but some time off for the horse. With all the qualifying a horse has to do today to get to the indoor shows, it's absolutely necessary to find some time to give him a rest.

The schedules are flexible at this point: one rider may qualify sooner than we expected, or a horse may have a good season and be able to take time off, to be turned out for two or three weeks. We reevaluate and adjust the schedules at the end of each quarter. Our individual clients have only themselves to think of. But we're thinking of fifteen or twenty people, including those who stable outside. Scheduling them all involves a lot of work.

Another gifted Cooney-Madden pupil, Lisa Tindall, rides Cadenza in the 1987 Kent School Horse Show. Photo: James Leslie Parker

Before the Florida circuit, we decide how a rider should be mounted and what he or she should be doing to prepare for Florida. The experienced horses and riders, those who are in the groove, can afford time off. For them, getting ready for Florida centers mainly on the horse's fitness. Three to four weeks before we ship, the horse is put in light work—walk and trot thirty to forty minutes four days a week. For new clients, lessons are usually the top priority. Some riders might need to get a Medal or Maclay win before leaving, because in Florida they'll face tougher, more seasoned competition than they will locally.

The typical schedule for a junior rider is two or three lessons a week and a horse show a month. One lesson might be on the flat; one on a school horse; and one on their own horse, over fences, right before the show. No one, however often he comes out, rides his own horse every day; we won't do that to the horses. The horses that have been to Florida and are in the groove never jump until they get to the show.

A lesson is an hour to an hour and a half, depending on the size of the group. For one rider alone, forty-five minutes to an hour is enough for the horse. We prefer group lessons though, because we believe the riders learn through observation and that the group creates a certain amount of competitiveness, which is healthy. Early in the year, we start gearing the riders' thinking toward the competitive option. We set up a line, and we give them a situation such as this: "Pretend you're at the in-gate before a class. There's a broken line to be done in seven strides with an option of the direct forward six. The six would win. Figure it out."

They learn to evaluate the option themselves, so when we're standing at a real in-gate, we look them in the eye and they look back, and we know it's going to work for them.

There are regular times for lessons: 11, 12:30, 3, 4:30. These are fixed times, no maybes. For someone coming after school from far away, we'll schedule an extra lesson at 6 P.M. It's hard on the grooms, but if the rider can make it, we can make it. We'll make time for whomever makes time for themselves.

Lessons consist of a lot of slow work, especially with young riders: work on a longe line to improve the seat, lots of work over cavalletti and low jumps, walking, trotting, cantering with and without stirrups to improve security. We work with basics, trying to improve the rider's foundation and build habits so that when they get to a show, they will only have to warm up. There's no such thing as a lesson at a horse show. If they've been well taught, they study the course, make a plan, and ride it to the best of their ability.

We have a set number of weeks before we leave for Florida to take a new horse and rider and put them together as a team. We want the new riders to spend as much time as they can with us, getting familiar with our system and picking up habits. They learn to be here on time and how to act in the barn and toward our staff. We want them to show up turned out for a riding lesson: neat, with a hard hat and either chaps and paddock boots or breeches and boots. They don't come in jeans and sneakers, with a pair of spurs over the sneakers. The habits carry over to their riding: when they're on their horses, they do as they're told. It all becomes one.

Once a rider has been with us for a few weeks, we can see the level of their commitment. For example, if someone has a weight problem, the first measure of their desire will be whether or not they lose weight. We also encourage them to ride on their own. They have to develop the ability to think on their own because when they get in the ring, they're all by themselves.

The Show Schedule

Florida is an example of how individual circumstances affect our schedules. It's only January, but we're aiming for the fall shows, thinking of them already. We normally do nine Florida shows in two months—two precircuit shows and the seven circuit shows. The one-horse rider has to economize. This horse might not do any precircuit shows, do the three Palm Beach shows, skip Ocala, do the two Tampa shows, and Jacksonville. The rider might skip some open equitation classes and concentrate on the USET, Medal, and Maclay, playing the hunters by

The gold medal Francesca Mazella is wearing is one awarded to the winner of the Maclay by the National Horse Show. The year was 1984, when Francesca, coached by Bill and Frank, scored a rare "double" by also winning the USET Medal finals. Photo: Budd

ear. For riders with more than one horse, we'd set up a schedule that was similar for each horse, depending on what that horse was up to doing.

Some of our people have tutors and stay down with us for the whole circuit. This is marvelous because they get a lot of exposure watching other good riders and professionals, and they have plenty of time with us and in the barn with their horses. About half of our riders stay in school and commute down on weekends, which isn't easy. We work the horses for them, and we might have a lesson Saturday morning for the riders who arrived Friday night; we'd be out there at 5:30 A.M. and the first class might be the USET at 8.

The riders are good about staying in touch, finding out what time we want them at the show, for example. If they don't talk to us, they check the work list, which is always posted the day before they ride. We try to give the young teenagers goals and responsibilities, but you can't want success for them; they have to want it for themselves.

After Florida, the two of us may split up and go to different circuits from April to June. We may decide to keep our more qualified horses at different shows from our greener ones. If we all go to the same shows, our riders are competing against each other. We don't worry so much about the riders who are in their last few years and are sure to qualify. But if the younger riders or the people with new horses go on a circuit where there's a softer touch, they can get more done.

Our choice of shows depends partly on logistics. We'd rather go to a show that's ten minutes from our barn than one that's half a day away. With both groups of riders though, we stick to the A shows. Sometimes there are thirty or forty people in the Medal and Maclay classes, and that's not easy with a young rider.

There are some shows that we all go to as a barn: Farmington, Connecticut, Devon, Pennsylvania, Southampton, New York, and Fairfield, Connecticut, for example. Otherwise, the schedules depend on where the horses and riders stand after Florida.

After Devon, at the end of the second quarter, we sit down and re-do each schedule, evaluating our progress to that point. One rider might need only one Maclay; others might need three and consequently have to go to more shows. We try to give the riders who are qualified and whose horses can be turned out for several weeks a nice summer with special clinics taught by top trainers from other disciplines. We'd give them some different work at home, such as schooling over natural fences, to broaden the base of their riding. We've had Jessica Ransehousen come to Hunterdon for dressage clinics, for example, and this is the sort of thing we'd like to do more of.

For the ones who haven't qualified, the third quarter can mean a lot of traveling around. They have to be ready to drop everything and go after the qualifying points and ribbons to reach the goals they set at the beginning of the year. We have two groups and we interchange: one of us takes a group to a major show, while the other goes to some smaller shows, and then we'll switch.

Before we know it, we're indoors for the fourth-quarter shows: Harrisburg, Washington, New York. We can't remember a year in which we haven't had about twenty qualified for these shows, and that takes work. Anybody can get two or three riders qualified, but twenty is a lot. Still, there have been times when our riders have gotten up to the wire and had to choose, for example, between continuing in the hunter division, where they had a chance of winning, or pushing for that last Maclay. Sometimes going after the Medal or Maclay is the wrong decision, because of the wear and tear it imposes on the horse.

Behind the Scenes

It's important to us that our riders understand what we're doing in terms of teaching, training, and caring for their horses. And from the floor up, the most important ingredient is the horse. One judge told us last year, "When your horses come in, the ring lights up." It's true that the horses look marvelous and are beautifully cared for.

Marion Hulick is with us now as an adviser in matters of care, selection, and training. Both of us have always respected her for the way her horses were presented. There was no such thing as a hose in her barn; her horses had a three-bucket bath, and the water was heated. They were covered, even in summer, with a Baker blanket and a sheet so that their coats would be perfect. The braid jobs were perfect, and they looked perfect. Marion was with us in Florida. One of the grooms said, "This horse is still shedding; what should I do?" And she said, "Keep on currying until there's no more hair coming out." The groom was there for two hours!

We have four full-time grooms for twenty horses, plus Debbie White, who manages the barn and pretty much runs the show as far as organizing the equipment, feed, bedding, and the like is concerned. We have other people who meet us at shows to groom, so on the road each groom has only three horses.

We prepare a work list and post it every night to let the grooms know which horses they should have ready in the morning. The work for each horse is based on his overall schedule. We start out with the year, break it down into months and weeks, and then work out the days. Most of our top horses don't go to more than fifteen or twenty shows a year. Others have to go more often, through lack of experience or because the rider needs Medals or Maclays. But except for the horse whose rider needs that last qualifying class, we try to give them all the month of August off, and most of them are also off in November and December, after the indoor shows. Only the ones that need work are kept on a light schedule. We also try to let them down before important shows like Devon so that they'll be as fresh as possible.

A horse might be off one week, work lightly on three days the next week, and the following week work three days in preparation for a show. While he's in work, he's ridden three days a week on the flat (one of them in the country) and turned out every day. He's not galloped or jumped. We do all the training ourselves because we want to know how each horse feels physically and mentally and because we want them to work a specific amount of time: if it's thirty minutes, then we want it to be exactly thirty minutes.

At home no horse goes in anything other than a plain snaffle and a martingale; but at the shows a horse goes in whatever works best. We don't believe in putting a sharp bit on a strong horse because it would only make his mouth really tender. If a horse has a problem, we figure it out in a D-ring snaffle; then with a twisted snaffle at a show, you're in heaven.

The grooms spend a tremendous amount of time with each horse; they work that rub rag every day. We insist that tack be immaculate and that the bits shine. For shows, the horses are always braided, just as the riders are always in jackets, no matter what the weather.

We don't do legs up, however, unless a horse has a particular problem. The key factor in keeping your horses sound is acute observation, really knowing what they look like. All the horses are X-rayed twice a year, but three times if we're following a problem. That way we know after Florida and before the indoor shows exactly what we have to work with. We have terrific vets and a wonderful blacksmith, and we make sure that all the basic things—worming, shots, and such things—are done on time and done right.

We know what our horses get fed to the pellet. We feed basic food, such as a mixed sweet feed, unless a horse has a temperament problem, in which case he'll get pellets and hay. The food has all the vitamins, so we don't supplement. But we add electrolytes to the water in hot weather, and if they don't have a weight problem, they have hay in front of them at all times. They get fed twice a day; rarely does a horse get lunch.

Debbie is there morning, noon, and night; she's a marvelous caretaker. The schedules showing which horses are going to which shows go to her, and she puts together all the vanning and equipment arrangements. She might have two tractor-trailers in the driveway at 6 A.M. with a complete set of equipment in each, because the two of us are going to shows in opposite directions. She vacuums the trunks, launders the rub rags, and takes all the blankets and sweat sheets to the laundry. She goes on the road with us to Florida; in the fall, she may be up all night, moving from Harrisburg to Washington. She was up for fifty hours straight during junior weekend in New York. We'd start riding the horses at 3 A.M., and after that she'd be there for feeding, mucking out, and the full day of classes. You have to be careful about burnout in your people.

We haven't taken a vacation in eight years. We take Christmas Day off, and we're back here the next morning to interview prospective clients for the following year. Every waking moment you're working, thinking about it, organizing it, or doing it.

Summing Up

There's no one way to ride or to teach. You can get a horse supple a thousand ways; you can teach a rider to wait at a crossrail a thousand ways. But first you must have a system. George Morris was incredibly good at building a system, laying a solid foundation. His idea of a quality product, of fine craftsmanship, coincides with ours. But he has always said to us, "Look, I'm not you and you're not me. You'll do things a little differently."

Now we're going on our own, as we always wanted to do one day, and George is doing what he always wanted to do: concentrate on jumpers. It's not so different for us after all, since we'd really been functioning like a separate entity for the last five years at Hunterdon. But it's a funny feeling to realize that Hunterdon will be strictly a jumper barn from now on. George gave us a lot to build on, and now it's a question of putting our stamp on it. As long as we stick with the solid foundation we have, we'll go in the right direction.

4

The Jimmy Williams Method

Jimmy Williams

Manager and riding master of the Flintridge Riding Club in California—where he has produced many champion riders and trainers, including five members of the USET—Jimmy Williams is one of the most colorful figures in the horse world, as well as one of the most knowledgeable and versatile.

His own life story is as picturesque as the Hollywood films in which he was once a stunt rider. His father was a horse dealer; his mother's family and his uncle were racehorse owners. While he never had a formal riding lesson, Jimmy was racing quarter horses by the time he was twelve and for many years held the title of Leading Short-Distance Jockey in California. Spotted by an MGM talent scout, he was hired to double for Tyrone Power in the riding scenes of his swashbuckling adventure films. When the studio didn't need him, he trained show horses for his father's clients and one or two for himself.

While serving in the army in Italy during World War II, Jimmy became acquainted with dressage. When he arrived at Flintridge in 1956, he had all his riders, whatever their specialties, teach their horses basic dressage movements, and he was one of the first trainers in America to do so. Flintridge then had a mixture of English and Western styles, and Jimmy was expert in both; he also showed stock horses, particularly cutting horses. Again fate intervened. A new zoning regulation excluded cattle from the area in which the Flintridge

Riding Club was located. In a final flourish, Jimmy trained Buttonwood to win the Pacific Coast Green Stock Horse Championship and then concentrated exclusively on English-style riding and hunter-jumpers, with equally outstanding success.

If decorations were worn in horse-show circles as in the diplomatic set, Jimmy Williams would hardly have room on his broad chest for all the medals he has won, including Horseman of the Year in 1960, California Professional Horseman of the Year in 1977, and no less than seven awards as California's "Leading Thoroughbred Breeder."

"Look, no hands . . . and no bridle, either!" Jimmy Williams on Livius, backstage at the Cow Palace in 1987. Photo: Courtesy of J. Williams

Hands and Legs

My biggest complaint with many riders is that they get too busy with their hands, jerking and snatching the horse in the mouth in an effort to control him. I have a pair of police handcuffs that I put on riders with bad hands. This device is worth a thousand words because it puts the hands in the correct position and forces the rider to use his weight influence to stop the horse instead of jerking with his hands. If the handcuffed rider tries to jerk the horse, it hurts his wrists. After two or three days of wearing the handcuffs, I get a lovely pair of soft and sympathetic hands. I'm always asked, "What if the rider falls off with the handcuffs on?" No problem. They will force him to fall in a ball and roll, instead of sticking out a hand to break the fall and ending up with a broken wrist or collarbone.

However, if I were given a choice between good hands and good legs on a rider, I'd definitely choose good legs. Good legs will overcome bad hands. If a rider makes a mistake with his hands, good strong legs will usually fix the mistake. It's far easier to immobilize the hands and make them softer than it is to develop strong and effective legs. Usually, a bad rider has bad legs. If I have a rider who is really having trouble learning to use his legs, I'll try to simplify things by working on one leg at a time. Since a rider often has one stronger leg, I'll place a spur on the weak leg and have him use only the spur leg. I tell him to think on one side only, and usually the other leg follows suit.

Not every rider can be elegant on a horse. I never try to fool my students. I explain to them that while they may ride as well as another person, they lack the natural elegance and poise of that person and, as a result, may be beaten by him. I want my students to know their limitations.

Taking the Pressure Off

I use a lot of what I call "cowboy psychology," derived from working with so many different kinds of people for so many years. I want my students to enjoy riding and not to be tense or nervous about what they are trying to learn. One method I've found very successful is to let the students teach each other. If I have a rider with a certain problem, I'll have him work with a less advanced student who has the same problem—

Susan Hutchinson, Jimmy Williams's former student and assistant, is one of the most formidable grand prix competitors on the West Coast, competing here in the Griffith Park Grand Prix. Photo: Hughes

let's say, bad hands. As the advanced rider works with the novice, he'll draw himself to his own problem and at the same time build up his ego by helping the other rider. Another method I'll use to teach my students is reverse psychology. If a rider is having a terrible time riding to a vertical fence, I'll tell him to try to put the horse in the worst spot he can possibly find. Usually this will take the pressure off the rider and he'll forget all the anxieties that are causing him to find a bad spot.

Judging Distance and Pace

I always try to teach students without "blowing their minds" or telling them too much for them to absorb in a session. Depth perception is a very difficult thing to teach, especially when a rider becomes too concerned about finding the "right" spot. I try to make a game of teaching depth perception (or timing) in order not to create any anxiety for the rider. I'll place a marker 30 feet away from a fence and have the riders try to put the horses' front feet right at the marker as they make their approach. By concentrating on getting the right distance to the marker 30 feet away from the jump, you eliminate all anxiety at the crucial spot, the takeoff spot. This is another good example of how I always try to make things easier for my students to learn. In this instance, since they have to "set up" the horse at the marker, they have two even strides and arrive at a good takeoff spot 6 feet from the jump.

Since depth perception works hand in hand with rate of speed, I do a lot of galloping without jumping while schooling at home. Judgment of speed is the most difficult quality to put into a rider. In small arenas, courses are generally set on a 12-foot stride, which should be ridden at the rate of 360 yards per minute. I have a game that helps teach a rider his rate of speed. I take a group of riders and mark off a distance of 360 yards. Each rider canters this distance while I time him with my stopwatch. The one who comes closest to doing the 360 yards in one minute wins the "contest." When they have mastered the 12-foot stride, I change the distance to expand the stride to 400–450 yards per minute or to decrease the stride. Another way I teach rate of speed is to have a very advanced student ride alongside a novice pupil at a certain pace so that the beginner can get the feel of that rate of speed.

I teach my students how to ride distance-related fences—that is, jumps set in a line at a measured distance—by what I call "counts." The count begins when the horse lands, so five strides between two fences is a count of six. I teach my students to ride jumpers the same way as hunters and at the same rate of speed. If the course is set well, a rider does not have to run his horse but can make up time in well-executed turns. The only difference in jumpers is that the rider is at an advantage if he knows how to compress the horse in order to prevent him from getting flat and how to maintain the horse's balance. A hunter, on the other hand, must be able to "rewind his own coil," because anything the judge sees is too obvious in a hunter class.

The Routine

I do not teach any riders exclusively. I have four people who teach with me: one for beginner riders, one for intermediate students, and two for advanced riders. I personally check every student the first time he rides,

One of many outstanding Jimmy Williams alumni, Robert Ridland. Founder of the National Grand Prix Riders' Association and an active course designer, he is riding Southside, with whom he scored many important wins during the 1970s. An equestrian jet-setter, based in New Mexico, he won the 1986 San Francisco Grand Prix with Karache, having competed a few hours earlier in the Harrisburg Grand Prix with Benoit, and expecting to ride in the Washington, D.C., International Grand Prix a few days later. Photo: Karl Leck

and then I assign him to the proper instructor. I have "raised" all my instructors, so they all teach the same way with my methods.

I expect a student's cooperation during a lesson, no matter who is teaching. One trick I use to "punish" an uncooperative rider is to send him back to a lower-level instructor. Then I check with that instructor to see if the student's attitude has improved. If it has, the student moves back up; if not, I'll drop him down to a still lower level. I don't have to do this too often, but my students know that I will if they make it necessary.

In a typical week's schedule, my advanced students jump quite a bit, although never without supervision. They never jump fences higher than 3 feet 6 inches at home; usually it's jumps of 2 feet 6 inches to 3 feet. Most of the show riders own several horses and lease one or two from me. Their show horses don't jump too often at home, but since I like my students to do a lot of jumping at home, they can use the leased horse. I am careful, however, not to drill, drill, drill, because I don't want my students to become bored. I concentrate on working on a rider's weakest points at home, as these are obviously what need to be corrected in order to win in the show ring. When I was on the AHSA Equitation Committee, I pushed for the rule change that would permit a rider to jump an entire combination if he had stopped in the middle of it. Usually a stop in a combination is the result of a bad approach, and I wanted my students to be able to practice correcting the weakness of a bad approach.

Before a big competition, such as the Medal finals, I'll deliberately slack off on my pupils. I want them to relax and feel enthusiastic about their riding, and I want their horses to be fresh. I figure schooling an advanced rider is like cooking a steak. It's ruined if it's overcooked, and it's best if it's just a little underdone. After all, you can always put it back on the fire. When I go to a show, I use the first day to let the riders and horses "sharpen up," and by the end of the show they are usually winning their fair share.

Communication

Many people are curious about the gadgets and so-called gimmicks I use. I enjoy teaching, and I'm always looking for ways to communicate better with my students as well as to make it easier for them to learn to ride. I'm constantly trying to come up with methods, natural or mechanical, that illustrate what I'm trying to teach. I have a walkie-talkie unit I frequently use at home. Basically, it's a small receiver that clips onto the rider's shirt collar and a small speaker that I talk into. I can talk to the rider as he goes around the ring without anyone else hearing me. I often use this device with a new student who has come to me from another instructor, so as not to embarrass him in front of the other students. It's a great confidence-builder too, because pretty soon a rider will become conditioned to what I'm going to say and his reflexes will become automatic, which is exactly what I want.

I also use an extensive loudspeaker system, and I have a cordless microphone I use at clinics or at shows. I have a portable microphone in my electric cart that I take to the shows so that my riders can always hear me without my having to yell at them. The electric cart is equipped with powerful headlights that I can use if we ever have to school in the dark. I always keep spurs, bats, and other teaching aids in the cart so that I can get to what I need when I need it.

Francie Steinwedell, trained by Jimmy Williams, won the Medal finals in 1976 and the Maclay in 1977. Photo: Budd

In conclusion, I must say that while my teaching methods have changed over the years, I still teach essentially the same style of riding, which is based on teaching a rider how to horseback and how to maintain a good base of support. I've always studied, read, and watched other instructors. When my students go to other parts of the country to compete, I tell them to watch not only the good riders but also the bad riders. They can learn what not to do, by watching other riders make mistakes. Also, it helps to build my students' egos to realize that other competitors are capable of making mistakes too.

While I am secure in my thoughts and in my methods of teaching, I will copy or try to apply the techniques of anyone I feel is successful. I will not, however, follow the crowd unless I feel it is the best thing for my riders. I've always followed the premise that communication is the most important factor in teaching, and I'll try anything and everything to get my ideas across to a student. I've always said that if you can't get through the front door, you should try the back door, the window, the chimney, or any way you can to get inside. This analogy applies to teaching successful riders. Both good riders and good instructors should never stop learning, and I've always tried to follow this tenet.

Finally, I must say that 50 percent of teaching winning riders depends on having the right kind of horse, while 25 percent depends on the support, financial and emotional, of the rider's parents, and 25 percent on the instructor. I can make a good rider, but I need for a rider to have good parents and a good horse in order to have that rider win in the show ring. I've been very lucky throughout my career because I have had talented riders who have had the right kind of support.

5

Handling Show-Ring Nerves

Lisa Castellucci

Since winning the Maclay finals at Madison Square Garden in 1981 (having finished runner-up the two preceding years), Lisa, a Paul Valliere pupil, has continued her show-ring activities in the Amateur-Owner Division.

Even though I have a lot of competitive mileage, my nerves can get the better of me unless I'm very deliberate and methodical about my preparation for the ring. For example, on the morning of the 1981 Maclay finals, I stuck to my routine. I planned how to ride each fence, but more important, I planned how to ride the course as a whole. That year it incorporated some long distances, demanding a forward stride, as well as some tight distances, needing a compact stride; there was even a bounce with no stride at all. It was a test of the rider's ability to adjust smoothly. To make my ride flow, I forced myself to stop worrying about single fences I didn't like the look of and to visualize my whole round.

Once I've ridden a course mentally, I watch ten trips at most, just enough to get the basic idea of how the course rides. If I sit around and watch a hundred trips, I see a hundred mistakes that I don't want to copy. Even worse, I see a hundred rides that I imagine are much better than mine will be, and I'm beaten before I go into the ring.

I never even glance around at the audience. I'm not one of those people who perform better when someone is watching. In the ring, I take my time. I make certain that I ride all my corners properly, and I don't try to rush my horse off his feet. I resist the urge to dash around the course. Anyone who's nervous hurries a little, so I make it a point to be extra deliberate. I tell myself that the judges aren't watching to see how fast I can complete the course; they're looking for quality.

I try not to concern myself with winning. My trainer, Paul Valliere, says to go in and have a good time. He tells me to take deep breaths, which is a lot more helpful than nagging me to relax.

In the finals that year, when I came back to work on the flat, I relaxed by concentrating on the rhythms of the gaits; and I actually did enjoy myself. I was called back in tenth place for the second jumping round. If I'd been placed higher, I'd have been more worried, but I made up my mind that I'd just give it my best shot. The pattern of dressage movements we had to perform in front of the judges' box as part of the second round was nerve-racking. I made sure that my horse had finished

Lisa Castellucci, 1981 Medal winner, rides Foreign Exchange. Photo: Courtesy of USET

each movement—halt, quarter-turn on the haunches, backing up—before I asked for the next one. I made my aids for counter-canter very definite. (A lot of finalists had trouble with this because they tried to rush.) When I changed horses with Lisa Tarnopol, I rode the course even more carefully, deliberately, and precisely, because I was on a strange horse.

6

Winning the Medal Finals

Francesca Mazella

In 1984 at the age of fifteen, Francesca won the two most coveted victories on the junior equitation circuit: the Medal finals in Harrisburg and the ASPCA Maclay finals at the National Horse Show in New York. Her double triumph rewarded years of effort, conscientious work with several leading trainers and a budget horse, and the help of supportive parents; her father is a doctor, and her mother raises ponies in the barn behind their home in Mount Kisco, New York. Since her equitation double, Francesca has continued her riding career in the Junior Jumper Division, as well as her studies at the University of Pennsylvania.

My parents made a final splurge on me for the finals. My horse Joe would travel to Harrisburg and New York with the group from Beacon Hill, where I'd been training for some time with Bill Cooney and Frank Madden; he'd be cared for by Evan, one of Bill and Frank's expert grooms. My mother, who'd done a terrific grooming job for me at many of the shows, was to be banned from the barn this time until I'd finished riding. She's a wonderful supporter, but she does get nervous! She agreed to sit in the stands and be a horse-show mommy for a change.

I had my final lesson the day before Joe shipped. Bill and Frank built another of their tough and varied courses. Some of the other riders did it over and over for practice, but Joe and I did two lines a couple of times and left it there. I was seeing consistently good distances; he was

Francesca Mazella in the 1984 Maclay finals. Photo: Budd

jumping well. If we did more, we might make him sloppy. As it was, he was good on the flat and he was fit. We were ready to go.

George Morris was both designer and judge for the competition. I'd seen the kind of equitation course he can create, so I was expecting an incredible killer with spooky jumps, bending lines, rollback turns. But what I saw early that Sunday morning was a hunter course. While the jump crew put finishing touches to the course, the nine other Beacon Hill riders and our trainers, Bill Cooney and Frank Madden, joined me, all of us wondering what George was up to now. As we made our way down to the in-gate for the 6:30 A.M. course walk, I reminded myself, "Take this seriously. It's not going to be as easy as it looks."

Bill and Frank have their riders walk a course alone at first before discussing it with them as a group. That way we learn to analyze for ourselves, rather than depending on them for the correct evaluation. I

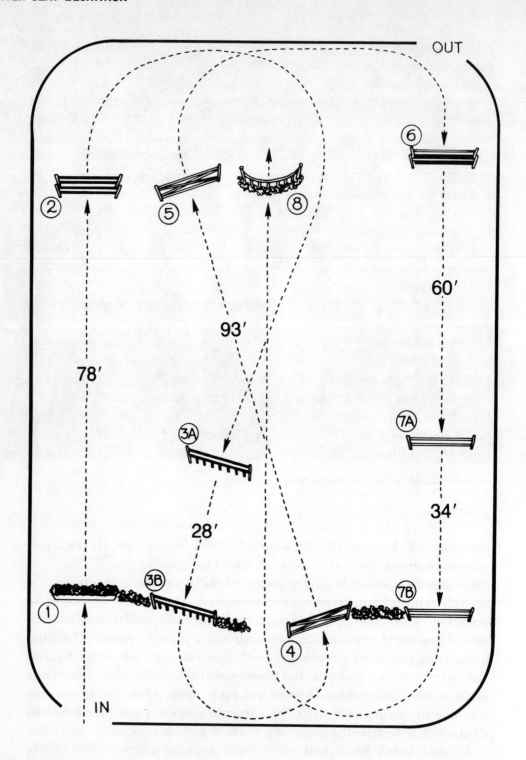

Course 1.

walked the course twice, first to assess the distances in each line and again to analyze the turns between them.

The first line—a brush to a rustic oxer—walked in a comfortable forward five strides, a flowing hunter pace that would show more riding ability than would a crawling, conservative six strides. I recalled George saying once that a judge always remembers a rider's first and last jumps more than his performance over the rest of the course. For my long-strided horse Free Union (known at home as Joe), the five wouldn't be a problem; but a horse with a short stride would have to be ridden strongly down this line. When we talked the course over with Bill and Frank later, they said that all of us were to do the five; there was no option. We were to establish a flowing pace right from the start of our opening circle and maintain it down the line. The wide oxer was not the kind of fence to mince down to.

From the oxer, the track turned right to the first diagonal line: a vertical-to-oxer in-and-out composed of two rustic gates. The one-stride distance between these two fences was also forward. The third line was a pair of white gates off a left turn. The first had a teeny gate for a ground line; the second had no ground line at all. I walked between them and found seven strides, which would ride a little steady with Joe's big stride. A forward six was possible, but I felt the seven was better for two reasons: we'd already have shown George that we could ride forward through the first two lines, and here a flowing pace could get you in trouble with the airy gates. The slightly steady seven would show an ability to shorten and would reduce the risk of knocking down the second gate.

From there, the track flowed right to the fourth line: an oxer followed by two verticals. The oxer was rather narrow, composed of a red wall with a white rail on the back. I thought the horses might spook at it. The distance between the oxer and the first vertical walked a normal to slightly flowing four strides, followed by a steady two between the verticals. Here, George would be looking primarily for a smooth transition between the flowing four and the steady two. I planned to jump in over the wall with enough pace so that I could ride forward for two strides and then just breathe "whoa" and balance for two before the vertical. That would let me show a flowing stride while still permitting me to jump into the in-and-out with the correct pace for its steady distance. If I steadied slightly all the way, I probably couldn't make the four, and I wouldn't show the forward hunter pace.

Coming out, the track turned sharply right into a long approach to the last fence, a Riviera gate near the out-gate. This was a narrow, flimsy-looking gate with a curved top and a bevy of little bushes in front that made finding the center of the jump hard. Here my accuracy would be tested: to make sure that Joe jumped the center of the fence without hesitation, I'd need to keep him in a well-defined chute between my legs and hands.

The distances established, I quickly returned to the beginning of the course to walk the turns. Lines of bushes connecting the jumps at the lower end of the ring restricted my opening circle to the area immediately in front of the in-gate. Since the gate opened to the left (the direction of the first line), I planned to walk in and around the gate, hugging the rail until I was near the first fence. There I'd pick up the canter directly out of the walk and make my circle using all the space available. The walk-canter transition would let me establish the flowing pace I wanted for the first line more quickly than if I took a few trot strides first. At the in-gate again, I'd look for a flowing distance that would let me jump the first fence out of stride.

After analyzing this approach, I picked up the track at the end of the first line. I'd need a right lead here; since Joe almost always lands on the right, I didn't anticipate a problem. As I walked the track to the in-and-out on the first diagonal, I could see that George had designed a fast-moving course that he wanted us to flow around. Since the in-and-out was a forward one-stride with a long approach, it seemed an excellent opportunity to show that I could gallop with control and jump out of a flowing, if not actually building, stride.

I would maintain my pace from the first line around the end of the ring, make a smooth turn between fences 6 and 8, and build slightly down the diagonal. I'd show much more technique this way than by taking back and crawling around. I'd need to find a distance out of this flowing stride. Since my eye is pretty reliable, I was confident that I'd see what I wanted as I passed between the two jumps. If I didn't catch the out-of-stride distance, I would have to shorten and opt for the medium one. I could still make it work, although breaking the flow would make the line not nearly as pretty.

The track from the in-and-out to the line of two gates on the second diagonal was a little tricky. Since the in-and-out and the first gate were set close to the end of the ring, the turn was short. The track flowed left—Joe's weaker direction, since he likes to cut left. Furthermore, it passed the in-gate, which usually distracts a horse's attention. To make a smooth approach to this line, I'd need to use all of the available space wisely.

Joe would probably land on his right lead, so my first job would be to get a lead change through the flowing pace he was in. I'd do this before reaching the rail; then I'd balance him and at the same time use my indirect rein and inside leg to prevent him from cutting left. With so little room, it was critical that he stay out on the track. When I balanced him, I'd want a shorter, animated stride—not fast, but with impulsion—in preparation for the steady seven. Hugging the rail, I'd look for a distance to the gate and turn as soon as I saw a comfortable one. I'd maintain some indirect rein and inside leg while turning, to be sure he didn't take a slice off the leftward approach.

I knew the seven would ride steady. But until I landed inside the line, I wouldn't know exactly how I'd need to ride it; the distance I found to the first gate would decide that. The important thing would be to balance especially carefully to the second element, the airy gate.

The track from this line to the red wall basically followed the rail. After the airy gate, it turned right (Joe's better direction) and then hugged the end of the ring. The wall came up three strides out of the turn onto the long side. Since the four strides to the vertical would not ride as forward as the first line, I'd need a medium flowing pace coming away from the gates. Joe tends to land with pace, so I'd only need to maintain his stride, not create it. I'd look for a distance to the wall out of this pace.

Inside the line, I'd need to act fast and fluently. I wanted to take two forward strides and then balance for two in preparation for the steady two-stride vertical combination. As I landed from the wall, my eye would lock into the distance; if I'd found a good one coming in, the four strides would be there. I'd ride forward for two; in the third stride, I'd say "whoa" under my breath, drop my weight back slightly, and close my fingers on the reins. In the fourth stride, I'd drop my weight back a little more.

Over the top of the first vertical, I'd say "whoa" again under my breath. I'd keep my weight a little behind the motion in the two steady strides between the verticals. Then, in preparation for the short 180-degree turn that followed, I'd say "whoa" once more over the second one. The turn into the long approach to the last fence was tight, but not unreasonable. It would help to be landing a little quietly from the short two-stride. Around the tight arc, I'd maintain balance with impulsion.

At the narrow Riviera gate, I'd have my second shot for a brilliant fence. Like the second line, this was an opportunity to show that I could gallop with control and jump out of stride. Since the fence was narrow, I'd also need to demonstrate perfect accuracy. To move up into a flowing stride, I'd lighten my feel of Joe's mouth, shift quietly into a slightly more forward position, maybe add a little leg, and allow him to gallop down to the fence. I didn't quite know how this would work out as I walked the course, but I knew I'd look for the flowing distance rather than a nicely balanced quiet one. This was the final fence, the moment to make a strong impression.

The out-gate was to the left of the last fence, so I'd need to hold Joe out to make a neat final circle. To show a little extra finesse, I'd break to a collected sitting trot before passing through the gate.

When we met with Bill and Frank, I found that my analysis matched theirs pretty closely. They warned us to be extra careful at the airy gate, where the horses wouldn't have a solid focal point to help them find the distance. In particular, they cautioned me to make sure I found comfortable distances to the gates and the fences in the fourth line, since Joe tends to rub rails if he gets sloppy. If he got deep at one of these, he could rub it hard or even have it down. Most of all, Bill and Frank both stressed that we must balance our horses, maintaining their impulsion around the 180-degree turn to the final fence, and then build to really show a hand gallop to it. To be successful here would be doubly impressive, they said, because the narrow gate, buried in all those bushes, would be much harder to ride out of a flowing pace than a normal one.

Armed with their advice, I walked the course twice again. First I concentrated on getting it down pat in my memory. Then, on my final walk, I pretended I was actually riding the course. As I looked for distances out of my pretend gallop and simulated balancing for a steady line, I probably got some stares. But by the time I reached the out-gate, I'd developed a real feel for the course.

On the order of go I was listed to ride ninety-seventh. Since there were 227 finalists in all, I probably wouldn't go until about three and a half hours after the 7 A.M. start. Several Beacon Hill riders were in the first fifty: Jenno Topping would ride eightieth; Linda Kossick, the previous year's Maclay winner, would be forty-fifth. After every fifty riders, George and the other judge, Marcia Williams from California, would release a standby list and then take a five-minute break.

After looking at the schedule, Bill and Frank told me to ride Joe on the flat at 8 A.M. and then return him to the barn. He'd be brought back to the warm-up area when there were twenty riders ahead of me.

I had time to watch some trips. Joie Gatlin, a very polished rider from California, had a beautiful round. She did the five in the first line and the seven down the line of gates, riding the whole course the way I hoped I'd be able to. Aaron Vale, whose riding I respected enormously ever since we'd both ridden in a USET training session with Bernie

Traurig the year before, also put in a flowing performance. Linda Kossick had a typically wonderful round. But less-experienced riders ran into trouble on many parts of the course.

As I flatted Joe for half an hour outside in the sunshine, with the class already started, I felt that we were going to do well. To keep my mind clear, I didn't think about the other riders except in terms of which horses I might have to switch onto in a ride-off. I'd seen most of the top contenders' horses all year, but I didn't know many riding details about them. The horse I knew best was Jenno's Charge a Count; but since we both trained at Beacon Hill, it was unlikely that I'd get him in a switch.

No one—Bill, Frank, my parents—had ever said that they expected me to win these finals. They didn't have to. I'd placed third the year before on Rugged Rule. With Joe for a partner, I'd improved in 1984. All year I'd worried that I wouldn't be able to match my 1983 performance, but now that I was here and Joe was going well, I felt psyched. I wanted to win. I believed I could. Of course, I didn't say this to

Linda Kossick, 1983 Maclay winner, was one of Francesca's leading rivals for the USET Medal finals in 1984. By 1987 she was a leader in the Amateur-Owner Division and reputed for her skill in Open Jumper speed classes. Here she is riding in the 1987 World Cup event of the Ox Ridge Horse Show. Photo: James Leslie Parker

anybody; that would have been obnoxious. But inside, you've got to want it.

I took Joe to the barn and returned to the stands to watch some more trips. The first standby list was out: Joie Gatlin was on top, with Aaron and Linda right behind her.

With twenty riders to go before my turn, I met Evan and Joe in the outside warm-up area. While I worked on the flat, I heard a great round of applause. Then Bill came out to warm me up over fences and told me that Jenno had had a pretty nice trip.

We trotted little fences and picked up the flowing canter pace I planned to use on the course to canter several fences from a long approach. We worked on one forward line that other trainers had set up. Then, in order to sharpen Joe's concentration without overdoing the jumping, Bill put up a Swedish oxer; its slanted rails made Joe look with new interest. He jumped it clean. Bill said to leave it there.

In the tunnel leading to the ring, I got off while Evan gave Joe a final grooming. Then Bill gave me a leg-up and a friendly pinch on my knee, wished me good luck, and walked away to the stands. Frank met me at the in-gate to go over the course one more time, line by line. He was very quiet and tried to act calm, but I knew he wasn't. Evan gave Joe a pat as the gates swung open.

I started my circle just as I'd planned and then hugged the rail as I came past the in-gate. Looking in to my first jump, I saw a distance out of stride, a medium distance with pace. Joe looked happy; his ears were forward and I felt him focus on the jump. He jumped in well. To maintain the flow down the line, I kept my leg steady. With Joe's naturally long stride, the five strides worked out easily; they were even, and my distance to the oxer felt great. Joe jumped out nicely over the back rail. And all continued to go well, practically as planned, from the first fence to the last.

I left the ring in a dressage-y sitting trot. Evan met me in the corridor that leads from the out-gate to the warm-up area. He gave me a big hug and told me we'd been wonderful. I dismounted and we walked along together. Frank met me at the end, picked me up and gave me a big hug and kiss. Bill joined him and told me I was great. They were especially pleased that I'd kept the flow down the long approach to the in-and-out in the second line and made a fluent transition between the forward four and the steady two.

Then I went into the stands to see my parents, who had been banned from the barn while I was competing. Both were ecstatic—and nervous. Just after I joined them, the announcer read the second standby list. I was on top; Joie was in second place; Mia Wood, another California rider, was behind her; and Jenno was fourth. Aaron was sixth, and Linda Kossick eighth.

My parents and I walked back to the barn, where we chewed over all the performances so far with Jenno and the other riders. While stuffing Joe with apples, Evan gave him a bath, wrapped his legs, and put him in his stall with fresh hay. My parents returned to the stands to watch some more—there were more than a hundred riders still to go!—and I went with a friend for a light lunch in the show restaurant. From there, I heard the third standby list announced: I was still on top, and the next four were also unchanged. Aaron had slipped to eighth place, and Linda to twelfth.

About an hour later, the fourth standby list was announced. There was a new leader: Chris Kappler from Illinois. I was second. I'd seen Chris ride once in a Junior Jumper class, but never in equitation. I hadn't seen his trip today, but someone at the barn told me that he'd done the line of two gates in a forward six—the line where Bill and Frank had insisted we should do it in seven. I felt a bit baffled about what George was looking for.

Aaron Vale, who finished just out of the ribbons in 1984, won the blue two years later, as shown in this picture. Now he is much in demand as a "catch rider" on the open jumper circuit. Photo: Courtesy of USET

When the fifth and final standby list was announced at the end of the first round, Chris was still on top, I was second, followed by Joie, Mia, and Jenno. Aaron was in tenth place, and Linda in eighteenth. Another of Bill and Frank's students, Alice Debany, was twelfth. We were thirty-three in all to be called back to ride the second course.

Bill and Frank were pleased that I wasn't in first place going into the second round. As the underdog, I could always improve, they pointed out; holding on to the top spot, a far more pressured position, would be more difficult. Their reasoning made me feel more positive too.

A few minutes after the final list was announced, the diagram for the second course was posted near the warm-up area. We'd all anticipated a very different one from the morning's hunterlike course, and we were not disappointed. This was a jumper course with hunter components incorporated.

Up in the stands, watching the ring crew build the fences, I saw the kind of course I'd expected originally. The first course had consisted of ten fences; now there were fifteen. But the crucial difference was in the turns between fences. These were not generous, flowing turns but rollbacks. One of them went from a narrow fence to another narrow fence. In another spot, the track turned sharply left and back between the fences of an in-and-out to a combination of two gates set at angles to each other. The end of the course was similar to the first one: a hunterlike line of three oxers, followed by a long approach to the narrow Rivera gate of the morning course.

As usual, we all walked the course separately and then with Bill and Frank. It was a trickier test than the morning one, demanding more from the rider and the horse. I had to plan my ride in view of Joe's ability as well as my own, also bearing in mind the impression we'd make on the judges.

For example, the final fence was the same Riviera gate as on the morning course, but I decided to ride it a little differently this time. I'd already shown that I could jump it out of a building stride; and after the preceding flowing line I could demonstrate versatility by riding to the last fence with collection. At this point in the competition, I wanted to play safe rather than take another shot at a dramatic building approach. I opted to land from the oxer, let the end wall collect Joe's stride, and then balance him around the right-hand turn. As I came out of the turn, I'd make sure he was straight to the fence, establish correct impulsion, and then ask for a flying change to the left lead to show a little extra collection and so polish an otherwise rather mundane approach. I'd look for a comfortable distance to the final fence and then

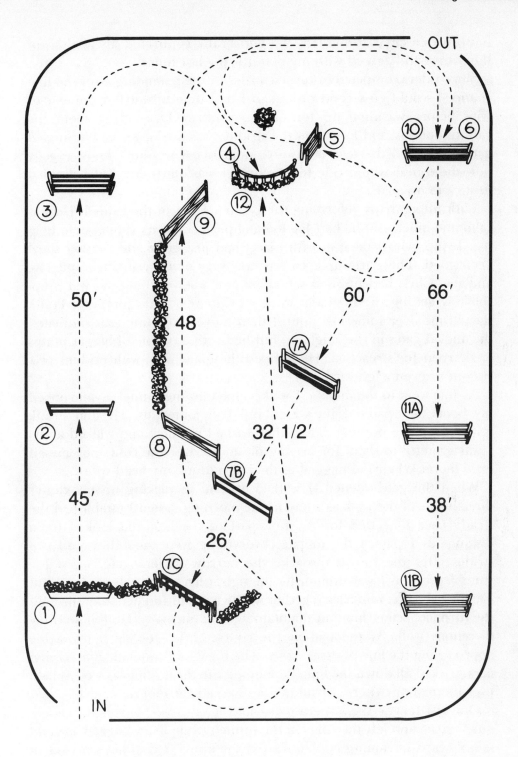

Course 2.

finish with a circle to the left. Bill and Frank confirmed my analysis of the course and agreed with my plan for the last fence.

Since riders competed in reverse order of their standing after the first round, I would go second to last, so I had time to watch a number of trips before warming up Joe. These confirmed my ideas about the various options, and I saw how the striding was working out. The angled gates produced the most awkward moments. I wouldn't know exactly how the course would ride for me until I was out there. But I decided to stick to my plan.

With fifteen trips before my turn, I met Evan in the tunnel. He was calm and quiet, and he had Joe looking perfect. Frank came out to help me. Jenno, who'd been in fifth place, had just gone and he said she'd been good. The warm-up area was now very quiet: just Chris and Joie and me. Chris had finished schooling and was watching my warm-up. Joe was getting tired, so we wanted to do very little jumping. Frank started me over some low jumps, then moved to a line that simulated the angled gates in the ring, and finished with a couple of bigger jumps to sharpen Joe's reaction. He jumped the gates well, with no hint of a runout or even a leftward pull.

As Joie went to the in-gate, I walked Joe into the tunnel. Evan rubbed my boots and painted Joe's feet. Bill had joined us. He and Frank watched, saying nothing. Then they wished me luck and walked away. I was grateful to them for leaving me to go over the course by myself once more. When I'm nagged at the last minute, my head spins.

When the gate opened, I walked around it, picking up my canter directly out of the walk as I had in the morning. Then I established the steady pace I needed for the first part of the line and looked for a distance as I passed the in-gate. Everything went smoothly until two strides after the fourth obstacle, the narrow Riviera gate, when Joe stumbled just as I was organizing the tight turn to the skinny oxer. But I managed to get him back together within a stride and bent him through the turn, collecting him but maintaining his animation. He followed my directions well. At the end of the course, I let Joe open his stride approaching the line of three oxers. The forward flow made him happy: ears pricked all down the line, he jumped the three oxers as well as he'd ever jumped anywhere. I couldn't have asked for more.

One last fence—the Riviera gate—and it was over. I landed, made a quiet circle, and left the ring. In the tunnel, while Evan hugged Joe and me, I heard screaming applause from the arena. I couldn't get back in time to see Chris's trip, but Bill and Frank said it was good. While we stood talking, the new class leaders were announced: I was on top, with

Mia Wood on Jacques at Culpeper, Virginia, in 1986. Photo: James Leslie Parker

Jenno Topping and her marvelous equitation horse, Charge a Count. Photo: Courtesy of USET

Chris second, Jenno third, and Mia fourth. Jenno's lovely trip had brought her up two places from fifth.

Now the four of us had to return to the ring for a ride-off over the same course, this time on another rider's horse. Mia was to switch with Jenno, Chris with me. We were to put our own saddles on our new horses and remount without help. I thought, "Oh God, I don't know this horse at all!" At the same time, I knew I was better off with Chris's made black gelding than with Mia's green horse.

As I mounted the black gelding, I admired the thoroughness of George's plan: he'd tested us over a hunter course and a jumper course; now he was checking our basic horsemanship.

Jenno had a lot of trouble with the green horse; the ringmaster was finally permitted to help her mount. Then we were told that we had one minute to practice on the flat with our new horses before jumping the course.

The last thing Frank had told me before I came back into the ring was, "Do the flying change before the angled gates, no matter what." So that is what I practiced first. I was pretending I'd just jumped the combination and turned back between its last two elements to set up for the change, when Chris and I nearly collided. Everybody laughed, including us, which let off some of the pressure. But the crowd noise made the black horse tense.

When Frank had told me to do the flying change, I'd thought, "Fine," little knowing that the horse didn't like to do lead changes. But he obliged me, if rather stiffly, so I knew that he was able to do it. Because he felt a little strong, I spent the few remaining seconds on stops and backs.

This time we didn't go in reverse order. Even before I reached the lineup, the announcer told me to start the course. My opening circle and the steady-to-forward-three first line went smoothly. As I jumped out over the oxer, a small voice inside me suddenly got very determined. Since I'd never ridden the horse, I knew I couldn't predict what he'd do through the S-curve, over the skinny jumps, or at any other tricky point on the course. So I decided to forget about equitation and just ride as if I were having a lesson with Bill or Frank.

The gelding was a little "looky" coming around the bush for the skinny vertical, but he balanced smoothly in the landing and turned well. Coming out of the rollback turn from fence 4, I saw a rather forward distance to the skinny oxer. I asked him to move up, he hesitated, and I came back with even more definite aids. He jumped across it fine and didn't falter when I asked him to land left of the shrub. I held out on the turn and caught the red wall out of a good forward pace, but I had to override the four to the triple in order to make the distance work. Coming out, I really said "whoa" under my breath. The long one-stride seemed extra long, but I thought he jumped out without seeming to make an effort.

Then came the part I dreaded: the sharp turnback between elements of the triple to the angled gates. I stuck to the same plan I'd followed with Joe: I would angle back to the left to set up for the lead change. I tried to make my aids more definite than those I used for Joe, but the horse failed to switch behind. I put my legs on stronger, and two strides later he completed the switch. The first gate was upon us. He twisted in the air and landed somewhat left of center, but the three worked out better with him than with Joe's longer stride.

By now I knew I'd really need to override the hunter-y forward line that came next. Coming to the red wall, I thought I had ample pace; but in the air the horse felt dwelly, as though uncertain that he could clear the back rail. On landing, I saw that the four wasn't locked in. To make it work, I moved into a much more forward position, driving him down to the in-and-out. He seemed to dwell in the air again, so I kept driving through the two-stride and out across the oxer.

Having moved up so determinedly, I now had the horse strong in my hand and on his forehand. The end wall helped slow him. He landed on the right lead, so I was able to concentrate on balancing for the snug turn. He was still strong as we hit the straight approach to the Riviera gate. I was glad I had to make the lead switch, since it would help steady him.

A moment later I saw a long distance to the gate. Since he'd seemed unsure of himself over the oxers, it would be a risky choice. I sat against him for another stride and saw the nice one. When the crowd cheered me on landing, he spooked and tensed up as he had earlier. I was doubly glad I'd chosen the conservative distance.

I returned to the lineup as Chris began his trip on Joe. He, too, had trouble adapting to his horse's stride, overriding the first line, so that the second three were almost too quiet. He didn't quite get Joe's eye on the skinny vertical and pulled a rail. The rest of his trip looked fine. Stride problems plagued Jenno too. Twice the green horse broke into a trot while on course. Then Mia went on Jenno's Charge a Count, giving what seemed to be a flawless performance.

The announcer excused us from the ring. While I remounted Joe, Bill and Frank told me that I'd ridden the black horse well. They didn't comment on where they thought I'd finished. Then the four of us returned to the ring with the seven other riders in the final standings.

There would be ten ribbons and a reserve. None of us knew for sure where he or she had finished. I thought I'd probably stayed ahead of Chris because of his override and the pulled rail. Since Jenno broke stride, she wouldn't have moved up. But what about that flawless trip of Mia's? It seemed unlikely that the judges would move her up three spots, but it wasn't impossible.

The ribbons are awarded in reverse order, starting with the reserve eleventh slot. The announcer gave each rider a big buildup, telling the audience about his or her past successes and who the trainer was. I felt faintly frustrated, anxious for the end to come and yet not wanting it to hurry. For a while I sort of turned off. Then I heard him saying that Jenno was fourth. That left three of us still in Limbo. I began to really sweat the next few minutes. Third place: Chris Kappler. I felt heat rising to the surface of my skin. The introductions seemed to lengthen as the announcer neared his finale. When he began, "And our Reserve Champion is . . ." I thought, "Oh my God." Then he pronounced Mia's name, and I felt tears of relief. "I did it!" I thought, "I really did it!"

With Bill and Frank beside us, the 1983 winner, Laura O'Connor, presented Joe and me with the AHSA silver trophy of a flying horse, and draped Joe's neck in a blue victory cooler. Then the spotlight was on us for the victory gallop. Just the two of us, flying along in that white beam of light. It was a magic moment.

III

Selecting, Riding, and Training Hunters

1

Horse Shopping

Paul Valliere

As one of America's leading trainers of horses and riders, Paul Valliere is always seeking promising mounts for the equitation students and show riders at Acres Wild Farm.

Here is how he screens a hunter prospect before investing in a vet exam.

I tend to act on my gut instinct when I try a horse. But I do ride the horse two days in a row and make a point of trying him in different areas—in an indoor ring and an outdoor ring, for example. And there are three things I look at closely.

The first of these is the horse's structure, along with his way of moving and soundness. Conformation is number one because it gives you a clue to the horse's future soundness; many, if not most, soundness problems develop from conformation faults. It can also give you an idea of the horse's ability. So the first thing I do is look at the overall picture, with the horse standing.

However, there are model horses that have no performance ability at all. That's why it's equally important to study the horse's movement, watching how evenly he goes, how his feet hit the ground, and how he uses himself over fences. Besides telling you about the quality of movement, this will give you a further idea of his soundness.

Soundness, though, is relative. Most horses have some problems, and a lot of those problems are things you can live with as long as the horse has talent and suits the rider. The key is whether or not the problem hinders his ability for the purpose you have in mind. In judging this, the best insurance is to deal with reputable people who will tell you frankly about the horse's faults. I usually have a horse vetted when I've decided to buy, although the vet's approval is no guarantee that there won't be trouble down the road.

My second most important area of concern is the horse's temperament. Again, what I'm looking for varies, depending on the purpose and the client I have in mind for the horse. For juniors and amateurs, for example, it's important to have a horse that's easy to work around the barn, with no kicking or biting streak. Under saddle, I want a horse that won't tense up. For that reason, a good, thorough trial ride is important; some horses become more and more excited the longer they work and the more fences they take, and that's a tendency I want to know about.

Third, I want to see a horse that has a healthy respect for jumps and an ample stride. A good stride is a critical factor, but I rank it third because in many cases, as long as the horse has good movement, structure, and temperament, minor stride problems can be worked out in training.

2

Progressive Education for
Hunters and Jumpers

Katie Monahan Prudent

One of the most popular stars of the grand prix circuit, Katie scored her first major show-ring success at the age of seven, when she rode her quarter-horse mare to the Illinois State Championship in the thirteen-and-under Junior Hunter Division. At fifteen, she won the Maclay finals. After an attempt to combine college with a riding career, she decided to devote herself full-time to horses and launched her own operation first in Upperville and then in Middleburg, Virginia, where she has trained and ridden many top grand prix jumpers, among them The Jones Boy, second in the 1979 World Cup finals; Silver Exchange, with whom she helped win the Nations Cup in Dublin, placed second in the grand prix at Dublin and Hickstead, and was selected for the 1980 Olympics; Noren, Grand Prix Horse of the Year in 1982, the same year in which Katie was named Mercedes Rider of the Year and Rolex Leading Lady Rider of the Year (a title she has won four times); and The Governor, a Holsteiner that she bought for Mrs. Averell Harriman in 1983 and that was American Grand Prix Horse of the Year in 1985. Among the many young horses she has developed are Special Envoy (with whom she won her third Invitational in 1988) and Bean Bag. Her most recent stable star is Make My Day.

Katie's training methods reflect the influence of her instructors during her equitation days: Chrystine Jones, Bob Egan, Bill Queen, Sallie Sexton, and George Morris. They also are typical of the best jumper training practices today.

Katie Monahan—Katie Monahan Prudent since her marriage to French show-jumping rider Henri Prudent—has made not one but two names for herself during her equestrian career. Photo: *Practical Horseman*

Jumpers and hunters must be total athletes. To jump through tricky combinations or put in a smooth, flowing round, meeting every fence accurately, a horse has to be balanced and responsive to his rider, and he must know without hesitation just how to handle his body and his legs. A talented horse—one who's naturally good with his legs, for example—has an advantage. But even a talented horse can't learn to jump a course in winning form in a week.

Most horses need several months of training just to perform well at lower levels, with another year or more of advanced work if they're going on to high-level competition. My program for training a young jumper or hunter is designed to keep a horse moving toward those goals by challenging him with progressively more difficult problems. I mix flat work with jumping, starting with basic gymnastics, moving on to lines made up of a variety of little fences, and, for the horse that's going on, returning to gymnastics for advanced schooling. Along the way, I look for signs that tell me the horse is ready to move up to the next level.

I'm on the road so much now that it's hard to have a regular routine at home; but in general I plan on jumping a young horse three or four times a week. I start a hunter and a jumper the same way; for the jumper, I gradually build the jumps a little bigger as his training progresses.

Basic Gymnastics

The first thing you want to do when you start a young horse over fences is to find out what his natural style is going to be—how he's going to take to jumping and what kind of form he's going to use. Gymnastics permit you to learn these things because they can be set up very simply, with normal distances between jumps, on stride for the horse. You don't have to try to find a distance to the jump, which can be difficult with a really green horse. You just steer for the center and leave the horse free to jump in the most natural way possible.

In addition to giving you an idea of the horse's basic instincts, gymnastics allow you to correct his faults. Before beginning, you should introduce your horse to single cross-rails and be sure he knows that he's supposed to go over a jump, not through it. Once he's got the idea of hopping over the poles, you can go on to two or three jumps in a row. Use simple standards and rails so that you can easily move the pieces around to make an oxer or a vertical, a cross-rail or whatever, where you want them. Start with a cross-rail, followed by another little one a stride or two away. Then gradually make the course more difficult: change the second cross-rail to a vertical; add another one or two strides to a second vertical; and later add an oxer two strides from the vertical.

Set up the fences so that all the horse has to do is to take a stride and lift his legs. For most horses, 18 feet is a comfortable one-stride distance, and 30 feet a comfortable two-stride distance. At the beginning, you should trot into the gymnastic. If the distances are set right, your horse won't have to make any stride adjustments and you won't have to intervene. At this point, your only responsibility as a rider is to teach the horse to go in a straight line through the grid, keep him at a medium pace, and observe his natural instincts.

When I first start a horse through this little gymnastic, I can usually tell right away what kind of form he's going to have. Does he hang his legs or snap them up? Does he seem to fall over a fence? Does he jump too low or too high? If you've had a bit of experience, you'll know when a horse is jumping too high, when he's making an appropriate effort. To know what his legs are doing, you'll probably need a person on the ground. In any case, when you school a young horse, it's always helpful to have a knowledgeable person there to give you ideas from the ground.

Once you know your horse's natural style, you can set up the gymnastic according to his needs. Always trot in over a cross-rail. The trot has a

Begin with a single crossrail to be sure your horse knows he's supposed to go over, not through. To encourage him, use wings and jump toward your barn.

When he can manage two crossrails two strides apart, convert the second crossrail to a small vertical.

Once he's comfortable with the vertical, add a rampy oxer two strides on.

Then square up the oxer. Now he'll have to fold his front legs faster or he'll clip the front rail.
Finally, add another vertical one stride from the oxer. Photos: *Practical Horseman*

shorter step and is more even a gait than the canter; it makes it easier for the horse to meet the cross-rail comfortably. The cross-rail is the setup point: it gets the horse into the combination at a comfortable distance from the first real fence. The learning begins inside.

If your horse is naturally good with his legs, you can ask him to start to think a bit more right from the beginning. Set up a cross-rail, one stride to a vertical, two strides to an oxer, and one stride to another vertical. He'll have to make a broader jumping effort over the oxer than over the vertical; this pattern makes him think about coming back, then going forward to the oxer, and then coming back again.

During the first few sessions, make the oxer rampy (lower in front than behind, say, 2 feet for the front rail and 2 feet 6 inches for the back). Until the horse knows what he's doing, the low front rail will give him a little more time to get his legs out of the way. Then square the oxer up. Now he'll have to pay attention and fold his front legs faster or else he'll clip the first rail. Continue to use distances that relate to his normal stride for the first week or two. You want to make jumping a pleasant experience for him.

If he's a "leg-hanger"—that is, lets his legs hang down instead of snapping them up, perhaps with one leg lower than the other—work more over rampy oxers. This type of jump gives a horse more time to fold his front legs and helps him get his front end up more than a vertical does. With a horse that hangs, I also start with two strides between elements rather than one; this gives him more time to study the jump and think about getting his legs up. From the cross-rail, go two strides to a rampy oxer 2 feet high in front and 2 feet 6 inches behind, and then go two more strides to another rampy oxer. For a leg-hanger you could set up three, four, or even five oxers in a row.

The cause of leg-hanging varies with the individual horse: some are so gangly as youngsters that they hang in the beginning and then naturally outgrow the habit. One of the most important factors in a horse's success at any level of competition is confidence. If you take a green horse that doesn't have great natural instincts and you set up tight vertical in-and-outs, you could easily destroy his confidence and develop a hanger for life. If instead you work over the rampy oxers at first, you give your horse a chance to learn how to handle himself over a jump, and he gains confidence.

A "dweller" stalls a little in the air; he also usually jumps too high. The remedy for this is to push the dweller on so that he gets the idea of going forward over his jumps instead of jumping straight up in the air and landing in a heap. Set up your basic gymnastic: cross-rail, vertical, oxer, with two strides between fences; spread out the elements, extending the two-stride distance to 32 feet. Then trot him in over the cross-rail and push him forward to the next element. He'll have to stretch a bit to make the distance.

If your horse is too aggressive, shorten the distance a little to make the two strides ride a bit tight, and square up the oxer. Now he'll have to wait or else he'll clip the front rail of the oxer. If he's speeding up, you've got to slow him down and keep him at a normal pace. Although this gymnastic is designed to let the horse learn directly from the exercise, you don't want a rusher to try to put one stride in a two-stride distance. You have to insist that he fit in two strides.

The theory behind correcting all these faults is very simple: always correct the horse with the opposite aids to what he wants to do wrong. If he wants to speed up, slow him down. If he wants to suck back and dwell, push him forward. If he tries to drift or pull to the right, hold him straight with the left rein; for a stronger correction, ask him to turn left in the air as he's jumping out over the last element.

Adjust your aids to suit the horse. If he's aggressive and has natural forward motion, you may need only hand, not leg, to get him straight in the air. A hot runaway who's already pulling doesn't need more leg; you just steer him into straightness. On the other hand, if he bulges to the right when you take up on the left to correct the initial drift, it's because he's not going forward. When the horse is almost stopping and sucking back as he goes to the side, you can't just keep pulling on his mouth; you must push him into straightness.

If you feel that the horse is sucking back and drifting to the right as you come to the cross-rail, the first thing to do is push him forward into a normal medium pace. Use your leg, cluck (horses respond very well to sounds), and carry a little stick on the side to which he tends to drift. Use the stick on the way to the cross-rail (it's hard to take your hands off the reins in the middle of a gymnastic); lay it behind your leg rather than on the shoulder, in order to reinforce the leg aid. Then keep pressing with the right leg to push him over and through the gymnastic.

There's not a whole lot you can do about a "twister" (a horse that lays on his side), aside from keeping him as straight as possible in the middle of his jump. I'm not much in favor of using devices such as poles laid out at right angles to the fence to hold a horse straight, because you won't have them to help you in the show ring. Straightness comes from training on the flat. You've got to develop a training system that allows you to straighten the horse with your aids, not with gimmicks.

Work on the small gymnastics might take a month or more—but

sometimes considerably less. Once your horse is jumping confidently and you've developed your opinion about his form and instincts, you can begin to introduce different types of single jumps.

Flat Work

All the time you're teaching your horse to jump, his flat work should be progressing: transitions from gallop to canter, strong trot to collected trot, canter to collected canter. A young horse has to learn this flat work and sharpen his responses to the rider's aids at the same time he's learning to jump. Gradually, you put the two together.

Thanks to the gymnastics, you should have an idea of what your horse's problems are: not just jumps, but ridability too. Is he a rusher, a sucker-back? Does he stay straight? You must start to correct those problems on the flat. You should be working on lengthening and shortening the horse's stride, getting him to respond to your leg: to move up when you close your leg, instead of pinning his ears, sucking back, swishing his tail. You should also be starting to develop your horse's mouth by gait transitions and collection, going from canter to trot, canter to collected canter.

Teaching a horse the collected canter is a constant effort; as you try to collect the stride, the horse often breaks into a trot, so you have to leg him again to get him back into a canter. Collection is one of the hardest things for a young horse to learn but also one of the most important. It allows you to position the horse where you want him in front of a jump. If he gallops to a fence in an open stride with no ability to adjust or shorten that stride, you have only a 50–50 chance of getting there right.

A good exercise for collecting the horse at trot and canter is to see first how slowly you can get him to trot without breaking into a walk and then how slowly you can get him to canter without breaking into a trot. Give a little tap with your stick or a little spur if he breaks, and teach him how to shorten his stride. Do a few strides forward and then come back, just a few strides at a time. Work on this day after day. Collection isn't something that comes overnight; it's something the horse has to learn. Collection is harder for some horses than others. But even if it's hard, don't be sloppy about it; struggle and work at it.

Little Fences and Lines

After a horse has learned to jump the little gymnastic, he has to jump the things that scare him, the things he's going to have to face during the rest of his life. I also want the horse to learn right from the beginning that he can't just plough through jumps. Once I'm sure he won't hurt himself, sure that he has the idea of getting over the fence, I move to small single fences and solid things that will seem a little scary to him, like logs or barrels.

When your horse has got over pecking at the gymnastics and goes through it easily—a month is the average time it takes to reach this point—he's ready to go on to the scary jumps and keep his mind occupied. We have barrels, a panel painted bright yellow, various plank jumps, a liverpool made of plywood painted bright blue, all little and low, but scary. And we don't always work in the ring. When the horse has grasped the basics, I'll take him on the trails and jump small logs, ditches, and so forth. After all, many horses that don't show learn to jump this way.

When you introduce the scary little jumps, start by trotting over them. The first goal is to make sure the horse goes over. With barrels, for example, you can add wings, carry a stick, and have a person on each side cluck in order to encourage your horse to hop over. If he stops, punish him mildly. Keep the jumps simple: no more than two feet high.

Once your horse is capable and confident over different kinds of fences, you can set lines which demand more of him. At the beginning, set them on stride. A normal stride is 12 feet long. To find out where your horse's stride fits, set up a line of two little fences. Measure the distance between them at 48 feet (a normal three strides, with an additional 12 feet for takeoff and landing). Then canter your horse into that line. Be sure to maintain a canter—not a trot, not a gallop.

If your horse clears the first jump, canters three strides, and jumps the second one comfortably, you can assume he has a normal 12-foot stride. If he jumps the first jump, takes three strides and chips in an extra fourth, you have to assume that his stride is short. If he jumps in, takes two strides, and chips in the third, you can conclude that his stride is long.

Start by setting the fences three or four strides apart. Now that you've introduced scary jumps, use any kind of obstacle: a little gate to a little wall, for example. In the beginning, it will be hard merely to maintain the proper pace. Some horses get anxious after they've learned how to canter over jumps; they tend to rush. But you want your horse to keep a steady pace as he goes around the course. The distance over low jumps isn't so important; if you don't find an ideal takeoff spot, it doesn't matter so long as the horse learns that he must canter to the jumps, not bolt and rush, not suck back and trot.

If he seems to be rushing and falling on his front end, you must teach him not to, perhaps by cantering the first fence, stopping him before the second, and backing so that he learns to jump into the line and wait. Or you might canter the first fence, come back to a trot for the second, and then stop again and back. You have to say through your aids, "Hey, wait a minute! I'm still up here and I'm in command. You've got to listen to me." So go back to practicing transitions and stopping.

If you jump into a line and the horse drifts way off to the right, circle around and come again. This time, turn him left in the air. The principle is the same as in your earlier gymnastic work: you correct the horse with the opposite of what he does wrong.

When you can keep him straight and keep his pace even through simple lines at home, he's ready to show—not show well, but get over a little course. At this point, you'll ride him around it at a slow hand gallop, slightly faster than a normal canter. Showing will further his education by introducing him to new jumps, new rings, new situations. If he doesn't show in perfect form, it doesn't matter at this stage; as his confidence increases, his form will improve.

Nevertheless, there are limits to how much you can improve a horse's form. If he's riding well, maintaining pace and adjusting stride, not rushing or boring down on the bit (all of which are corrected by transitions, turns, and lateral work with your leg on the flat that teaches him how to balance himself), then he has the best chance of jumping in his best possible form. A horse is going to jump the way his natural instincts dictate. You can deal with straightness, keep him at a good pace and in balance, and prevent him from leaning on the bridle—but you can't perform miracles.

If the horse jumps flat, you can stress a nice release in the air to make sure you're not on his mouth. But I'm not into gimmicks. For a horse that is jumping flat or holding his head up in the air, the only other thing I do occasionally is to put a rail on the ground anywhere from 9 to 12 feet in front of the fence and another the same distance beyond it. The rails encourage him to stay round in the air. He looks down and sees where he's landing and thinks about putting his head down instead of stargazing.

If the horse doesn't outgrow the tendency to hang his legs, you can go back to gymnastics. You can also try to help him lift his front end in the air by keeping a feel on the mouth during the takeoff and keeping your shoulders back a little behind the vertical, in order to balance him. Since horses tend to hang more at verticals than at oxers (because the jumping effort is more vertical), the rider sometimes needs to support his horse's mouth more at a vertical.

Introducing More Difficult Lines

As your flat work progresses, you'll find that your horse begins to listen to you when you see a distance to a jump and ask him to shorten, for example. Now you can make the lines a little trickier. Very rarely will you find a course where every distance looks perfect as you come out of the turns. The best riders adjust all the time—but they do it imperceptibly. The horses have to learn to adjust to the rider's signals.

Set up a line of three fences three strides apart. Between the first two, take your normal distance and shorten it a foot or two; between the second and third, lengthen it 5 feet. You'll ride this line back and forth, so that the horse goes from short to long and from long to short. He has to learn not only to adjust his stride, but also to listen to the rider: short or long, he has to get to the next jump in three strides.

It's much easier to go from short to long than from long to short, because it's easier to get a horse to move up than to come back. So a line that is, say, 47 feet to 53 feet—a short three to a long three—should be fairly easy. You canter in slowly, do the short three, and, as you jump the second fence, begin to leg the horse and push him on so that he goes forward a little faster and a little longer and gets the forward three to the third jump. Most horses will lengthen nicely. If your horse gets quick, coordinate a little leg with a little feel in the mouth so that he goes forward without rushing.

When you have this down pat, make a half turn and come back down the line the other way. If you're approaching a long line, the first thing you have to do is open up your horse's stride. Many riders hold coming out of the turn and look for a big distance to the first fence; they want a big jump going into the line to get the long distance all the way through it. You'll have a better chance of finding a forward jump if you let the horse lengthen or open his stride through the turn and on the approach to the line. Then, even if you don't get a perfect first distance, your horse will still have enough momentum to cover the long distances inside the line.

Get your horse going a little more forward, open up the stride, and

A rampy oxer gives a leg-hanger extra time to fold up his front end. First time through, this young horse drops one knee . . .

. . . but he soon catches on and pulls up both front legs.

Later, with a horse that doesn't entirely outgrow his tendency to hang, you can help lift the front end by keeping your shoulders back a little during takeoff and keeping a feel of his mouth.

If your horse sucks back, cluck, apply leg, and use your stick behind your leg as you approach the crossrail.

If he dwells in the air, lengthen the distances between elements a little and move him forward. He'll have to stretch to reach the fence comfortably.

For a horse that jumps flat, place a rail on the ground 9 feet in front of the fence and another rail 9 feet out on the landing side. The horse will look down at the landing rail and stay rounder in the air.
Photos: *Practical Horseman*

look for the first jump. Then push him forward to get the long distance to the second fence. Now you have a short distance right away, so your horse must respond to your hand. Close your fingers, take a feel on the mouth, and use your arms, bringing your upper body back a little just as the horse is landing. Don't wait a stride or you'll be too late. Keep that pressure until he starts to decrease his pace. If he doesn't, it may be that his training on the flat is insufficient. Go back to working on lengthening and shortening his stride.

Perhaps your horse shortens fine on the flat, but you still have trouble with the line. You jump in boldly, do the forward three, jump the middle fence, close your fingers—and nothing happens. You do two strides, chip in and pop up over the third fence, and say to yourself, "Rats! What went wrong?"

What went wrong is that your horse didn't respond quickly enough. So repeat the line: do the bold three, and then, as you land to put in the steady three, lie right back and wrench him to a stop. Now your horse says, "I'd better listen in this line." The next time you close your fingers, he'll come right back and put in the three.

There are times when a rider must be strong to educate the horse, but strong doesn't mean rough. Temper should never enter into your training. It's simply a question of teaching the horse to respond. I expect my horses to do this sort of line badly the first few times, even to forget between sessions. A horse that does it well right off the bat is very rare. It's a constant, gradual process. Training a horse is like educating a child: you don't send it to first grade and then immediately to college.

Often when the horse goes from long to short, he won't handle the jump coming out very well. It's hard for him to shorten his stride in a tight space. He may knock the fence down, twist over it, or even stop if he thinks he's getting in dead wrong. Through repetition, doing various lines and distances, he'll learn to handle his body from different spots and at different paces and get used to a whole range of demands from you.

Meanwhile, you should be dabbling in a variety of exercises. Constantly mix flat work in with the jumping. Do the short-to-long line; then, depending on the lead you land on, do a counter-canter through the turn. Or work on the flying change. Or come back to a trot with the shoulder-in. Educating the horse with jumping and flat work mixed together from the start is very important. Bending, leg-yielding, and lateral exercises are particularly valuable for hunters and jumpers. By increasing your horse's responsiveness, you better your chances of keeping him straight and in balance through a line of fences.

A horse needs a full year of basic hunter-level education before he's ready to go on to serious hunter competition or as a jumper. Even if you see from the start that your horse is bounding over his jumps effortlessly, you can chalk up the first year to practice: getting him to listen and come back, to go forward, not to be afraid of the strange surroundings of a show. He has a baby mind. The jumps are spooky, the rings are spooky, the flowers are spooky.

Preparing for Higher Levels

Eventually—perhaps well into your horse's first year of showing, more likely into his second—you reach the point where he's unafraid of any jump. He's riding around a course of fences. If it's a long line and you ask him to go forward, he goes right forward; if it's a tight line and you ask him to come back, he comes right back. Now you have to teach him to handle his body and legs like a gymnast or a figure skater who's going on to the highest levels of competition.

When the horse has reached this point in his training, you can start riding him through advanced gymnastics. This work is useful for hunters and jumpers alike because it teaches the horse to judge his fences for himself in all sorts of situations. It also gives you practice in helping your horse to meet his fences right.

The hardest part of a jumper course is the triple combinations. The horse has to know how to measure the distance inside the combination himself. When you're in a triple combination, you're working with two strides at the most—often just one stride—and you can only do so much. The horse has to be clever; he has to want to clear the jumps.

There are no triple combinations on hunter courses, and the striding is usually consistent through a line; but a hunter must still approach each line with the proper pace, length of stride, and balance. If it's a long line, you are responsible for moving up around the turn and looking for a distance out of that pace. If it's a steady line, you must collect during the turn and approach at a slower pace. While working through your gymnastic at home, you should gradually present your horse with every type of situation he might find in the show ring.

At this higher level, you'll canter rather than trot into the gymnastics in order to make the exercise more difficult. Work on adjusting your horse's stride during the approach. At first you merely steered him to the gymnastic and let him figure it out for himself; now it's your job not only to ride him well inside the gymnastic but also to see that he approaches the combination properly.

How you design the gymnastic depends on the horse and his individual problems. Let's take The Governor as an example. He's an extremely careful horse. When I got him from Europe, he'd just come off a bad ride and was very scared. When he gets scared, his stride gets really quick: it's like a little drumroll; you can't even hear his hooves touching. He'd get in trouble in combinations by being so quick and panicking his way out. In the beginning, I worked him through tight combinations at a very slow pace, making him take his time and go slowly. As he began to respond, I gradually lengthened the combinations and spread them out. I finally got him to the point where he'd lengthen his stride instead of doing his drumroll. But this was only after weeks and months of practicing slowly. I'd usually set the fences anywhere from 21 to 22 feet for one stride and from 33 to 34 feet for two strides. I'd do one stride and then two, back and forth. And I varied the work constantly: sometimes one and one, sometimes two and two. I'd use different types of fences: oxer to vertical, or whatever, so that he'd see and know everything without anticipating. This schooling was really all he needed to regain his confidence. For example, this year on the morning of the Tampa, Florida, Invitational (which he won), all I did was set up a triple combination: oxer, vertical, oxer, with one stride between each pair. I started at 3 feet 9 inches and built it up until it was 4 feet 9 inches or 5 feet, just to continue building his confidence.

When you work your horse over advanced gymnastics, you should offer him different types of problems over a long period of time so that he gradually learns how to handle himself in every possible situation. Instead of setting the fences at perfect distances, use distances that force him to adjust: for a jumper, a tight one stride to a big vertical, where he has to slow down and rock back on his hocks and jump up, or a long one-stride to a big oxer, where he has to go forward or else get in trouble and hit the back rail. Again, work tight-to-long, long-to-tight, long-to-long, tight-to-tight. For hunters, most course designers work off a stride that is a little longer than 12 feet, more like 12 feet 6 inches or 13; in the beginning, school slowly out of a canter, moving up into a hand gallop.

You can't teach these skills in one day, one week, or one month. For example, suppose you set up a wide oxer with a tight one-stride to a tall vertical. Your horse may catch the back rail of the oxer in his attempt to suck back to clear the vertical. You have to repeat the combination often enough for him to get the hang of it.

It also takes an experienced rider to teach these skills. If you set up an oxer with a very tight one-stride to a big vertical, you can't come barreling in at a mad gallop, because that's not fair to the horse. You have to ask for a rather collected slow gallop in order to give him enough impulsion to make it over the oxer—but not so much that he can't fit in that one stride and make it over the vertical. It's your job to meet the first jump with just the right speed, balance, and impulsion to negotiate the combination.

Introducing a horse to the skills required to deal with triple combinations involves a minimum of one year of advanced gymnastics, after the first year of basic hunter-level training. The AHSA's program is pretty realistic: at least one year in the Preliminary Division with heights of 4 feet 3 inches to 4 feet 6 inches—although an exceptionally good horse can move up to Intermediate during his first year. It takes another year to move up to the higher level, and only a handful of jumpers make it. The others progress laterally to become junior jumpers or amateur horses when they reach their peak.

3

Conversation with a Conformation Hunter Expert

—

Kenneth Wheeler

Kenneth Wheeler, who operates Cismont Manor Farm in Virginia with his wife, Sallie Busch Wheeler, is equally expert in buying, breeding, training, showing, and judging working and conformation hunters, although he is most renowned for his extraordinary success with the latter: Cismont Manor entries have dominated the Conformation Hunter Division for a good many years and won numerous national championships and Horse of the Year awards. The stable is also active in the Fine Harness Division, breeding and showing hackney horses and ponies as well as American saddlebreds.

How did you come to be one of the few hunter trainers associated primarily with the Conformation Division?

I've always liked the pretty horse. I get great satisfaction from picking out a colt, having him grow into a good-looking horse, and then showing him.

What do you look for in a conformation hunter?

A pretty head and a pretty front. He should have a fine throat latch and his neck should come out of his shoulder properly. A nice-necked horse is appealing even when he's standing in his stall.

You need a straight hind leg in a strip horse. The hock should line up with the point of the butt. You want a horse with a good topline, preferably a close-coupled, short-backed horse. Naturally, a conformation horse must have good clean legs with good bones, short cannons, good length to the pastern, and straight feet.

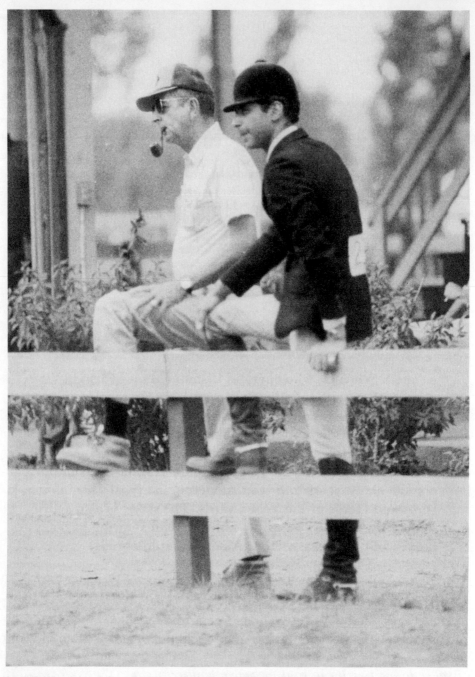

Kenneth Wheeler and Cismont Stable rider Tommy Serio watch preceding rounds in a hunter class in which Tommy will show a Wheeler-trained entry. Photo: James Leslie Parker

We look for medium-sized horses: 16.1 hands is a good average size. People go crazy over tremendously big horses, but when a horse gets too big, it's difficult to find everything in proportion. The medium size is usually your nicest horse.

Since you probably won't find all of these qualities in any one horse, which ones do you consider indispensable and which can you do without?

A conformation horse must have a straight hind leg. And these days you really need a horse that moves well. He should walk straight, front and back, and move out from his shoulder. You've seen horses that just flip their toes out. This is a good characteristic if they move from the shoulder at the same time they send the toe out.

Presence means a lot, as when the judge walks down a line of ten horses and there is one that suddenly looks at him in a way that catches his eye.

What about blemishes? Does a horse have to be absolutely clean-legged to be a strip horse?

There aren't many blemishes allowable on a conformation horse if you're showing him strictly on the line. He has to be clean. In a performance horse, however, if a horse has a little splint but still has a nice trip, the splint might set him back in the judging, but it wouldn't eliminate him.

Do the qualities considered desirable in a conformation horse also contribute to a better athletic performance?

A horse that is built correctly usually makes the best horse, but certain slight variations—a hind leg not perfectly straight, a less than perfect shoulder—don't mean that the horse won't be able to perform well. Hind legs, except for a badly sickle-hocked horse, don't bother performance. The most important ingredients of a successful performance are ability and disposition. If your horse has a good temperament, you can teach him anything.

Where do you look for strip horse prospects?

I go to some of the sales, especially Timonium, Maryland, where I've bought a lot of nice yearlings. I also contact a good many of the other professionals I know. Often if they think they have an exceptional strip horse, they'll call me.

We generally buy about ten young horses a year, ranging in age from weanling to four-year-old. We prefer buying the four-year-olds, but they're much harder to find, so we've had to go on to the younger ones.

To what extent can you tell what the mature horse is going to look like by looking at the weanling?

Some things don't change. If the hind leg, head, and shoulder are good in the weanling, they'll stay that way. When you buy a weanling, you want a lot of quality and especially a very long neck. A six-month-old colt may be adorable, but if he's a little too compact, too mature-looking, he won't have enough scope when he fills out. Sometimes your

Even the best-mannered hunter needs an occasional distraction during a long class. Photo: James Leslie Parker

better horses, particularly the bigger ones, don't look like very much until they're three or four years old.

When a yearling has an average-length neck and a finished look to his structure, he'll probably make a nice horse but not an outstanding one. If you see a two-year-old with a neck bordering on coarse, you can usually predict that he'll be too thick in the neck at the age of three.

It's hard to tell about the fully grown size of a colt very far in advance. If he's average-sized, and if his dam and sire are both of a nice size, then he should be big enough for any judge to accept. An average-sized weanling should blossom as a yearling. The great big ones, which we call overgrown colts, generally take longer to fully develop their best proportions.

How much can you tell about a colt from his bloodlines?

I don't place too much importance in breeding, except in terms of disposition. I prefer to know that a particular stallion's horses are quiet. I do believe that certain stallions get better-looking horses than others, but it could be because they stand in an area of the country where higher quality mares are available.

When you buy a weanling or yearling, do you hope to resell him right away, or do you raise him and show him?

We try to sell them as soon as they're in topflight shape, which is why we prefer the average-sized weanling that will blossom as a yearling to the larger horse that is a slow developer. Generally speaking, you can sell them more readily when they're yearlings and two-year-olds.

Although I think it's good for the stable to have winning horses, all of our stock is for sale. If we have a proven winner or one we think will be rather special, we try to sell him to one of our own clients in order to keep him in our barn. But he'd still be available on the open market.

How much should the buyer expect to pay for a yearling with enough quality to show in hand?

They've really gone up in price these past few years. A horse capable of winning immediately at top A shows would obviously be much more expensive than one that couldn't be shown until he was older. But it's virtually impossible to quote specific figures.

When you buy a weanling or yearling for resale, how do you go about getting it into condition?

A weanling should get about 8 quarts a day of crushed oats and sweet feed, along with good mixed hay. As he grows, I increase the amount of feed accordingly.

I like timothy and clover hay, or timothy and alfalfa. Some people feed straight alfalfa, but I think that's a bit too much protein. I also often use a blood tonic supplement, and I think it's a good idea to run blood counts regularly, as well as to maintain a good worming program.

We keep our colts in stalls and turn them out for exercise. Young colts need lots of exercise, much more than older horses. Of course, if you're trying to get a colt ready to show, you can't leave him out as much as you can if you're just trying to raise a nice, healthy colt.

We put a shine on our colts with good feed and by rubbing them every day. After they're groomed, we usually bring them out, stand them up, and admire them ourselves. By getting used to standing up every day, it comes pretty easily to them when they get in the ring.

When do you start teaching them to jump?

In the fall of their two-year-old year, after the indoor shows are over, we start them jumping. We worked with about ten or twelve young horses last winter, some of them conformation prospects and others working hunters. We chose them because they were nice-looking, moved well, or seemed to have obvious potential.

We hope they will all ultimately have good dispositions. If a colt is quiet, there will always be a place for him somewhere in the world. But if he doesn't have the necessary disposition or desire, he'll never make a successful show horse.

Do you school the conformation prospects differently from the working horses?

No. I school them all the same way and just hope they aren't injured. Actually, they get hurt in the paddocks much more than they do during schooling. Sometimes one will suddenly turn up with a scar or a splint, which of course immediately puts him in the Working Hunter Division.

What about condition? Do the conformation horses need special care to keep them in good flesh?

You have to put them in peak condition. A working hunter can afford to be a little drawn from a long campaign, and if he still jumps well, it's no handicap. But when a conformation hunter drops even a little weight, he doesn't look as good as he has to in order to win. You start out in the spring with your horse big and fat and in good shape; then you continue to feed him well and take care of him in order to maintain his appearance.

Perfect working hunter form: Kenneth Wheeler rides Gozzi, one of the most outstanding horses he has trained and shown. Photo: Budd

Sometimes it doesn't work out that way. You think your horse is sufficiently filled out at home, but when you get him to a show and compare him to the other horses, he's not fat enough to win. When he's not carrying quite as much weight as he should, he's going to look a little high off the ground, as if he didn't have enough middle or depth.

Is there a bigger demand for conformation horses than for working hunters?

There's a good market for conformation horses, but I wouldn't say it's greater than the market for working horses. So many working hunters eventually turn into amateur or children's horses. As a rule, however, a conformation horse brings a slightly higher price, since they're harder to find. Frankly, I think that if a horse performs well and is also attractive to look at, then it's only natural that he should be worth more.

4

Selecting, Breaking, and Training
a Show Hunter

Bucky Reynolds

Son of the top judge, dealer, and trainer J. Arthur Reynolds, Bucky has specialized in producing top conformation hunters at Merryweather Farm in Warrenton, Virginia. As co-owner of this leading show stable, he has discovered and developed many champions, including Henry the Hawk, Early Light, Flashlite, Rocky Raccoon (later a successful show jumper), and two Horses of the Year, Stocking Stuffer and Gozzi. At a recent National Horse Show in New York, all of the four Hunter champions had once been trained or owned by him! He is also an active Hunter judge, and a prominent figure on the Thoroughbred sales scene.

In order to produce a top conformation horse, you have to have a good one to start with. Sounds simple? Actually, I think it is—provided that you've picked the right horse. Selection is the key to success.

There are countless ways to train a horse successfully, as long as your methods remain within the realms of good judgment and common sense. I think anyone training within that wide range could have produced such champions as Gozzi, Henry the Hawk, and Square Lake. I was just lucky to find them. I gave them some guidance and exposure, and tried not to get in their way, and they did the rest. To say there weren't some problems and anxious moments along the way would not be entirely true, but by and large they made it awfully easy.

I've seen some problem horses turned into star performers mostly through sheer perseverance and skill. But these are exceptions to the rule, and I don't like to gamble on exceptions.

During the past five or six years, I've scoured the country and attended sales in a dozen states from Virginia to California, looking for young horses to buy. Most are yearling sales, as well as a few two-year-old sales in the spring.

From a business point of view, it doesn't make sense to buy green working prospects as young colts unless they are exceptional bargains. You won't have an opportunity to sell them until they are three years old and starting to jump. So you'll have to wait for a year or two, and this increases your investment considerably. And there's still no guarantee that they'll turn out to be good jumpers.

But with the breeding division now being offered in horse shows, there's a ready market for conformation prospects. So I don't hesitate to buy what I consider to be a good-looking colt, because I know that I can always find a buyer for him. Marketability, then, is the difference between buying green working prospects and green conformation prospects at a young age.

The biggest problem in buying conformation prospects is that I have to look at literally thousands of colts in order to find enough of them to support my business. A really outstanding conformation horse is a rarity.

Selection

I go to about a dozen sales a year and follow the same procedure at all of them. The first thing I do when I get the catalog is to cross out all the pedigrees that are beyond my price range. Then I go to the sales grounds in the morning and take a look at all the colts I haven't crossed out. I don't look at any fillies—not that I have any particular dislike for them, but because my customers prefer colts.

There are certain bloodlines I'm partial to, and some that I don't care for because of past experience with temperament or ability. For example, I like Bold Ruler breeding. They are the best-looking and best-conformed horses in the world. But for the most part, I look for conformation rather than bloodlines. I'm also very particular about how a horse moves. Any horse that I'll consider purchasing must have a good rhythmical walk.

When I see a horse that interests me, I always go back and have a second look. I like to talk to the owner or the person who cares for him. During our conversation I might discover something about the colt's temperament and disposition. Whether or not he has brains is all-important to me.

Once I've decided that I'd like to buy something, I decide how much I'll spend, although I often wind up paying a little more than I had planned to pay.

Breaking

When I bring yearlings home, the general program is to break them in the fall—October or November—and then turn them out for a full year. I think that turning them out at this age (as opposed to stall confinement) is conducive to producing athletes and horses with mental stability. They learn to take their licks and to stand up for themselves. I like the kind of horses I get from this practice.

Gordon Fishback, who makes his living breaking colts and is an expert in his field, breaks all of my yearlings. He comes with his exercise saddle and a snaffle bridle and plays with them in the stall, and before you know it, he's riding them. It never takes him more than three days to get on one, and even three days is exceptional. Usually he has them tacked and is on their backs for ten minutes or so within the first two days. And that's as long as he spends with any colt. He's on and off before they've had a chance to get annoyed.

When they can walk, trot, canter, turn a little, and stop—all of which happens very quickly, during a total riding time of about three weeks—he stops riding and they're turned out again. In the fall of their two-year-old year, Gordon returns and gets on the colts for a day or so to remind them of their lessons as yearlings. Then I begin to ride them.

When I start working with the two-year-olds, they're still turned out in the field. We bring each colt in individually, clean him, and ride him for about twenty minutes, and then back out he goes. The colts benefit not only from the riding but also from the routine of being handled and groomed each day.

These twenty-minute riding sessions for the late two-year-olds are usually identical during the first two or three weeks. At the beginning of each ride, I spend eight or ten minutes just letting them unwind a little. I try to be indulgent, keeping in mind that it's only natural for them to be lively and cheerful. After walking, trotting, and cantering both ways of the ring, most colts will settle down to a point where they are receptive to a few things that require concentration. Their lessons at this stage are very elementary: responding to leg aids, turning, stopping, and backing a couple of steps. I never try to push colts into the bridle. They seem to get there soon enough.

Every effort is made to adapt the duration of these training periods to the colt's attention span, which unfortunately is very brief. If you exceed the span, young horses become disinterested and aggravated, which is the first step toward making them dislike their work and so must be avoided at all cost. The last few minutes of each ride are spent walking around the ring on a loose rein.

The colts I'm working with continue to live out until the latter part of February or March, when it's time to decide whether a colt will be shown as a three-year-old or whether he'll be given an extra year and brought out at four. If he is to be shown, he must be brought into the stable in order to get him in show shape by the beginning of the season.

All the horses that are kept in the stable are turned out in the paddocks for at least half an hour before they are ridden. There's no substitute for freedom. I've often thought that if I were faced with the choice of giving up my paddocks or my ring, I might just let my ring go.

Jumping

I usually start jumping my colts after they have been in work for three or four weeks. By that time they should be responding adequately to the leg and hand aids, so that their approach to the fence is controllable. If all the variables in the approach are correct, once a horse reaches the fence he's in a position to display his natural ability as a jumper. After that, jumping is merely a matter of exposure to the fences.

My first step in schooling over fences is walking and trotting over rails placed on the ground between standards. When the colt is performing quietly, I go on to cross-rails with ground lines on both sides so that I can jump back and forth. At the end of a couple of weeks, I'm jogging over little individual fences around the ring. Eventually I progress to some comfortably spaced in-and-outs. At this stage, the colt's responses to the aids are not refined enough to deal with distances requiring any adjustment of stride. In the approach, I trot freely forward on a very light contact. As the colt leaves the ground, I make sure that my seat is well off his back and remains so until after landing. This encourages him to use his back. I also give him complete freedom of the mouth over the fence to encourage proper use of the neck. I continue to jog over fences for about a month before I start to canter. Even when we've reached this point, I start each schooling day with some trotting fences.

My jumps are as simple as possible, but are built with a lot of material to encourage the horse to jump them. All too often a horse is tempted merely to "step" over something that doesn't seem to be very solid. So from the beginning my horses are taught to respect the construction of the fences.

The early schooling fences are built to follow the horse's jumping arc. An oxer with the front side slightly lower than the back or a vertical with the ground line set well back allows the young horse ample time to gain altitude before encountering any difficulty. Should a horse make a mistake over one of these fences, he's likely to hit his coronet band or his hoof. Almost invariably, his reaction the next time he jumps is to bring his knees up and out of the way. I never try to get a colt deep to the base of the fence until I'm absolutely sure that the habit of bringing his knees forward has been firmly established.

Because Virginia winters are severe, cross-country riding and training are impossible then, so I go to Southern Pines, North Carolina, in the latter part of January. Down there the sandy footing is ideal, and I can

Bucky Reynolds demonstrates Square Lake's form over fences at the Sedgefield Charity Horse Show. Photo: Linda McFarland

get out almost every day. The trails are filled with little logs and Aikens, the best possible types of jump for a young horse. We usually go out in groups of three or four and just pop over the fences as we come upon them. There are various rings available for schooling too. I prefer to hack to the ring in which I've chosen to school, so that by the time we get there the horses are all calmed down, which makes everything much easier. Nothing creates jumping faults more readily than schooling a horse who is too high.

After all my experience with young horses, the thing I still find the most difficult to combat is the urge to overschool. Unless a horse is doing something grossly wrong, schooling sessions should be kept short. Young horses are going to have good days and bad days. That's only natural. If your schooling sessions get progressively longer, the first thing you'll discover is that the bad days are beginning to outnumber the good days.

If you have a really talented jumper, it will be hard to hold his attention at 3 feet 6 inches throughout the first year. The newer things look to him, the longer he'll remain interested. If he's not looking to the left or right by the time he gets to his first show, he's already done too much. I'm willing to sacrifice the early part of the year so that by the time the most important shows come along in the summer, I have a horse that's still interested.

All the time I'm working with the young horses, I'm trying to evaluate them. Because of past experience, I'm very leery of the horse that is always nervous about his work. He usually gets worse, not better. Form faults in jumping are also of great concern to me. Sound training methods can help correct jumping faults to a certain extent, but if the horse's basic instincts aren't right, the faults will always be there underneath. I like to see a horse canter in good balance too. This is one gait that can be improved, but will never be really good unless it's natural.

To sum up, my training credo is a simple one. First, you select a horse you think has the potential to be good. If your selection is good and if your training is commensurate with the horse's physical and mental capabilities, then the end result is bound to be good.

5

How to Develop Proper Head Carriage

Rickey Harris and Ray Francis

An open jumper is not penalized for faulty head carriage—except to the extent that it's a handicap in producing the best possible jumping effort. With a hunter, however, head carriage simply has to be right (or at least look right) if he's to have any chance of a top ribbon in the show ring; a horse that holds its head too high (the most common fault) is severely penalized.

What can be done to improve a horse's head carriage? Two hunter experts describe their methods. Rickey Harris, a prominent Illinois-based trainer, produced many winning hunters and jumpers, as well as many top junior riders, before turning her attention to the training of Thoroughbred racehorses. Ray Francis, an English-born trainer, instructor, and judge who specializes in training and dealing in young hunter stock, is now based in Doylestown, Pennsylvania.

Rickey Harris

Much of the "look" of a hunter is due to the way his neck comes out of his shoulder. I like to see a horse's head and neck come out of the withers in a nice curve, with the head held fairly low. I like an almost straight line from the back to the withers, to the head, but the neck should have an upward curve to it and the horse's face should be perpendicular.

Certainly for the Under Saddle classes, horses with the most naturally correct head carriage are the easiest to work with. You can almost always get a horse to carry his head in the proper place with proper schooling, but most horses with inverted necks will revert to their old habits when they get nervous in the show ring. The longer the neck, the easier it is to set it in the right place.

When I'm buying horses for clients, I try to avoid conformation faults they'll have to fight with. But you can do a lot for a horse's head and neck with the use of a bitting rig and draw reins and with proper flat work. If you do your homework, a very good rider can control the horse's head position.

To work on a head carriage problem, I use a bitting rig in the stall or longe the horse in it. The adjustment depends on the individual horse. If he likes to stick his head up and has a very hard mouth, I adjust it rather short. If he is very solid on the bridle, you can tighten up and draw his head right in. I usually use the bitting rig for about half an hour a day in the stall or for as long as necessary when longeing. Some horses get the benefit in ten minutes; others have to be longed for thirty or forty minutes. You don't want to overdo it though, or they'll drop way behind the bit. If a horse won't take the bridle at all, I don't like to put him in these things until he comes up to the bit properly. Also, with very young horses, I wouldn't work them so long in the bitting rig, because their attention span is shorter.

With an experienced rider, I like to do a lot of work in draw reins because it's a slightly quicker method. With a horse that really likes to carry his head up, I use the draw reins under the chest, between the front legs. If a horse gets very hard in the corners of his mouth on his turns, then I use the draw reins to the side, under the saddle billets.

I like to do a lot of walking, shoulder-ins, serpentines, and exercises in which the rider uses his legs to drive the horse's head down, but not so strongly that the horse gets excited. I like to do a lot of exercises that teach the horse to accept the rider's leg and hand. Most often, horses put their heads up because they haven't accepted the rider's hand and leg. I sometimes even jump in draw reins, but, of course, only with a very competent rider up. And never big fences. Fairly little ones will do.

I never use running martingales on hunters, although I do occasionally on jumpers. But I'm a great believer in standing martingales. They're not a cure-all, but a lot of other problems are caused by not being able to get a horse's head in the right place, and a martingale will do that. The goal, of course, is eventually to get the horse to go on a slack martingale or none at all. But some horses never will. In these cases, I don't hesitate to tie the head right down.

Ray Francis

Proper head carriage isn't so much a matter of angle as degree. Almost every horse will have a slightly different head carriage. The natural head carriage the horse would have when walking free is to me the most attractive in a hunter.

Horses with a tendency to be high-headed are often rather thick through the shoulder, short and heavy through the neck, with the neck muscles a little more tied into the shoulder. It's interesting to note that high-headed horses also tend to have more back problems. This figures, since their back is under so much more strain.

The high-headed horse is very difficult to deal with, and I wouldn't recommend buying a horse with that particular problem if it could be avoided. Nine times out of ten it was caused by a rider with too-strong hands combined with a very strong seat and leg, which pushes the horse's head up. After a while the horse gets in the habit, and then it is almost impossible to correct completely.

Working on this problem is more a matter of perseverance than of drilling, since drilling is probably what caused it in the first place. Perhaps with patient retraining, the horse can be persuaded to drop his head, but he'll probably revert right back when he is under tension. I can't recall ever seeing a high-headed horse that was cured of the habit and wouldn't revert back to it under stress.

This being said, I think the best way to attempt to remedy a high-head problem is with normal draw reins, run down between the horse's front legs, used with very soft reins and soft legs. A snaffle bit must be used, of course—preferably of soft rubber or, next best, a thick-mouth snaffle. I'd do lots of work on the flat, lots of circling and figure eights, in the draw reins. To start with, I like to hold the draw reins and bridle reins in different hands, because I think you can be a little softer, a little subtler, in playing with them that way. A bit later I'd hold them together, separated by just one finger, but only when the horse is more relaxed about the whole thing. It's very important to work with very soft hands and without a great amount of driving with the legs, in order to get the horse to relax and drop his head. No matter how severe the problem, almost any horse will react to draw reins by dropping his head; but as soon as you take them off, he may pop it back up again. The draw reins exert pulley pressure to keep him from raising his head in toward his chest. He soon finds it easier to let his head drop to a natural position.

We're forced to use a standing martingale with a high-headed horse over fences, but it has to be short enough to be effective. Personally, I abhor running martingales and never use them. I think they do no good at all.

When schooling over fences, I set up a gymnastic consisting of cavalletti, followed by a no-stride in-and-out, and ending up with an oxer with a rail on the ground 3 feet on the far side. The distances should be rather long in order to encourage the horse to extend. Instead of emphasizing verticals in my schooling, I'd emphasize square oxers with a rail on the far side to encourage the horse to reach out and look.

6

Planning the Career of a Show Hunter

Leslie Burr Lenehan

From her home base at the Fairfield County Hunt Club in Connecticut, where she joined the famous father-son team of Bruce and Emerson Burr (no relation) in 1976, Leslie Burr, now married to Brian Lenehan, has helped develop the careers of many show hunters and a number of outstanding jumpers, including Chase the Clouds. When that great gray gelding died suddenly of colic in 1982, he was succeeded by three young horses—Albany, Boing, and Corsair—who carried her to the most successful year's record in the history of the American Grand Prix in 1983: six grand prix wins in a single season (a record); three grand prix in a row (another record); a sweep of the first three places in the grand prix at Upperville (an unprecedented achievement). She was American Grandprix Association (AGA) Rider of the Year, a member of the gold-medal-winning U.S. team at the Pan-American Games. In 1984 she rode on the gold-medal U.S. Olympic Team at Los Angeles, and in 1986 she won the World Cup finals in Sweden.

A consistent winner on the international grand prix circuit and in the Hunter Division, she also finds time to judge and to train young riders. In 1985 six of her students won ribbons in the ASPCA and AHSA medal finals.

Most of our Thoroughbred show hunters start under tack as late two-year-olds. While we're not bound to a rigid schedule, they'll be ready, if all goes well, to start showing over fences at the pre-green level by the summer of their three-year-old year.

The two-year-olds go off to another farm to be broken while I'm busy at the fall shows. I pick them up when I come back home either late in the two-year-old year or early the next year. I concentrate on teaching them to go forward, to regulate pace, and to work on a circle. I use simple direct rein aids: a pull on the right rein means turn right, a pull on both reins means stop. They're not ready at this age for real flexion or lateral work; the main thing is to maintain a relaxed attitude.

As soon as a horse can walk, trot, and canter, I start trotting him over small cross-rails and very low single jumps. When he is confident or seems a little bored, we progress to slightly bigger jumps and simple combinations.

Leslie Burr and her unforgettable show jumper, Chase the Clouds. Photo: Budd

Every young horse stops at a jump once in a while. If it happens frequently, it's a sign that you have to go back to something simpler to restore confidence. But if you advance too slowly and baby a horse too much, you can create a sour attitude. If you show your horse every fence and if you pat him every time he stops at something new, you'll make a spook out of him. He'll think he's supposed to stop.

A lot of three-year-olds start showing pre-green in Florida early in the spring. But ours are still at home, where they can be turned out for several hours of playtime a day.

By the time a horse of ours reaches his third birthday, he's cantering around small courses and he's ready to handle flying lead changes around the turns. But I gauge his attitude carefully. If the lead changes upset him, we go back to simple changes through a few steps of trot for a while. A horse that is tense about flying changes never learns to do them properly.

In most cases, our horses are ready to begin a light show schedule by summer. We show them pre-green or in the three-foot divisions offered in some eastern states. Horses these days need a year of unrecognized

Leslie Burr and Albany won a place on the U.S. team in the 1984 Olympic Games and shared in a team gold medal. Here they are clearing an obstacle on the much-praised Némethy-designed course. Photo: Courtesy of USET

showing before they're ready to go first-year green. Hunter courses are more sophisticated, and there's not usually time to school in the ring before morning classes, so that the first pre-green year is absolutely necessary for developing relaxation and ring discipline and for accustoming the horse to the horse-show atmosphere.

Although most of the horses I introduce to the show ring are young, I'd follow the same procedure with an inexperienced eight-year-old. Age doesn't dictate rate of advancement as much as the physical and mental development of the individual does. Some horses progress much faster than others. Ponies, for example, mature quickly, so a two-year-old Welsh pony might be the equivalent of a three- or four-year-old Thoroughbred. On the other hand, the European-bred horses I've worked with are much slower to mature than are Thoroughbreds. Some aren't even broken until they're three or four.

I use my time schedule only as a sort of yardstick to measure my horse's progress against what I know are reasonable expectations.

IV

Showing a Hunter

Packing for the Horse Show

Stables that spend a large part of the year traveling design their tack rooms to be functional as well as decorative. Trunks hold blankets and coolers, saddles and tack. Draped tack rooms provide a place for riders to dress and rest, and occasional sleeping quarters for grooms. When each item has its specific place, setup time is kept to a minimum.

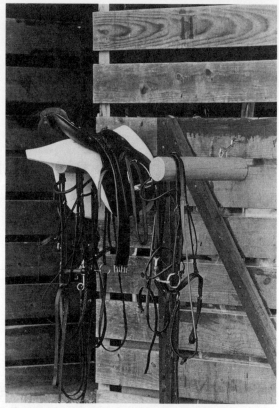

Above: A horse show setup needn't be fancy to be functional. A small sawhorse padded with scrap carpet serves as a saddle stand. Any trunk that can be locked will store miscellaneous tack and grooming items. Put your saddle away overnight, however.

Right: Two-foot sections of round fence post, painted in stable colors, provide a convenient way to keep each horse's tack handy between classes. They require only one screw eye for installation and are easily taken down at the end of each day.

If you show out of a van or trailer, you'll want all your equipment within easy reach. This bridle board is 2 inches by 4 feet, with ordinary coat hooks.

Some stables carry out the tack-room motif with matching partial drapes on their stalls. The dress halters with neatly rolled shanks look smart and are handy for emergencies. Coolers, blankets, and equipment trunks are spaced the length of the shed row for convenience.

This groom solved the problem of keeping her grooming tools handy for last-minute polishes at the in-gate. With a screw eye on her dandy brush, she can hang it from her belt loop by a double-end snap. Towel tucks into her waistband. Photos: *Practical Horseman*

175

1

Packing for the Horse Show

Checklist

In your vehicle

hammer
screwdrivers: large and small, Phillips head and flat
pliers
wire cutters
electrical tape
nails of various sizes
several screw eyes
double-end snaps
jack, either scissors or hydraulic type (Bumper jacks
     provided in autos are not safe for changing a tire
     on a horse trailer.)
spare tire properly inflated for both trailer and tow
     vehicle

In your tack trunk or carrying box

grooming tools: brushes, curry combs, hoof pick,
     sweat scraper, sponge, and bucket
body wash, if you use it
fly spray and/or wipe
hoof dressing
braiding kit: scissors, yarn, puller, and mane comb
bandages
bandaging cotton
sheet or cooler
towels
saddle soap and tack sponge
shoe brush for rider's boots

Vaseline, mineral oil, or glycerine for use around
   horse's eyes and nostrils before he goes in
   the ring
hair spray, for rider and for horse's braids
antiseptic dressing for minor wounds
special medications for your horse: electrolytes, etc.
tack: saddle, bridle, spare reins, martingale, at least
   one saddle pad, girth, breastplate, extra halter,
   and extra shank
boots for the horse, bell and/or galloping
longe line
crop
spurs
hair nets, for women

For the rider, in the car or trailer

coat
breeches
boots
socks
extra shirt
stock or tie
hat
gloves
raincoat
jeans to wear over breeches between classes

In the glove compartment or in your purse

Coggins Test copy
AHSA membership card
copy of registration papers if you're going to a
   breed show
emergency money, cash and change

If you'll be away overnight

feed
hay
hay net
stall screen
water bucket
feed pan
hose and nozzle
rake
pitchfork
broom
extension cord

2

Setting Up Your Horse-Show Stall

Whether you're stabled in a strange barn or in portable stalls under a tent, these tips from the manager of a top show stable will help you create an environment that's safe for your horse and convenient for you.

Start with a thorough check for hazards. Remove any nails protruding from the walls or rocks sticking out of the floor. If there are gaps between boards, you'll have to take measures to make sure your horse doesn't put a foot through. You can nail up sheets of plywood around the lower half of the stall . . .

Left: . . . Or you can hang up sheets of heavy material. These plastic tarpaulins, available at boating supply stores, fold up for travel and come equipped with grommets for easy installation.

Above: Hang them with 1½-inch staples (known as fence nails), hammering one end of each staple through a grommet and the other end directly into the stall board. Staples are safer than nails because nothing protrudes that might injure the horse or catch in his halter.

Staples are handy for hanging water buckets and feed tubs too. They're easier to install than screw eyes, and you can hammer them in anywhere.

With two staples and a length of chain, you can make a blanket rack for the front of your stall.

Above left: Most temporary stabling provides the doorway, and the user provides the door. Half-height iron-mesh stall screens are convenient to travel with. Be sure you hang yours high enough to prevent your horse from reaching passers-by in the narrow aisle, but not so high that you invite him to "graze" underneath.

Above right: Stall screens are easy to install: they simply drop into screw eyes on the door frame. If a horse gets caught under the door, he can easily free himself by lifting the door off the hinge. But the screw eyes on the door frame are hard to install and have to be spaced just right to accommodate the hinges on the door. If you often use temporary stabling, it's worthwhile to travel with prefabricated hinges. These consist of screw eyes, appropriately spaced, installed on a ¼-inch strip of steel. Three nail holes on the steel strip allow it to be quickly hammered into place. (A metal shop can do the work for you inexpensively if you don't have the tools yourself.)

Nail up the strip on an angle so that the door slants. When you open the door either way, it will stay where you put it and you won't have to worry about its swinging shut as your horse is passing through. Photos: *Practical Horseman*

3

Winning Horse-Show Strategy

Christina Schlusemeyer

The horse-show world is so organized that there are suitable shows and classes for virtually every kind of riding horse. But selecting appropriate shows and classes is just as important for hunters and jumpers as selecting the most favorable events is for a Thoroughbred racehorse.

Christina Schlusemeyer, who knows the horse-show world as well as anybody, describes the possibilities offered from the bottom to the summit, along with astute advice on how to make the most of them. Owner of Quiet Hill Farm in Ocala, Florida, where she prepares horses and riders for Junior and Amateur-Owner divisions in A shows, Christina has trained more than fifty AHSA high-point champions. She is also an AHSA judge of hunters, jumpers, and hunter equitation.

Since her article appeared in 1979, there have been various changes in the AHSA rules, which do not, however, affect the validity of her basic strategy. Prices, alas, have escalated. Those mentioned here might be increased by 50 percent in general. For a top grand prix jumper, the sky's the limit: The Natural was sold in 1986 for $1 million! Nevertheless, the relative cost of showing at one level or another remains basically the same.

It isn't true that in order to compete in the show ring you must have an expensive horse and pay astronomical bills every month. Most of the people showing today are doing it on limited budgets. Some of them don't even own a horse.

If you can afford to take riding lessons on a regular basis, you can probably afford to do some showing. Happiness is choosing the right horse show for your ability, and the right horse for the show.

I divide horse shows into ten levels, ranging from the very smallest private riding club shows to a handful of what I call "super-A" prestige shows. First, you must find the level that suits your riding skill and your pocketbook. Next, you must mount yourself on a horse that is suitable for that level so that you can, at the very least, have some fun and win a few ribbons.

There are all kinds of ways to evaluate horses, but for the purpose of matching the horse to the level of showing, it boils down to two factors: reliability and quality.

The reliable horse may be plain-looking, he may have some age in him, he may not be a very good mover, and he may not jump in the fanciest style; but you can count on him to put together eight pretty good fences if the rider gives him half a chance. The quality horse, on the other hand, has all the looks, snaps his knees, and floats over the

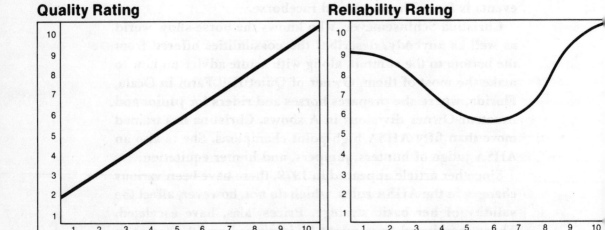

To get the most out of any horse, you have to show him on the level at which he belongs. This is partly determined by the ability of his rider but also by two factors that I call quality and reliability. On a scale from 1 to 10, a big, good-looking horse with a beautiful way of moving and classic style over fences approaches 10 in quality. A horse that can be counted on the make eight good jumping efforts in a row every time he enters the ring, earns a 10 for reliability. These graphs illustrate the minimum requirement for each factor at each level of showing. First, rate your horse objectively. Then consult these graphs to determine his competitive level. You can show him anywhere from his level down with success. But if you show him above his level, you won't do much winning.

ground, but he may blow up in the hack and stop at every fourth fence if he isn't very well trained and ridden.

At the lowest level of showing, reliability goes a lot further than quality. But as you rise through the ranks to the rated shows, quality is a must, and you may be able to give a little in the reliability department. At the very top, there's no getting around the need for both quality and reliability. So in every showing situation there are three elements to work with: the level of the show, the ability of the rider, and the reliability-quality factor of the horse.

Usually at least one element, the rider's ability, is already determined, and often the rider already has a horse. In this case, there is probably one level of competition best suited to the pair, and success hinges on finding it.

However, the same rider at the same stage of experience given a horse rated higher on the reliability-quality scale might be able to move up a notch or two with no loss of success. By the same token, a low-ranking horse given a more experienced rider might also move up the competitive ladder.

To achieve the best results, you have to analyze each level of competition in terms of the opportunities it offers to various horse and rider combinations.

LEVEL 10: The Private Club or Riding School Horse Show

Many riding schools and clubs hold occasional in-house shows to give their students a taste of formal competition. If you are taking lessons regularly, your instructor may ask you if you'd like to take part in one of these events.

The chances are that your competition will be the other members of your riding class and that your mount will be the school horse you've been riding during your lessons. Any horse that can jump 18 inches will do. In fact, these shows usually include lots of classes on the flat, so that you can compete even with a horse that doesn't jump at all.

Your only expenses for participating in a show at this level will be entry fees, plus perhaps a training fee to the instructor who coaches your performance during the show. If your horse for the day is of a little better quality than the average school horse, you might have to pay a daily or weekend rental fee of around $25.

At this level, you can find out whether you like horse-showing enough to go further, without making a major financial investment. The owner of your riding school knows that if you decide to become more involved, you'll take more lessons and may buy a horse of your own, all of which is good for his business.

LEVEL 9: The Semiprivate Boarding Stable Horse Show

Sooner or later as your riding progresses, you'll find that you're bored by the cute, wonderful, stubborn, placid, lazy school horse mentality of Old Brownie. So when your instructor tells you that there's a little schooling show at the stable down the road and asks if you'd like to take Whitey, one of the more advanced horses, you'll be eager to go.

It's going to cost $25 to transport Whitey, and the entry fees will be a

This green prospect was a beautiful mover but a mediocre jumper, carrying his knees unevenly. With a good rider, he might have competed successfully at the middle-level shows, but it soon became evident that he didn't like to jump. Quality: 5. Reliabilty: 1. He is now a successful dressage horse. Photo: Judith Buck

little higher. You may have to mow a few lawns to help pay your expenses. But going 5 miles down the road is certainly a lot cheaper than going 250 miles away on an overnight excursion involving stabling fees, motels, and long-distance vanning.

These shows serve as stepping-stones to the larger schooling shows. You might meet up with some polished riders giving their green horses experience. But on the whole, there's not much competition at these little shows, so you'll probably come home with a few ribbons, which is always encouraging, not only to you, but to the bill-payer too.

LEVEL 8: Local Schooling Shows with High-Score Awards

There are series of shows—usually sponsored by a local horseman's association or club—that offer awards to the horses in each division earning the highest number of points during the series.

To horsemen further up the scale of competition, points for a local

An honest school-horse type; she jumps safely, but her performance has been somewhat marred by a succession of inexperienced riders. Quality: 2. Reliability: 5. She's suitable only for level 1, small in-house horse shows. Photo: J. C. Totton

series may seem like no big deal. But it *is* a big deal, because for the first time you have a goal aside from just getting around the course and hoping that your trainer won't tell you that you goofed at the sixth fence.

There are several ways to take advantage of these shows. If you are an inexperienced rider on an inexpensive but very reliable horse, you can gain a lot of experience at not much expense. You can go in your own trailer or a friend's, and depending on your horse's durability, you can perhaps cram seven or eight classes into one day. With that kind of repetition, you'll polish your performance without breaking your family financially. You might even have a crack at a high-score award. For this, you really need a horse of your own. But a glorified school-horse type, in the $1,500 range, will do.

If you're a rider with two or three years of show-ring experience under your belt and a trainer to help you, you might take a young Thoroughbred or quarter-horse prospect for which you'd paid some $2,500 or $3,500, go to fifteen or twenty shows and give him mileage over 3 feet 6 inches without breaking his first-year green status. At the end of the year, you could have a very nice horse for which one of the leading professionals might offer you $10,000 or even $20,000, depending on your luck. This is the level at which it starts to make sense to sacrifice reliability in favor of quality.

At a series like this, you sometimes see a child with limited ability mounted on a high-quality horse that, with a better rider, might be capable of winning at the larger recognized shows. In this company, it wins consistently, despite the limitations of the child, who gains confidence and enthusiasm for the sport.

LEVEL 7: Quality Unrecognized Shows That Avoid AHSA Rating

These shows are primarily for trainers who want to give mileage to high-quality green horses without breaking their first-year green status. They are confined mostly to the few parts of the country where there are enough young hunters to support them, like New Hope and Middleburg, Pennsylvania; Warrenton, Virginia, and Southern Pines, North Carolina. Even though they are unrecognized, these shows are well run, provide nice facilities, good footing, and well-built jumps.

Here you see the horses that in two years' time will be competing for national high-score awards. But you'll also see horses suitable for lower levels of competition. The trainer may bring some of his students along.

This mare is absolutely honest, kind and willing though not the fanciest with her knees. Quality: 5. Reliability: 9. Well qualified to carry novice riders at levels one through five, or to campaign locally. Photo: Bob Foster

He thus fills up the empty stalls in his van and gives his students a chance to compete. Since these are nice shows, they also attract the local nonprofessionals with horses of various levels.

For most exhibitors, the shows in this category serve a purpose in developing their horses' abilities or their own riding skill. But they are not an end goal. Nobody buys a horse specifically suited to this level. If you have a horse whose chief virtue is reliability, you can come to a show like this to gain experience without looking ridiculous, even though you may really belong at a lower level. And if you have a quality horse, you can use these shows as a training ground for competition at the higher levels.

LEVEL 6: Local-Member AHSA-Rated Horse Shows

When the AHSA devised the local-member rating, the idea was to guarantee a competition meeting certain minimum standards, where you'd be sure to find eight decent jumps and safe footing. While most local horse shows were offering makeshift courses consisting of rusty barrels and 1-inch rails, the local-member show attracted good entries. But today, most horse-show organizers know that if they want to draw enough entries to make a profit, they have to meet certain basic standards.

This level, like the next one, plays such a temporary role in your advancement as a rider that your reliable fancy school-horse type is still perfectly serviceable, even though you'll meet some quality horses there. When you trade up, you'll be looking further ahead, for a horse capable of carrying you through the C-rated level and probably to B-rated shows too.

LEVEL 5: AHSA C-Rated Shows

As you become a more competent rider, there's nothing wrong with taking your "golden oldie" to a few C-rated or even B-rated shows for the experience. But very soon it will become evident to you that you need another horse.

Even when you're a year or two into your riding career and ready to move up on the quality scale, you're still a learner, so you still need the reliability factor too. Your new horse is going to cost more because he has more training, he's more attractive, and he may be a little bigger, younger, even sounder. He's a better mover and he's probably a better jumper.

For the first time, you have to buy a certain amount of quality, along with reliability, if you want to be a real contender. The price range for a horse suitable for this level (plus a level or two above, since you'll soon pass through this one) is $5,000 to $10,000 or even $12,000. Very rarely will you find a suitable horse without a serious problem for as little as $3,500.

This doesn't mean that you have to lay it all out in cash. If you're still affiliated with the stable that sold you your present horse, he'll probably be passed on to another student and you'll recover your initial investment, or you can trade him in on a suitable new horse.

The reliable school horse is often a surprisingly good investment. I had a pony I sold six times for $2,800 during the course of nine years. That pony taught a lot of children to ride, and each of the owners recovered the purchase price when it was time to move up to something fancier.

The C-rated shows are primarily for riders who need mileage. As long

Main Event. He was hot, but tended to suck back at his fences, so the two factors combined to give him steadiness. A good jumper, but not an easy horse to ride. Quality: 9. Reliability: 7. Capable of winning at the top level shows with a good rider. Photo: Judith Buck

as you're missing three out of eight takeoff spots, you belong at the C level, where you can get experience and bring home a few ribbons to keep the bill-payers happy. It's discouraging to fork out almost $200 for one weekend, not counting meals and motel, and never even see a sixth-place ribbon.

At C-rated shows, you'll find mostly intermediate riders, but some of them are getting started on B-quality horses, getting schooling under experienced riders. These are green horses brought to C-rated shows to improve reliability, which will make them much more valuable. They will quickly move on to higher levels where prospective buyers will have an opportunity to see them.

Since there aren't very many C-rated shows, and a lot of B-quality horses show at them, the horse you buy should be suited for the B level as well.

LEVEL 4: AHSA B-Rated Horse Shows

Now you have about three years of riding lessons behind you. You've traded up from a fairly inexpensive first horse to something a little fancier, a legitimate show horse. You know you won't be doing the indoor circuit, the Florida shows, or campaigning for an AHSA high-score award. But you're ready for a little more competition. You're even taking on some of the A-level exhibitors who are rushing around to two B-rated shows in a single weekend for the sake of points.

Your horse is capable of being successful at the B-rated shows, and he won't disgrace you at the A-rated shows. With entry fees up to $10 a class, you can easily spend $60 a day in entry fees alone, and the prospect

Mandarin. Jumps in classic form, even for a rider of average ability, despite the fact that he's a stallion and was a five-year-old in this picture. Quality: 10. Reliability: 9. Capable of winning at the top levels with a good rider, and at levels 5–8 with an average rider. Photo: Winning Photos

of earning some of it back in prize money becomes an important consideration. My rule of thumb is that a horse is successful when he's capable of winning back his entry fees, including warm-up classes and schooling classes. And he is *very* successful if he earns back his stall fee and part of his training fee too. A horse that doesn't manage to earn back at least half of his entry fees isn't adequate at this level.

The B-rated shows are the last outpost for the exhibitor who wants to lead a fairly normal life. They are for the most part one-day shows, which means that you don't have to be away from home for a week at a time, missing work or school, rearranging vacations, and living in motels. However, there aren't many straight B-rated shows anymore, because most horse-show managers find they can make more money if they upgrade the most popular divisions to an A rating.

LEVEL 3: Mixed A- and B-Rated Horse Shows

There are probably more of these mixed-rating shows than any other kind of AHSA-rated hunter-and-jumper show. They are generally two-day shows, where the average nice horse can win championships and sometimes even qualify for the super-A shows.

Here, some divisions will be much tougher than others. In most parts of the country, the Junior Hunter, Pony, and Green divisions fill best. A B-rated show that attracts thirty-six junior hunters will probably add to the prize money and split the division so as to qualify for the A rating, knowing that next year another dozen entries or so will be attracted by the higher rating.

On the other hand, if the A-rated Working Hunter Division, with $1,000 in prize money, draws only six horses, next year the management will probably reduce the prize money and drop the division to a B rating. If entries are still light because of having lost the people who supported the A rating, it may drop another notch to the C rating the following year. At that point, it's bound to draw more entries because the local exhibitors will come out of the woods, knowing that they won't lock horns with A-level competition.

The quality of horse you need for a mixed show naturally depends on the division you're competing in and whether it's particularly strong in your area. In general, horses and riders at this level are pretty polished and get around the courses pretty well. When the prize list says fences at 3 feet 6 inches, you can count on a solid 3 feet 6 inches. You may be able to get by in some divisions with a horse of modest quality, but to be successful in the toughest divisions, you need a horse capable of jumping a solid course with distance variations, and the sky's the limit as to what you may have to pay for him.

LEVEL 2: Regular AHSA A-Rated Horse Shows

Some people think there are too many A-rated shows. Cheap horses with astute management can duck the competition and still pile up records at the A level. I don't agree.

There are lovely horses competing in A-rated Hunter divisions in every major horse-show area of the United States. The horses that win at the big indoor shows come from all over the country. Even in the

Murmansk. No matinee idol, he jumps with his legs level, but what a great coper! He covers up his rider's problems through his natural instincts to round himself over the fence, no matter where his rider asks him to take off. Quality: 8. Reliability: 10. Winner of the 1975 ASPCA Maclay finals and the 1976 and 1978 AHSA Junior Hunter championships. Photo: Judith Buck

remotest areas, it takes a very nice horse to win consistently at the A level.

A horse who can manage that—and it doesn't matter where he does it—commands a big price. Twenty-five thousand dollars won't buy you much, and even at twice that price there's no guarantee. It's a question of supply and demand. There are simply too many people wanting to show at the A level for the number of horses capable of doing the job.

My personal feeling is that if we have to operate in this crazy horse-show world, it should at least make some financial sense. Sure, a top horse is a necessary investment if you're going to show at the top level of competition; but if my customer has to fork out $40,000 for a horse, I want him to beat one that cost $70,000, and when I'm through with the horse, I want the customer to sell him for at least $55,000.

This business today—six figures for a top horse!—is crazy. I've sold some horses at prices so high that even I have been amazed. But I've bought a couple of horses for half their asking price because I've been tenacious.

When one of my horses wins a class and all the others jogging for the ribbons cost considerably more than mine did, I feel that I've really achieved something.

LEVEL 1: Super-A Prestige Horse Shows

These are the three fall indoor shows: Harrisburg, Washington, and New York—plus Devon and the Florida winter circuit. They don't count for more points than other A-rated shows, but they generally give more prize money than the minimum required for an A rating. And often they're the only game in town. During the Florida circuit, for example, there's simply no other place for a top horse to go.

The super-A's attract 700 or 800 entries, horses that have qualified by winning ribbons at other rated shows. You can't be champion at one of these shows by ducking anybody.

The riders at this level are extremely competent, but that doesn't mean they can sacrifice reliability in their horses. The successful horses are not only full of quality; they're good every time. These aren't the cute five- or six-year-olds that snap their knees and have one good trip out of a dozen. These horses can be depended on for the same eight good fences, the same excellent Under Saddle class, at virtually every show. They're the diamonds in the pile of semiprecious stones.

In order to compete at this level, however, it isn't simply a question of buying a fancy horse. The horse itself, no matter how expensive, doesn't guarantee success. There's a tremendous team effort on the part of the rider, the rider's family, the trainer, the blacksmith, and sometimes the veterinarian—in other words, everyone involved—to make the horse competitive at the very top. These people make a commitment that requires them to sacrifice many of the elements of a normal life.

At this level, an investment of $50,000 or more in the horse is only one of many factors that contribute to success. In fact, if you buy one of these horses and, through team effort and sacrifice, continue to win with him, you'll probably enhance his resale value.

However, if you want to compete in A-rated shows, if you're willing to put in the effort and make the sacrifice, but if you can't swing the $50,000 for the horse, there are other ways.

If you become a good enough rider, you may be asked to show for owners who don't ride themselves. Some are professional trainers, hoping

Sneak Preview. This young prospect looks like a super jumper, and at this early stage I'd have rated her 9 for quality and only 5 for reliability, as she needed a lot of experience at the lower levels. (She went on to become a consistent winner at the highest levels and a five-time AHSA national champion.) Photo: Judith Buck

to develop top horses for profit. Others are private owners who just like to watch their horses compete at the big shows.

There's another route you can take if you're an experienced rider. It's a long-shot gamble, but it can pay off. You take every cent you have and buy quality without reliability. Buy the pretty horse that showed ability in a jumping chute or over a cross-rail. Or perhaps one that doesn't jump at all yet. Take a beautiful mover with a nice temperament, and invest three or four years of your time in training him. Don't let anyone else but your trainer touch that horse! And resist the temptation to sell him for a short-term profit. Who knows? You might succeed in the super-A's with not very much money after all.

4

Horse-of-the-Year Specialist

Walter ("Jimmy") Lee

One of the most coveted titles in the horse-show world is Horse of the Year, awarded by the AHSA to the horses that have amassed the greatest number of points in shows throughout the year, the point value of a win or ribbon varying according to the importance of the show and competition, and to the zone.

Due to the prestige of these year-end awards, some major stables go to great lengths, traveling great distances if necessary, to accumulate a maximum number of points. One of the most successful experts at this game within the sport is Jimmy Lee, who has trained and masterminded the careers of horses in his charge to over 100 high-score awards, including six AHSA Grand Champion Hunters, an all-time record.

It isn't talent alone that sets the high-score award-winning horses apart from any other good show horse. It's primarily their consistency. A high-score horse has to go pretty much the same way class after class under all kinds of conditions.

It's not too difficult to go out and buy a horse and pick your spots. Go to only eight or ten shows a year where you know the judge likes that type of horse, where the competition is easy, where you run the show, or where your client is a member of the committee that selects the judge. That sort of thing is happening more and more often.

But if a horse is going to be high-point Horse of the Year, he has to

Jimmy Lee poses a model for the judge at Devon in 1987. Photo: James Leslie Parker

earn well over 1,200 points. He has to go to 20 or 25 A-rated shows, be a good solid champion at 15 at least, and win about 50 out of 100 to 125 classes.

There are only seven horses in my barn right now, and seldom are there more than ten. Anyone who has half a dozen genuinely nice horses has a very, very good stable and is very lucky.

I buy only about half a dozen horses a year, and two of those might turn out to be not really what I'm looking for, but still pretty nice horses. I don't believe there's safety in numbers. You spread yourself too thin, and you have to end up spending more time on a mediocre horse, trying to bring him up to the level of competition. You slight your better horses, and the whole operation suffers.

If I buy a horse I like for my own account, I try to sell him in my own barn. If I still think he's a nice horse after having schooled him for a while, I'll sell him to a client for around $10,000 or $15,000. That's if he's unproven. People are paying $30,000, $40,000, and more for top proven show horses now.

I drive some 40,000 miles a year all over the country looking for nice horses. I call a professional whose opinion I respect and tell him to scout his area for me. Obviously, he expects to make money on the deal. I just decide whether I think the horse is worth that much. His commission is the best investment I can make.

Generally speaking, I'm not interested in horses I can't see jump at least over a small fence. I'm not a fortune-teller. I can't look at somebody's two-year-old and say, "That colt's going to be a good jumper."

If you can see a horse over a 3-foot jump, you certainly can't predict that he's going to be a high-score horse, but I think you can distinguish the horse with no talent from the one that might be useful.

Right now we're in a cycle where everyone is thinking jumper. It's kind of hard to look at a young horse and say, "I think this horse has tremendous scope." I don't think all that scope is necessary. I think a horse that is going to jump 3 feet or 3 feet 6 inches in good form is very possibly going to make a nice first-year horse, and you have to worry about first things first.

I look for style, athletic ability and attitude. A horse has got to be able to use his back well and get his legs up pretty well. Maybe he doesn't fold exceptionally tight over a 3-foot fence because he doesn't have to, but if he has major faults, if he hangs his legs or jumps with a hollow back, you'll spot them and you'll be able to rule him out.

If I see a horse I like jumping a 3-foot fence, I'll usually buy him. I'm not going to get hung up if the horse is not 16 hands, if he's not a super mover, or if he has some conformation fault. I couldn't care less if a horse has a stable vice, and I wouldn't rule out age either. I'd buy a three-year-old or a late two-year-old; right now I'm interested in an eleven-year-old that's a good jumper and hasn't been used too much.

While I don't want to take on a horse I've got to medicate, a splint or curb doesn't bother me. A lot of people systematically have a horse they like vetted. The vet comes up with some crystal-ball verdict, such as "In two or three years, you may have problems with his back or with this knee." People miss a lot of nice horses that way. There are so many new people buying horses who aren't sure of what they really want, and I think they give too much importance to some small defect the horse may have. The vet is on the spot, because he naturally has to protect himself from legal problems. I'm very fortunate in having an excellent vet, and if a horse has faults, he tells me whether I can live with them or not.

Now temperament is something I do get hung up on. I won't buy a horse that needs tranquilizers. Other faults bother me less or not at all. If a horse has a decent temperament and is a good jumper and if he wins blue ribbons, I don't care if he's a cribber or not a good enough mover to win every Under Saddle class.

Even so, it's tough to find the horses I seek. Lots of them can jump 3 feet 6 inches quite well, but not many make really good show horses. Very few, in fact. You go to a big horse show early in the season, and there are 120 green horses, but maybe only fifteen good rounds, and maybe only two or three horses you'd want to buy for a client.

Horses get into bad hands or get hurt. A horse may have a bit of spook in him or be unable to concentrate. Some horses aren't as smart as others and don't learn as quickly. Some can't handle certain kinds of footing. Many horses can be taught to jump 3 feet 6 inches. It doesn't take a super talent to do that. But to be a winner, he's got to be consistently good at 3 feet 6 inches. Maybe not tremendous jumping, but consistent good form at that height.

You can develop a horse's native talent. You can take a horse with ability that for some reason doesn't suit somebody else and turn him into a good horse. But I don't think you can take a horse that has a major jumping defect and make him into a useful horse. At least I've never been able to do it.

You don't train a high-score horse differently from any other average show horse, but you work on a longer-range program. You don't press him quite so hard for any individual show or particular class as you would with a horse that you were taking to only ten or fifteen shows a year.

It usually takes me until about May, after I've been to Florida and a number of schooling shows, to make up my mind as to whether or not I've got a possible high-score horse. A colt that looks good at home, where there's nothing to compare to him, sometimes doesn't seem quite as outstanding when he gets to a show.

By May, I've made up my mind as to whether he's the sort of horse I can train to a certain level of performance that can be maintained throughout the season. A high-score horse has to adapt well to being on the road a lot, to changes of environment. Some horses thrive on it, while others don't adjust well and their performance suffers.

The horse-show public has to like your horse too—not only the judge but also the trainers and everybody else. Many trainers are also judges, but even one that isn't a judge can hurt your horse. If word gets around that he doesn't like him, other people aren't going to like him either.

It's a good sign when a lot of people try to buy your horse at the early shows. It doesn't affect your opinion of your horse, but it tells you that the public is beginning to like him. The horse-show world is a very closely knit group of knowledgeable people, and a nice horse gets talked about. An inferior horse may win at a particular show, but a lot of exhibitors will see that he is not a very nice horse, just one that had a good day. When people really like a horse, there's a certain atmosphere. The word gets around and everybody talks about him.

But the most important thing is for *you* to like your horse. You can't sell a horse to the public unless you honestly believe in him. Horse-show people can't be fooled very long.

When someone tells me they have a super horse, I study it more critically than if they say, "I have kind of a nice horse; why don't you take a look at him?" I'd much rather have another horseman tell me that he likes my horse than have to fish for a favorable opinion by saying, for example, "I've got a nice horse, don't you agree?"

Some people say a horse doesn't necessarily have to be the best horse in the country to be a high-score award winner. Of course that's true. But he does have to be the horse that can best maintain a high level of performance over an extended period of time, under all kinds of conditions and all types of judges. In my opinion, any horse that can do that deserves the title. Furthermore, he has to be a horse that really tries for you, because if you have to be strict with him in the schooling area, he won't last through the campaign, mentally or physically.

You can't keep pressing on a horse, pulling out all stops week after week. But during a year-long campaign there are certain wins that mean more to you than others. Personally, I'd rather win at New York than at any other show in the country, and—perhaps because I'm from Virginia—being champion at Upperville is important to me. I aim to have my horse sharp for those shows and for the hunter classics. The rest of the time I just try to keep an even keel. If I kick my horse too often during June and July, I've got no horse left in November.

You can't let yourself catch the winning fever in every class. At each show there are trainers who are going all out to win a particular class, and they often do so. But if you're interested in the high-score award, you can't be inveigled into staying with them step by step. It's simply impossible to keep a horse that razor-sharp all of the time.

So you maintain a normal level, with a win here and there, but you settle for second or third when you have to. You're moderate in the schooling you do before each class. When conditions are bad or the judge doesn't happen to like your horse, you know when to stop showing. If the footing for the Kentucky Derby comes up bad, they're not going to run Secretariat. But the man who's there just to be there, he'll run his horse. What difference does it make? With Secretariat, there's too much to lose. In showing, too, if you let the competition press you, it's your horse that's going to crack.

I have a small outfit, all my eggs in a small basket, and I can't afford to lose my good horses. It's very hard for some people who have braided and paid their entry fees to say, "I'm not going to show in this class after all." But it doesn't bother me. I could be one point ahead for the championship at Devon, and if there were pouring rain and the conditions didn't suit me, I wouldn't show. I want a horse for the fall shows too.

A year's campaign toward a high-score award costs an owner between $15,000 and $20,000. With luck, they'll earn some of that back in prize money. But I campaign only a selected few. No way would I lug around a lot of horses just for the boarding fees. I like to take horses and win with them. The only way I can do that is to take a few nice horses and not get greedy.

5

Warming Up a Hunter

Charlie Weaver

The advice of Charlie Weaver, star rider of the Hunter Division, is well worth heeding, since he has warmed up for winning rounds numerous high-score award winners, including working hunters such as Ruxton and conformation hunters such as Eastern Shore, Stocking Stuffer, and Early Light.

A hunter needs to be soft and very adjustable, which means that he must be relaxed. How I create this state of mind in my horse during the warm-up depends on the individual horse. I may need to wake him up a bit or calm him down. Since I often ride several horses in a class, I don't have much time to work out a problem or wear down a horse that plays too much. If my horse tends to be a little stiff in one direction, I'll try to ride him a bit in the morning before the start of the show. If I have a very fresh horse, I'll make sure he's longed or ridden in the morning.

I've trained my horse at home. All I'm doing in the warm-up is limbering him up and preparing him for the ring. I spend a minute or two trotting and cantering around the warm-up area; then I start to jump.

I like to trot over something low to begin with, but if the schooling area is busy, I might have to start over a 3-foot jump. In any case, I always start at a height lower than what I'll be jumping in the ring, gradually increasing it to 3 feet 6 inches. After jumping the vertical about four times, I move on to an oxer, again starting small and building

Charlie Weaver shows Ruxton at the Sedgefield Charity Horse Show in 1977. Photo: Linda McFarland

up to 3 feet 6 inches. On a casual horse that needs a little rub to sharpen him for the ring, I'll finish up with a fence about 3 inches higher than he'll compete over. For example, I might go into a regular working hunter class off a 4-foot-6-inch fence. But a naturally careful, clean jumper doesn't need a rub. He needs a confidence builder. I wouldn't warm him up over anything bigger than what he'll meet in the ring.

If my horse has a bad habit such as jumping to the right, I use the warm-up to remind him to jump straight. I might even make him jump to the left in the warm-up so that if he drifts a little in the ring, he'll end up in the center. But I don't make such an issue of the problem that the horse gets rattled. The warm-up is not the moment to resolve basic training difficulties.

The average warm-up takes five to ten minutes, although it can vary. I might start extra early if I'm riding a particularly nervous horse, leaving time to stand quietly at the gate for a few minutes before going into the ring. I might even dismount at the gate to let the horse really relax. With an experienced horse, I try to time it so that I ride from the warm-up area straight into the ring.

When the same horse has several classes back to back, I'll do a pretty extensive warm-up before his first class and then maybe jump only one or two fences before the others, just enough so that he's looking for a jump when he goes into the ring.

At a big show, the warm-up area can get pretty crowded. By getting the major part of my work out of the way early, I avoid the heavy traffic and keep my horse relaxed.

6

Riding Hunter Courses

Bernie Traurig

One of the top professional riders in America, Bernie Traurig attracted attention as a USET recruit when he won the Medal and Maclay finals. He would have competed in the Three-Day Event of the 1964 Olympics if his horse had not incurred a bowed tendon. He was then invited to train with the U.S. Jumping Team.

At the end of six months, practical considerations obliged him to turn professional. After working with steeplechase trainer Mike Smithwick in Maryland, he set up his own sales and training barn, Bloodstock Farm, in Pennsylvania. Among his finds were Idle Dice, which he bought for $3,500, and Sloopy, a horse with a $1,300 price tag and a questionable tendon. Idle Dice went on to win three American Gold Cups, and Sloopy, a silver medal in the 1972 Olympics.

Noted for his smooth style with hunters, his versatility with all kinds of jumpers, and his skill in puissance events, Bernie was a member of the USET jumping team at the fall indoor shows in 1978 and 1980; with Eadenvale, he represented the United States in three successive World Cup finals and in the 1982 World Show Jumping Championship in Dublin.

But in 1986, Bernie abandoned his position as a leading show-jumping rider and switched to dressage. He was soon winning grand prix in that division too, including the Fédéra-

tion Equestre Internationale (FEI) Dressage Grand Prix at Tampa in 1986, thus performing a marvelous exploit very few horsemen have ever accomplished—reaching the top in all three of the traditional Olympic equestrian disciplines.

Even while I'm riding a course in the ring, I'm conscious of keeping my horse supple and balanced. While I'm jumping a line of fences, I'm preparing to have the horse bend the proper way around the turn. Maybe more than any other rider, I'm conscious of the way my horse moves between fences and around turns.

In New York, for example, the ring is very tight. You have two fences and then a tight turn. A lot of riders let their horses cut the turns, pop their shoulders, and canter around the turn with their head turned the wrong way. I think the way a horse goes between fences is just as important as the way he jumps. Too many hunter judges overlook the turns. A horse that jumps well, that is beautiful between the jumps and beautiful around turns, should be placed over a horse that jumps just as well but isn't as smooth in between. This may seem obvious, but you'd be surprised how often it doesn't turn out that way.

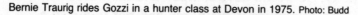

Bernie Traurig rides Gozzi in a hunter class at Devon in 1975. Photo: Budd

Today, most hunter courses are computerized. They're held in such small areas, with the fences so close together, that the number of strides between fences in a line is set. As a result, hunters need much more schooling and training than they did a few years ago. Jumpers used to be in small rings, and hunter classes were held on outside courses where the jumps were so far apart that it was impossible to judge the number of strides between them. Within the past few years, this has been reversed: they've moved the hunters into the small ring, and the jumpers out in the fields in preparation for grand prix courses.

On a long course, when you have more than eight strides between fences, the most important factor is the rider's eye. The rider has to rely on his eye to meet the jumps as if they were all the first fence in a line. The horse doesn't have to be as well schooled. As long as he isn't going to get strong and tense, you've got a lot of room in between the jumps to get there right. When all the distances used to be more than eight strides, the rider had to use his eye ten times for ten jumps.

Riding is easier nowadays with the computerized course. All it boils down to is being very accurate with your eye to meet the first jump of a line and then ride in a predetermined number of strides smoothly. The trainers stand at the in-gate and you hear them tell their kids, "It's six up the first line, four to the in-and-out, a long five down the next line, and a steady seven home."

Pamela Carruthers, one of our leading course designers, makes very few rider problems. Her courses are dead on stride, allowing 12–13 feet to a stride in a small ring: 60 feet is a four-stride distance, allowing for takeoff and landing; 72 feet, five strides; and 84 feet, six strides. Every course in New York one year (1974) utilized a combination of four-, five-, and six-stride distances. The only way to win that kind of class is to know exactly how many strides there are between the fences. Sometimes the distances are printed on the course diagram posted at the in-gate. Or you can tell the distances by watching some horses go. Distances generally range from five to nine strides. By watching horses go in front of you and knowing your own horse's stride, you know exactly how to ride the lines.

A distance of 84 feet, for example, an average six strides for the average horse, will be tight for a horse with a big stride and also will be tight if you jump the first fence of the line very forward. But with a distance of this sort, you have no options. It must be done in six strides. This is where training pays off. When you take a horse with a big stride like Riot Free (the horse I show for Eddie Spruance in the Working Division) through an 84-foot distance, it is very tight for him and you've got to jump the first fence of the line conservatively and very smoothly

Bernie Traurig's smooth performances in the jumping arena are based on solid preliminary work at home. Photos: *Practical Horseman*

"Personally, I like to ride jumper courses on stride. Even on a jumper, I like the performance to come out looking somewhat like a hunter." Photos: *Practical Horseman*

shorten each of the six strides in order to get to the next fence accurately. If Riot Free weren't trained properly, when I go to shorten the six strides it might end up looking very rough, with his head up and his mouth open—and he might drag me right underneath the second fence of that line. New York was almost impossible for him because of the tight courses; but he came back so well and so softly in between the jumps that he made it look smooth.

All of this works the other way too. Sometimes course designers set up lines that ride very long. Your horse has to go forward just as smoothly for the six, seven, or whatever strides as he has to come back for the tight distances.

Very occasionally, you'll get a line on the half stride—say, six and a half strides, or 90 feet. Then you have to decide whether to ride a long six or a tight seven. But at least you know about it before you go into the ring, and you can make a decision depending on where that option line is on the course, and how you meet the first jump of the line. A tight six, heading for home, is almost impossible; I'd definitely think about leaving out a stride. But going out, my horse is not warmed up yet. If there's an option line at the beginning of the course, I'm better off adding a stride, because it keeps my horse softer and quieter for the rest of the course. Sometimes I won't make a decision about how to ride a line until I've jumped the first jump of the line. If I jump it really forward, I'll go ahead and leave out a stride; if just average or a little on the deep side, I'd certainly add a stride.

Most of the jumper courses are now computerized in the same way hunter courses are, and that's why riders walk them on foot. Even in a big field there are more jumps, so that the majority ride on a set distance. The rider in a jumper class has the option of adding strides between the jumps and getting away with it, because he's not penalized if his horse is rough between fences, if his head comes up, or if he's unattractive-looking.

Personally, I like to ride jumper courses on stride because I think it's a smoother way to ride; even on a jumper, I like the performance to come out looking somewhat like a hunter. Sometimes, if there's an option to a big vertical, I'll add a stride to put my horse back on his hocks, to slow him down and collect him a little. Leaving out a stride to a big vertical is a bad idea because the horse has a tendency to get flat. But unless there's a special reason for breaking a stride up in order to add a stride to a fence, even a jumper should remain balanced and smooth throughout the course. Just because you're riding a jumper and jumping big courses, there's no reason why it shouldn't be beautiful.

7

What the Hunter Judge Likes

Steve Hawkins

During more than twenty-five years of judging hunters, jumpers, and hunter seat equitation, as well as many Western divisions, Steve Hawkins (who is also Secretary of the AHSA) has presided at all of the big shows from coast to coast, including Devon, Washington, D.C., Harrisburg, and New York.

In Hunter classes, I like to see both horse and rider enter the ring in a positive manner, with an air of authority that makes me feel they know what they're doing. The round should then begin in a businesslike manner with a decent circle confined to the lower third of the ring. It's annoying when riders utilize more than half of the ring for their circle, especially at a show with a large number of entries. They should trot about halfway around the circle and then break off smartly into a canter before straightening out to head for the first fence.

The first fence on many courses is traditionally the brush. While I personally do not particularly like it as a first fence, as long as it's there it should be treated with as much respect as the other fences. All too often riders take the brush fence for granted, as a result of which they end up with a bad first fence. Of course, it's more impressive if the first fence is a good one; but if you make a mistake and have a poor first fence, it doesn't necessarily mean that all is lost. As long as the round is under way, you should try to get something out of it and not go to extremes by either yanking the horse back off the pace or by driving

Steve Hawkins judges a Hunter class at the National Horse Show in Madison Square Garden.
Photo: Budd

him strongly forward in an effort to get the trip over with as quickly as possible. You should at least try to make it a good school for the next class.

For a green horse, I like to see a slow, modest pace that is more or less hand-ridden. Second-year horses can move on a bit, but in my opinion should still remain rather conservative. Working hunters can move on stronger, but should maintain a steady rhythm. I prefer a horse to move on and jump, but only if he can handle it well, jumping easily and out of stride without chipping or reaching. There are no circumstances where I want to see a junior or amateur horse moving too strongly. These horses more than any should display a willingness to be rated by their riders; I'll penalize a horse that seems to be out of control in any way.

Some juniors have no idea of pace and consequently have bad trips—not because of the horse's inability to jump well or in good form but because the riders don't try, or don't know, how to maintain a suitable, even pace throughout the course. We've all seen trips that look like parts of two unrelated rounds instead of one trip by one horse: a steady flowing rhythm for perhaps the first three jumps and then around a turn, whereupon momentum vanishes and the rest of the course is completed at the speed of a turtle. If, however, the horse can move on and jump well in good form and if the rider looks comfortable and is right there for every fence, then the entire picture looks as if it belongs together; it's beautiful to watch.

I prefer to see the horse and rider approach every fence in the same way—that is, at the same pace—and jump from approximately the same spot. They should land gracefully going away, not in a heap (although you can forgive it if the footing is particularly bad). I like a horse that wears his ears well and displays a good attitude throughout the entire trip. He can be slightly on the bit without trying to take over; he should look as if he's enjoying what he's doing. I don't like to see a horse carry his head too high or too low, open his mouth, wring his tail, or show signs of ill-temper or displeasure. After all, an important part of this performance is manners. A resentful or sour disposition is unacceptable.

With regard to actual jumping form, I look for a horse that folds his front legs well and evenly and is well balanced over the top of his fences. I don't like a horse that hangs, doesn't look as if he knows what he's doing, or, worse yet, looks as if he never learned how to fold and is therefore potentially dangerous. I prefer a horse who is athletic and well balanced, who uses himself well during the entire performance.

While not in favor of anything extreme, if I had to choose between horses that jump from a spot too close to the base of the fences and ones that stand too far away, I'd have to select the first kind. Horses that habitually stand too far back from the jumps sooner or later are going to meet ground conditions that they can't handle from that distance and they'll end up in a wreck.

I don't like to see a horse rub a lot of fences, even if his basic form is good. I'll forgive one or two touches if the jumping form is right, but I don't like to call back a horse that has rubbed six or seven fences on the course. You've got to penalize him in comparison to other horses who've had equally good trips without the rubs.

Under certain circumstances, I'd pin a horse that chipped in front of a fence or two, although I'd never place him over a horse with a perfectly smooth round. A horse that gets himself out of trouble by shortening his stride at the last minute instead of refusing or diving at the fence from a stride and a half away, is thinking for himself and taking care of his rider at the same time; if I need a horse to place behind some smooth, well-done rounds, this one would be eligible for the spot. Chipping in at a fence coming off a fairly strong pace is preferable to jumping out from under a rider or leaving out a stride, either of which is potentially dangerous.

To my way of thinking, a refusal is the worst fault a hunter can commit, and a knockdown is the second worst. A judge does not traditionally pin horses with refusals or knockdowns over those who got around without either, even though you know at times that you're pinning an inferior horse over a better one who had an unlucky rub that brought a rail down or who stopped once because he knew that if he didn't he'd be in trouble.

People who show ought to remember that everything in horse shows and in judging them is relative. I've heard people complain about ribbons that they didn't win but thought they should have or that they did win in classes where they thought they didn't stand a chance. What they fail to realize is that in the first instance the entire class may have been of super quality, so that even their horse's round (the one that was the full realization of his maximum ability) would not have been good enough to earn a prize. The second instance might have been a very poor class in which lack of disaster was sufficient to guarantee success.

The Hunter Under Saddle class is an important part of the Hunter Division, although people tend to discount it and even neglect to really show their horses. In order to win this class, a horse should be first of all a good mover, with a nice long trot, but not one that is obviously difficult for the rider to sit on. More specifically, the trot should "belong" to the horse and not seem forced. The canter should move close to the ground with a flowing stride and definite rhythm, as should the hand-gallop, but with a little more extension and a slightly faster pace. The hand gallop is very important. Many riders throw away classes simply because they don't hand-gallop. Instead, they assume the hand gallop position by standing up in their irons and then allow the horse to continue to canter. I prefer a horse to move on as he would behind hounds; since there are only eight horses on the rail at a time, there's no excuse for them to wind up in a boxed position or at close quarters with the others.

I definitely do not like to see flapping sloppy reins in an Under Saddle class. The class requires a hunter being *shown* under saddle, which to me means being *ridden* at the walk, trot, canter, and hand-gallop, not being permitted to wander around the ring half asleep. I want the rider to show me how the horse can move. That's what they're out there for. While I think manners are important, I'll pin horses that buck or play around a little when they're feeling good, if it's not exaggerated.

8

Judging Jumping Style

Victor Hugo-Vidal
with Robin Serfass

A horseman of many talents, Victor Hugo-Vidal is a leading equitation instructor, a popular horse-show announcer, a sought-after giver of clinics, and a highly regarded hunter and equitation judge. Horseman of the Year in 1971, he was voted Best Hunter-Jumper Judge in 1980 for the thirteenth consecutive year!

These photographs were taken at his farm in Southern California, To and Fro Farm, in collaboration with his partner, Mark Mullen, and two outstanding students, Cece Durante and Lynn Hansen.

It doesn't matter how a jumper or an Event horse jumps a fence as long as he clears it. But in the Hunter divisions, it's not enough to have a horse that can get over the fences; he has to clear them in a way that pleases the judge's eye. Jumping style alone won't guarantee success either. A horse with a good jumping style can make mistakes in other aspects of his performance that put him out of the running. But a horse with a poor jumping style won't do much winning no matter what else he does right.

Every part of the horse's body contributes to his style over fences, each one playing a changing role as the jump evolves from takeoff to landing. But throughout the jumping effort, one thing remains the same: at any stage in the jump, the horse's body should conform to a smoothly curving imaginary line, passing from the point of the hock through the point of the hip, through the withers, to the base of the ears. Any flat spot in this line, any hollowness or lack of symmetry, indicates a fault of style.

In the following series of photographs, we've stopped the action at many stages from takeoff to landing in order to analyze the contribution of every part of the horse's body to jumping style. In some pictures we'll see examples of what I consider A-plus jumping efforts. In some we'll discover elements that are merely acceptable. And in others we'll see elements of style I score as faults.

As we zero in on style, bear in mind that other aspects of performance, such as the way the horse travels between fences and the uniformity of all his jumping efforts taken together, also contribute heavily to the success of his round.

Photo: Robin Serfass

I like the way this horse is preparing to leave the ground. The smooth curve connecting his right hock via his hip and withers to his ears is a good indication that he'll still be round at the apex of the fence.

I suspect that he was nicely balanced in the approach and that he's pushing himself off his hocks as he should. If too much of his weight were on his forehand, his hind feet would be planted farther behind him now and he might be leaning on the rider's hand for balance.

Most horses plant their hind legs some distance apart for the push-off, a natural continuation of the galloping stride. At the moment, this horse's right hock is supporting most of his weight, but in a fraction of a second, the left hock will be equally bent and the right forearm will rise to the level of the left forearm.

I believe this horse's front legs will achieve at least a minimally acceptable degree of folding because even here the bones forming the shoulder have already risen. Shoulder motion is the key to good folding; a horse that draws his scapula up and back and closes the angle of the shoulder well is likely to close the other leg joints too.

This horse is holding his tail away from his body as a balancing rod. Some horses do this; some don't. At this stage of the jump, it's neither a plus nor a minus. But the horse that flips his tail above the horizontal over the fence will probably put it in the air or wring it while he's galloping on the flat. It's a sign of discomfort that I penalize.

I don't fault a variation in takeoff spot from a little long to a little close to the base of the fence, provided that the horse makes good use of the parts of his body, as this horse is doing, and provided that it fits well with the round as a whole.

Photo: Fallow

Another good takeoff, similar to the previous one, except that the horse is jumping from a deeper spot and the fence is an oxer. The bend in the right hind leg is even more pronounced. The pastern is flexing really well, with the fetlock nearly touching the ground.

Since the wider fence requires more scope, this horse has dropped his head and extended his neck more than the first horse.

He's using his tail for balance, but it's not above the horizontal and it doesn't look rigid, so I don't expect him to flag it in the air.

In an instant, his left forearm will rise to match the right.

He, too, shows the curve I like from point of hock to base of ears.

Photo: Howard Schatzberg

At first glance, a pleasant picture. But the form here is less than adequate. This horse happens to be a jumper, but he is demonstrating a style that would be faulted in a hunter.

Our curved line is spoiled by an elevated head and neck and a flat back. His back isn't hollow; it simply isn't sufficiently rounded, probably a result of the position of the head and neck. They in turn, I suspect, have been affected by less-than-adequate performance on the part of the shoulders. As a result, the forearm is below the horizontal. The horse's knee's should be more tightly flexed to prevent his lower leg from dangling. And I'd like to see more curl in the pastern and ankle too.

Photo: Fallow

This horse is producing an adequate-plus effort: rounding his back, with forearms well above the horizontal and with ankle and pastern joints flexed, although his lower leg is not very tightly folded. But his expression and ears are optimal.

This mare demonstrates an A-plus effort with her forearms, knees, lower legs, fetlocks, and pasterns. I'm not saying that the position of the forearm is the crucial factor. Roundness throughout the jumping effort is of equal importance. But it is a winning trait, and this mare displays it beautifully.

Photos: Fallow

A barely adequate performance. This horse is achieving the minimal acceptable level of roundness. The head and neck could be a little lower, the back a little rounder, and the forearms a little higher. There is nothing about this horse's jumping that I could fault. It's simply not an A-plus effort.

Photo: Fallow

This horse will touch down with his left front leg, which means that he is intending to canter away on his left lead. He's maintained his roundness over the fence, giving us a nice curved line from the point of his hock to the base of his ears. He still hasn't begun to raise his head.

His hind end is following in a straight line behind his body, but in terms of flexion, I classify it as adequate. I'd like to see more bend in stifle and hock, which would bring the gaskin closer to the vertical and fold the cannon more tightly against the gaskin. However, as long as gaskin and cannon form an angle of not more than 90 degrees, I can't consider it a fault. (Any greater angle constitutes trailing.)

The angle of the hip joint is just what it should be for a hunter. If the hip were closed any tighter, the lower legs would be drawn forward under the flanks, jumper-style.

The tail is somewhat elevated, but not with the rigidity that qualifies as flagging. You can see that there's a bend in the tailbone. If the tail stuck straight out behind at this stage of the jump, I'd expect a buck or a wringing tail on landing.

Photo: Fallow

This is an A-plus effort of the hind legs. They're drawn up in a bunch. The angle between gaskin and cannon is very small, the fetlock and pastern are tightly curled (even half as much flexion would be acceptable), and the hocks are raised above the lower contour of the flank. (Just to the stifle would be acceptable.) The hip is still open, holding the legs out from under the horse and preserving the roundness of the bascule.

This photo was taken a fraction of a second later than the previous one. The right front leg is touching down, and the head is starting up.

Photo: Fallow

The first front leg is firmly planted and now it's obvious that the head and neck are rising. The angles of the hind legs are acceptable. The hocks are above the stifles; the pasterns and fetlocks are nicely curled. It's not as outstanding an effort as the mare's in the previous picture, but the fence is lower too. A small fence, requiring less push off the ground, is less likely to produce the tight bunching we like. As the fences get bigger, this horse might improve his use of his hind end.

Photo: Fallow

This is the same horse as in the previous photo, during the first stride after landing. You can see by the rider's position and loose rein that he knows his horse is relaxed and so he is simply balancing in the saddle while his horse carries himself. This is the way I like to see a hunter canter away from a fence.

I wish I could rank the faults of style we've seen in order of importance, but judging is very much a matter of degree. How much less than adequate was his horse's front end relative to how much that horse failed to drop his head and neck?

Style itself has to be weighed against other elements of the round— the way of moving, for example. A bad mover must be an exceptional jumper and very well mannered to prevail over a good mover. A very good mover can be forgiven one fence that is slightly out of context with the others in the round, provided its jump didn't endanger the rider.

Bad manners on the flat can detract from a perfect round over fences.

225

I hate to see a horse come out of a turn with his head bent so far to the outside that he doesn't even see the fence until the last stride.

The division is a factor too. In a pre-green class, I'd rather see a horse go kindly, even if he's lacking a little polish, than to see eight perfect fences with a tense, uptight way of going between them. A slight error, such as cross-cantering for a few strides, won't eliminate a pre-green horse from consideration for a ribbon.

In the Junior and Amateur divisions, the "packer" gets the edge. I favor the horse that looks as if he'd carry someone's mother-in-law in the hunting field over the one whose skillful rider is finessing him around the course.

Judging is the process of evaluating the relative importance of faults. Of course, before you can evaluate the faults, you've got to spot them. Now that we've frozen the motion and analyzed each stage of the jumping effort, you know what I and most judges look for. By watching horses in motion, you can train your eye to pick out the faults and the good points. That's the easy part. Deciding what to do with what you see is where judgment comes in. It's skill, born of experience, that sets the good judges apart.

9

Winning Strategy for a So-so Mover

Brian Lenehan

A regular competitor on the East Coast hunter-jumper circuit, Brian (who is married to Leslie Burr) is also an active AHSA judge in the Hunter, Jumper, and Hunter Equitation divisions.

You don't have to have the best mover to win the Hunter Under Saddle class. When I judge, I try to look at the whole picture: the horse's condition, turnout, and attitude are important elements. If the prettiest mover is a little underweight, pins his ears back, or froths at the mouth, he may easily be upstaged by a horse that's not as good a mover but is beautifully conditioned, carries himself properly, and has a pleasant attitude.

Make sure your horse is in show-ring condition. At the top shows, people understand that they must have immaculate turnout if they expect to bring home a ribbon. However, once you descend one rung in competition, this aspect of showmanship is too often ignored. The judge has only a few minutes to make his decisions, so the more you can make your horse stand out, the better his chances will be. Especially if he's not the best mover, he'd better be in good flesh and properly conditioned, with his mane correctly braided, tack clean, and stirrups and bit shining.

Remember that the judge is probably watching from the moment you enter the ring, so advertise your horse's good point as soon as you have the opportunity. For example, if his trot is unexciting but he has a

The phenomenally gifted Sloopy with Neal Shapiro up, the individual bronze medal winners at the 1972 Olympic Games in Munich.

particularly nice canter, work in that gait as soon as you enter the ring, making a couple of good passes in front of the judge before the class starts. Once the class is under way, you can sometimes hide in the crowd while your horse's weaker gait is being judged and then separate yourself from the other riders so that you'll be noticed at his better gaits. (But a good judge will find his top horses in any crowd.)

I like to see a horse that's pleasant and quiet, especially one that's using his ears properly, pointing them forward. Today, horses often have so much show mileage at a very early age that attitude becomes a decisive factor. If I can spot five horses in a hack class that look as if they're enjoying themselves, I feel lucky. A horse that looks happy can often move up over a better mover.

Think about your contact and your position. Your horse should be able to carry himself on his own. While I don't like to see huge loops in the reins, I certainly don't want to see a rider taking hold of the horse's mouth and making him flex around turns. A good hunter is athletic and balanced, able to go forward on his own without his rider's help. If you're sitting upright and straight, so that the horse is out in front of your leg, you'll make it easier for him to stay balanced and off his forehand.

When you're analyzing your horse's movement, remember that it's not always the daisy-cutter or the horse with the longest reaching front legs that makes the best mover. I want to see a horse that can cover a lot of ground at the trot and canter, of course. But I also want to see a horse that moves evenly in front and behind. Too often, the horse that uses his hocks correctly, well under him, is overlooked in favor of the horse that's flashier with his front end.

10

Performance Faults That Lower Your Score

Practical Horseman *Magazine Staff*

Jumping with a flat back.

Uneven folding.

Twisting behind.

Dangling the forelegs.

Diving.

Stiff jaw, high head.

Trailing the hind legs.

Cross-cantering.

Meeting fence off center.

Standing off too far and reaching.

Boots in a Hunter class.

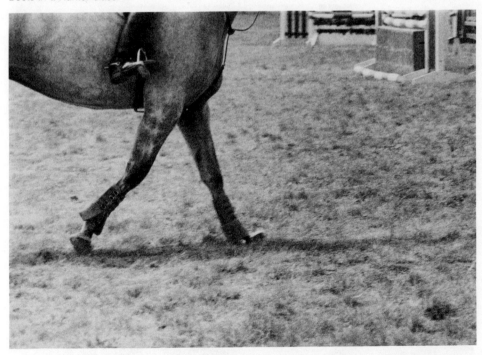

Wrong lead around the turn.

Getting under the fence and hanging.

Refusal. Photos: *Practical Horseman*

11

How to Keep a Show Horse Sharp
During the Entire Season

———

Patty Heuckeroth

Timing is a critical element of all sports, and not only during competition. Timing during schooling and conditioning, timing so that the athlete's peak of form coincides with the most important competitive events and the most demanding efforts and timing the season's program to avoid fatigue and boredom are vital to a successful competitive career in sports.

Patty Heuckeroth, who was Horsewoman of the Year in 1970 and who operates a successful stable in Southern Pines, North Carolina, buys, sells, schools, and campaigns hunters for field and show. She describes her methods for keeping a show-horse sharp, in form, and in a frame of mind to do his best whenever he appears in the show ring.

The best way to keep a horse sharp is by not doing too much with him. At home, this means doing as little schooling as possible, working only on those aspects of his performance that are in need of improvement. One horse, for example, might need a little sharpening up on tight distances, so you do some work over short combinations. Another might need just the opposite, a reminder to stand off and come forward, so you do long combinations. Essentially, a made horse should do only as much as necessary to keep him in good athletic condition and fit to jump; the rest of the time he ought to be turned out or lightly exercised.

Green horses should be handled in the same way, except that there may be a few more points to work on at the beginning of the season.

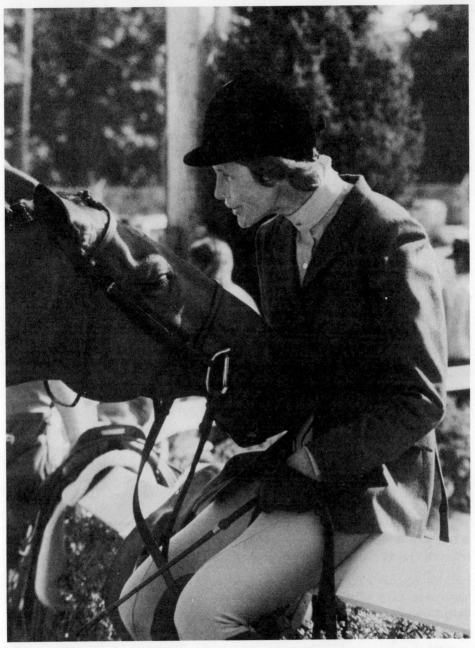

Patty Heuckeroth, an all-round horsewoman, was to the saddle born: she is the daughter of Otto Heuckeroth, who managed the Ox Ridge Hunt Club in Darien, Connecticut, for over forty years.
Photo: James Leslie Parker

Ideally, you hope you won't have to do more than two schools before a particular show, assuming that your horse is in condition. Once the show season is in full swing, you really don't want to jump even one fence more than is absolutely necessary.

My show season runs approximately from May to November, after which the horses are let down completely. In the spring, I give them a month to six weeks in which to get ready, generally no longer than that, because I don't want to start out the year with a very fit horse. The showing will get them there soon enough, and I've found that a month of slow, short rides, skipping a day from time to time, gets them ready for their first shows.

As the season progresses into summer, I try to back off a little and go to no more than three shows in a row, because more than that really can take the edge off a horse. With conformation horses especially, you have to pick your shows and stick to schedule to make sure they're holding the condition that you want and that is indispensable for winning.

You really have to plan a special schedule for each horse, taking into consideration his level of education and experience. No matter how experienced a horse may be, I don't want to start out with Devon as my first show of the season, so I'll make sure he's been to two or three shows before it gets too near to Devon. On the other hand, I'd just as soon not show the very week before. I'd rather go to Devon a little fresh after a week at home.

A horse will tell you when he's getting somewhat disenchanted with the show routine and needs to get away for a while. He'll begin to rub a lot of fences, get careless and a little flat over his jumps, lose the better part of his form, or perhaps get quick. All of these symptoms mean that it's time to back off and give the horse a chance to find a new perspective.

A complete change of scene and a break in the showing program are as much a part of training as schooling on the flat and over fences. After a horse has been shown for a while, no matter where the show is or what the fences look like, he's easily bored by the monotony of the whole procedure. He may show a bit of interest the first time around a new course, but the novelty wears off quickly. The only solution is to leave it behind for a couple of weeks.

If a horse is going well and has no major problem and if there are several shows where I'd like to take him, I use the week or two between the shows to turn him out. I won't ride him at all until the last couple of days before the next show, and then I keep it to a minimum.

If a horse has a problem, I still try to limit my rides and rest him as long as possible. Then when I do ride him, I don't try to solve the problem in the short space of time between two shows. There really isn't enough time to do it correctly, and I'd be risking my horse's condition.

When I school between shows, I jump mostly bits and pieces of courses. Then when I'm getting close to a show, I like to give the horse a complete course to make sure that both of us are as sharp as I'd like. When you jump fragments of courses all the time, you can run into problems just when you want to put it all together, such as the horse's gathering speed or not turning well, problems you hadn't noticed before because you'd been pulling up in straight lines. So I like to try a complete course at least once before heading for a show, just to be sure I haven't overlooked something that might develop into a problem later.

V

Selecting, Riding, and Training Jumpers

1

Jumper Talent Scouts

Dianne and Steve Grod

Where and how do you find a good jumper? The most usual, least risky way is to deal through a professional horseman and to benefit from his experience, contacts, and eye for evaluating a young horse's potential. Dianne and Steve Grod combined Dianne's hunter-jumper riding experience with Steve's showing experience as manager for the legendary Ben O'Meara, in operating a successful training stable and sales barn in California, where they produced a number of top open jumpers, including The Godfather, Texas, and T.R.

Since this article was written, Steve has turned his attention to training race horses. Dianne continues to train and show hunters and jumpers.

We're always looking for potential jumpers. We often go to the racetrack to look at Thoroughbreds that simply aren't fast enough to win. We also visit breeding farms to look at young Thoroughbreds or perhaps at a horse with an injury that finished his racing career but won't affect his jumping ability. However, our major source of jumper prospects is other trainers who have horses showing in the Hunter divisions. We probably buy 80 percent of our jumper prospects from professional trainers who don't have the inclination to turn a hunter into a jumper, who want to sell a horse, or who simply do not realize their horse's potential ability.

Of course, there's a big difference between a good show jumper and

Texas, a Grod discovery, ridden by John Simpson. Photo: Karl Leck

a grand prix jumper. While 65 percent of the horses we try can make it as show jumpers, only 5 percent will make it to grand prix level. With a show jumper, you can get by with a shorter mover because you're showing in a smaller area with tighter distances and shorter turns over smaller fences. A grand prix jumper has to be able to consistently gallop over long distances and jump big fences over long courses, which requires a great deal of stamina and ability. Needless to add, we expect to try a lot of horses before we find a really good one.

A horse's conformation is important in evaluating an ideal jumper prospect. We prefer a big horse, at least 16.2 hands, because a small horse has to be terrifically athletic to jump big fences.

We look for a long shoulder with a 45-degree angle from the withers to the shoulder. The horse with a long shoulder will usually cover a lot of ground in his stride, which is desirable in a jumper. Horses with straight shoulders tend to be short movers.

We also look for long, powerful hips, because the horse's thrust and power come from his hind end. You need both good hips and a good shoulder in a jumper. We've generally found that good hips don't compensate for a bad shoulder angle, and vice versa.

Over the years, we've seen that the majority of the stronger, more successful jumpers have long backs. A horse with a long back tends to be more supple and athletic. But we're more flexible about this point of conformation than we are about the hips and shoulders.

We've had successful horses who were exceptions to our ideal rules. For example, Bommalla Bobby was a small (16 hands) quarter-horse mare, definitely not built according to our ideal; but she was a very good speed horse and won her fair share in grand prix competition on the West Coast. However, she was retired at the peak of her career, and it's doubtful that she could handle today's grand prix courses as easily.

Another important requirement is that the horse be naturally well balanced, that he carry himself well and move underneath himself. We study the horse standing still to see if he has a straight hind leg, one within his point of balance instead of behind it. A horse with sickle hocks or cow hocks or one that doesn't have straight hind legs will stand with his hind legs behind him. When we see a horse move, we look for one that carries himself well, which to us means that he is off his front end at the trot and the canter and that his impulsion comes from his hips and hocks. A naturally well-balanced horse will almost always make a good jumper. Again, there are exceptions: The Godfather is a perfect example. He's a big horse (17 hands), and he has a tendency to be a little too much on the forehand. However, he became balanced, thanks to hours and hours of flat work.

Soundness and injuries must be considered, but if a horse will pass the vet, we'll take a chance on him. A bowed tendon doesn't bother us if it's old and tight; we don't worry about buying a horse with a splint if it doesn't interfere with the horse's movement and if it's not located in a place where it can be hit and cause future problems. We'd take a chance on an animal with a splint in the middle of the cannon bone, but not if the splint were located near a joint. As far as osselets are concerned, they won't bother a horse unless they're recent. When osselets are set, they cause no problem unless there is inflammation in the joints—in which case the horse would be lame when we looked at him anyway. Bad suspensories and large bog spavins are definitely weaknesses, although not necessarily unsoundnesses. We don't take chances on horses with knee problems either. We give a lot of weight to our vet's opinion of a potential prospect; he has the final say as to whether or not we should risk buying a horse with a weakness or injury.

The horse's attitude is important too. We prefer a jumper to be kind but just a little cocky, definitely not a deadhead. If a horse has an attitude problem—stopping, for example—we try to determine whether or not the rider was the cause of it. If the horse seems to have some ability, we'd be willing to take a chance on him. However, we wouldn't pay a big price, because we'd be taking a greater risk than usual.

When we go to try a horse, we both prefer to see someone else ride so we can watch. If no other rider is available, Dianne will ride, but we don't consider this essential.

We like to see a horse go over two fences, a vertical and an oxer, preferably a combination. Most horses will jump a big single fence, but a big combination is more demanding and reveals more about the horse's ability and attitude. A vertical fence is indispensable. It's a test of the horse's style, while an oxer is a test of his scope.

When we're testing a horse, we try to detect his weakest points. Depending on how weak they are, we make our evaluation. If a horse doesn't jump the vertical combination too well and needs improvement over the oxers, he's not what we are looking for.

We ask ourselves qualifying questions: (1) Does the horse struggle with the distances in the combinations? Can he cover the distance between the two fences easily? (2) Does the horse use his back and does he round his back over a fence? Could the horse be helped by specialized schooling to jump with a rounder back? (3) Does the horse have a tendency to use one shoulder more than the other, and is it because he's used to landing on the same lead all the time? This is one of the biggest problems we run into. If we see a horse that is uneven in front, we try to determine whether he is truly one-sided. We can correct this weakness by trotting to small vertical fences, landing on whichever lead we want.

When a jumper prospect can jump a five-foot square oxer combination and a five-foot vertical combination fairly easily without any of the glaring weaknesses just mentioned, we'll usually buy him. It isn't necessary to see him jump a big fence. We seldom jump a horse we're testing over a fence any higher than five feet. Most of them are green hunters anyway, and we can't test them beyond their present capabilities.

We don't insist on "classic" good form, because we've learned that the horses who jump in the best form do not always make the best open jumpers. T.R., a very successful grand prix jumper, used his shoulders but didn't always get tight with his lower leg. When he'd "feel" a fence coming off the ground he would get really snatchy in the air because he didn't like to hit fences. Sundancer tended to jump slightly inverted with a hollow back, but he still tried to jump clean and get his hind end out of the way.

Barney Ward bought T.R. from the Grods as a last-minute replacement for Taggart to ride in the Ox Ridge Grand Prix. After only four days of work together, Taggart and T.R. jumped like this and won the event. Photo: Budd

Of course, we've made a few mistakes in selecting our jumper prospects. Once when we were at the Caliente Race Track in Mexico, we saw a horse in a race jump over the rail after throwing his jockey. We bought him that very day, took him home after the required quarantine, and put him in the jumping chute, where he looked like a potential superstar. Unfortunately, he couldn't jump over a stick with a rider on his back. Obviously, that horse had a freak problem, because normally if a horse can jump free, he can jump with a rider in the saddle. He was also a bit of a rogue, and his attitude didn't lend itself to consistent work. In general, however, we've been pretty successful with the horses we've "discovered."

Once we've selected a potential jumper, we prefer to begin his show career in the Hunter Division in order to give him the necessary experience; but if the horse is exceptionally brave, we'll put him right into the Preliminary Division. It depends on the individual horse.

249

If you buy a jumper prospect for a customer, as we often do, it's necessary to educate the customer to understand the importance of mileage for a jumper. You need good owners to bring along a jumper, particularly if the horse is not a super hunter, because lots of money will have to be spent in hunter classes to give the horse experience in the show ring. We think the ideal campaign for developing a good jumper starts with a year or even two in the Hunter Division. Then the horse needs one year in Preliminary or Intermediate jumpers, depending on how much experience he's had as a hunter. You run a terrible risk of burning out a horse's desire to jump clean if you push him too far when he's still green.

If a horse seems to have the ability to make it in the Open Division, we'll take as much time as we feel necessary to bring him along. We have a horse now that we've deliberately kept in the Preliminary Division, even though he's capable of jumping bigger fences, because we don't want to have to run him in jump-offs at this stage of his career. He needs the mileage for his mental development. We'll continue to take it slowly until he's ready to move up.

The Godfather, a big chestnut jumper we'd been showing quite successfully in grand prix competition, is a good example of a horse who had lots of mileage, both as a hunter and a jumper. He was shown as a hunter in the East for two years without much success and was tested as a jumper prospect by several well-known professionals; but he never got to the show ring in the East as a jumper. As is often the case with horses of exceptional ability, The Godfather was probably too eager in the Hunter Division, too impatient with the small fences. When we brought him to California, we knew he'd had sufficient hunter miles, so we began preparing him for jumper classes right away. His first year of showing was in the Amateur-Owner Jumper Division; the next year, Dianne started riding him in Preliminary. He jumped out of Preliminary at his first two shows, and at the second show he took second prize in the grand prix. Even though he didn't have a lot of jumper mileage before winning as a jumper, he'd cleared a lot of fences in the show ring during three years prior to his debut as a jumper. The ability and attitude were always there; he never had to tax his ability, not even in the preliminary divisions.

At the opposite end of the mileage spectrum, A Little Bit, Buddy Brown's gray jumper, is a rare example of a successful jumper that never had any green hunter experience. He showed enormous ability and began his jumping career in Europe in the Open Division. Of course, the horse probably had several months of intensive training with the

USET (although this is only an assumption). But it is most unusual to see a horse that has been started so quickly and has kept on winning in the Open Jumper Division without having had the benefit of the background we consider essential.

Once we've selected a jumper prospect, we estimate what we feel the horse is worth and set a price on him. We'll always sell a horse if our price is met, even though Dianne would often like to keep him and show him herself.

2

What I Look for and Look Out for in Selecting and Training Jumpers

---

Csaba Vedlik

During more than a quarter of a century, Mr. and Mrs. Carleton Blunt's Country Club Stables has been prominent in the Amateur-Owner Division. At its Florida headquarters (and a summer place in New Jersey, where some breeding for its own show prospects is done), their accomplished equestrienne daughter Carlene maintains the family reputation for excellence and true amateurism: in 1983 she was awarded the Walter B. Devereux II Memorial Sportsmanship Trophy by the AHSA. Csaba Vedlik (pronounced sháh-bah) is her trainer, coach, and manager.

Throughout the years, the eminent Hungarian-born horseman has helped Country Club Stables produce some outstanding jumpers: Silver Lining (his all-time favorite), Navara, The Hood, Tinker Toy, Altmeister, Pill Box, and Passe Partout, among others.

What do I look for in a jumper prospect? I agree with the racehorse trainers who say that "a good big horse will always beat a good little horse." I go for size because of the size of the courses today, the distances. A little horse is put to a tremendous test trying to negotiate them. It's less intimidating to look level at a big fence than to look way up at it.

As for breed preferences, I adore the American Thoroughbred. I think it's the best horse in the world. But it also requires the best rider in the world. It takes much tact, much finesse, much tender feeling, to

Carlene Blunt and Silver Lining. Aged seventeen in 1975, when this picture was taken, Silver ranked second in the AHSA Amateur-Owner Jumper standings. Photo: Budd

handle Thoroughbreds, since they're bred for a completely different purpose than jumping. But they are the most superb animals in the world—if we can harness their atomic power.

Nevertheless, the best horse I ever had, Silver Lining, was half Thoroughbred and half pony, so I'm certainly not at all opposed to mixed breeds. I recall another good one from way back: Altmeister, which was a Hanoverian. I don't object to any horse that can jump a nine-by-nine oxer.

I look for disposition, because I deal mostly with amateur riders, and I put the greatest emphasis on a sound mind. This is an absolute necessity for a jumper, unless you are willing to use unorthodox or illegal methods to straighten it out. However, I remember an old Hungarian master sergeant saying that if you have a rogue and you can get him to put all that energy into jumping a fence, you usually end up with a very decent jumper. During my own career I've tried to look for those, found some, and discovered that the old soldier was absolutely right. But the horse must be handled by a professional. It's not a horse for everybody.

A horse that is perfectly put together has an advantage over a horse with serious conformation defects. However, with jumpers I don't mind a long back at all because it makes it easier to cover the long distances, even though it's also more difficult to keep them round and to hold them together.

I won't fool around with a horse that is basically unsound in mind or limb. I don't believe in showing a horse that is in pain. I try to stay away from unsound horses because a jumper is put to a most grueling test, exceeded only by that of the racehorse and the Three-Day horse. I try to stay away from an unsound horse no matter how well he jumps.

Although there are many excellent jumpers that hang their knees, I wouldn't consider buying a horse that doesn't fold properly. I like the type of horse that practically bruises his chin every time he jumps a fence. There are excellent jumpers who hang from the shoulder down and therefore jump much higher; but I don't like that type of jumper myself. I really don't think you can reform horses that hang their knees. They can't fold properly either because of their physical makeup or (as I believe) because of some kind of insecurity from long ago. When they started jumping, they got worried; and when they get worried, they hang their knees for the rest of their lives.

I don't seem to have the gift for recognizing outstanding jumping ability in a yearling, although some people do. I prefer to see a horse at the age of three—broken, trotting over little cross-poles, gradually working up to oxers and in-and-outs. I observe his mental and physical attitude toward a fence, measure his ability and courage, and see how he handles his body, how he balances himself at takeoff and at landing. Some people can assess all that at the age of six months, but not me. I try to find my jumper prospects at the age of three or four, when I can see them as first-year green hunters. I really consider the entire Hunter Division just a preliminary to finding a good jumper. To jump 3 feet 6 inches or eventually 4 feet—almost any horse can do that. Anything over 4 feet takes exceptional ability, and you find that in the Hunter Division.

I don't believe in starting a horse out in the Preliminary Jumper Division at the age of four because at four he's not yet fully mature. Geldings mature at the age of six, mares at the age of five. At four, their mental and physical abilities are not quite up to jumping 4 feet and 4 feet 6 inches. At the age of five or six, you can get by with it. But I wouldn't consider showing in the Jumper Division any earlier than that.

When I start young horses, I give them a lot of flat work to make them flexible and responsive to moving forward and coming back. I take pride in being quite well known for having my horses well broken, and

I don't jump a fence with them until I have complete control at a walk, trot, and canter. Then I start them over little fences.

I'm a great believer in cavalletti, where everything is set and the rider doesn't have to influence the horse at all. They enable me to find the horse's natural ability on the shorter and longer distances and see how he takes to them. The cavalletti are a very good tool if you know how to use them, but they can be quite dangerous if you don't. I adjust the length to suit the individual horse. If I want to lengthen my stride, if my horse wants to hang back a little, I'll set the distances a bit longer but no more than the horse can trot over comfortably. Then we go on to individual fences, little in-and-outs, little water jumps, banks, and drop jumps. If I have a problem, I go back to the cavalletti and try to correct it without any influence from the rider, letting the horse figure things out.

Having a European background, when I say that I "break a horse" or "school a horse," I mean that I teach the horse elementary dressage, which consists of stopping and trotting and taking the proper lead. As soon as horses have learned that, at the age of three or early four, I start to bend them. I teach them the shoulder-in, haunches-in, a little two-track, and, depending on the type of temperament and cooperation I find, I might even take it further. Well-broken horses usually have a basic dressage background. You can use different terms, such as "schooling on the flat," but it's all the same. If someone knows how to "bend a horse" or how to "flex a horse," you can call it "dressage."

I always introduce a variety of fences during early training. My three-year-olds trot over cross-poles with a little brush in front or behind, giving them something to look at, a groundline. I use little oxers, little walls, little coops, little solid-looking things, natural-looking things. I believe that horses can distinguish different colors, no matter what the scientists say! So at the end of the second or third month, I start to mix natural rails with painted poles. Then I gradually introduce bigger walls, ditches, wider dry ditches, and little water jumps. By the age of five or six, they'll come to a bank with no problem at all because they've already trotted up and down little banks as three-year-olds. I think it's very important to vary the fences. If you have nothing but poles and rails at home, you ought to go where your horse will see something else: different colors, different obstacles, walls with holes in them, and so on. If they've had this experience at three or four, you won't have any problem when you take them to a horse show and they see some of these things.

I train my horses in a plain thick-snaffle bridle. When breaking them, I like to use a standing martingale—if only to protect my nose. Later on, when I go to competitions course after course, and my horse is getting stronger and more spread out, more eager, then I'm very open-minded about using different bits such as the Pelham or even a wire snaffle. I've had no experience with Kimberwickes; and I never use a double bridle, because I don't think it's good for jumpers. It's fine for riders with hands of silk, but I don't have them and don't know anyone that does. Because of the long shanks, the severity, a double bridle can do much harm with an untimely release, making the horse afraid to jump, afraid to use his head and neck, particularly the very sensitive, highly strung horse on which you'd probably want to use it anyway. I don't believe in gags either, unless the rider has such a tremendous pair of hands that he can turn the head loose at the appropriate moment, and this is unlikely. Gags seem to be very popular these days, but it all depends on the rider who handles it. It is equipment that should not be used by everybody.

When I'm bringing my horses along, teaching them, I don't like to use martingales. But when I run into a problem, I don't hesitate to put on a standing martingale, adjusted to the proper length. On the other hand, I'm dead set against using running martingales if they're not perfectly adjusted. A running martingale is really just to dress the horse

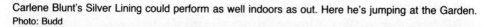

Carlene Blunt's Silver Lining could perform as well indoors as out. Here he's jumping at the Garden. Photo: Budd

up, for appearance. If it's adjusted too short, breaking the line of the rein, it acts like a pulley. If it's too long, it's ineffectual. And if it's just right, the horse doesn't need it anyway.

I'm very much opposed to things like side reins and draw reins, because few people know how to use them. Enforcing equipment might be used to overcome a particular problem for the time being, but it won't have any lasting effect. Draw reins on the side can be useful in flat work, making a horse bend, working out a shoulder problem; but they have to be used with a tremendous pair of legs and very soft hands. I'd never use them for jumping.

While many problems that arise with jumpers can be solved, some of them practically defy solution. Stopping is the worst habit in the world to try to cure. I'd certainly never consider buying a horse that was in the habit of stopping. To cure it, you have to be very determined and sometimes even cruel. Of course, every horse will stop at one time or another if the rider gets in wrong. But a genuine stopping problem is practically incurable.

Another common problem is the horse that charges his fences. We have to remember that the horse is a grazing animal; his instinctive defense is to run away. When I'm on his back he can't bite or kick me, so he runs. If he charges up to fences or charges around, it's a sign of fear. If I can overcome his fear, he'll stop charging. Of course, you can't suppress fear in a week or two. It's a long process.

When a horse carries his head up in the air, it's usually possible to bring it down. It takes a lot of flat work, using a martingale and so forth, unless the horse has an unusually high stargazing type of conformation—which I avoid. The horse that carries his mouth in his chest is a very difficult problem. Since I can't affect his mouth, he goes wherever he pleases, takes off from wherever he pleases. It takes a long time to solve this, and I'd rather get rid of him.

If a horse is careless only with his hind legs, he probably has a problem arching his back over the fence, using his hind end. We can teach him to use his back, but if he's careless in front as well as behind, he's not going to make it as a jumper. We can set up false groundlines, we can put up tack poles, we can put up iron poles; but if a horse is intrinsically just plain careless, he's never going to be careful. That's why I said I look for a horse that bruises his chin with his knees. He's naturally careful. If the horse doesn't mind hitting the rail all the time, even so hard that it falls down, he might do very well as a field hunter or even as an equitation horse, but not as a jumper. Careless horses shouldn't be confused with hanging horses. A careless horse can be careless even when folding really well, but not minding if he has rail after rail down. A hanging horse, on the other hand, might care enough to jump higher and produce one clean round after another. The two cases are quite different.

Bucking and bolting are resistances indicating stiffness somewhere in the horse's body. I can live very well with a bucking horse as long as I can stay on him, as long as he doesn't buck in the middle of a triple combination. They seldom do. But a bolting horse is a serious problem and one should not even enter the ring with a horse that is likely to bolt. This problem has to be worked out at home or at smaller shows until it is overcome. You can get bucking out of a horse by galloping a lot. But bolting is dangerous. You might as well send that one out to plow a field. I don't like to fool around with bolters, but I don't mind buckers at all. In fact, I rather like them.

3

A Professional View of
Buying and Training Show Jumpers

Barney Ward

——

An all-round athlete who has excelled in football, tennis, and golf, Barney Ward is one of the most successful trainers, riders, and dealers of open jumpers in America; he buys, schools, shows, and sells some 400 high-class horses in a typical year. He's also collected an impressive number of show ribbons, including four grand prix wins in 1985 alone; twice he has qualified for the World Cup finals.

From his headquarters at Castle Hill in Brewster, New York, Barney scours America and Europe (particularly Germany) for likely jumper prospects, evaluating them with the experienced eye of a shrewd professional who must put practical considerations first.

First of all, I look for horses that are good movers. In order to win a grand prix these days, a horse must be able to cover the ground. He must have a good stride, which does not necessarily mean that he's a daisy-cutter; but he has to be really free with his shoulders. In fact, he has to be a really free mover everywhere—in his shoulders, his back, his joints. Short, choppy-striding horses simply can't handle today's distances.

Obviously, no horse is perfect, and you often have to compromise. You might see a horse that is good with his shoulders, but a little late with his legs. If he had a good disposition, I'd take him anyway because a good attitude can often overcome something like that. An excellent example is A Little Bit. He's super with his shoulders but not very good

Barney Ward and Taggart perform during the 1974 American Gold Cup. Photo: Karl Leck

with his arms. Nevertheless, he has so much ability and such a strong desire to jump clean that he's able to overcome his technical shortcomings. But he's an exception to my belief that you can never correct basic defects in a horse's jumping style or technique on a permanent basis.

I'll buy a stopper—a horse that will jump, say, six good fences and maybe stop at one or two, but is essentially a good jumper. I often work with such horses, provided that I think they are victims of bad riding,

The horse-show arena is a showcase for Barney Ward, who is also a professional horse dealer, and he doesn't show his jumpers for long before they're sold. Here he's riding The Houstonian.
Photo: Karl Leck

lack of confidence, or something like that. In these cases, I can build up the confidence and get them jumping again.

As far as specific jumping faults are concerned, all I can say is that I won't buy a bad jumper. Some people will buy a horse that hangs his legs and think they're going to improve him. I don't believe you *can* improve him. You can get him to jump higher, but he's still going to hang his legs. I won't bother with horses that jump really flat and don't use their back either. I want a horse that's very supple with his back and is well underneath himself all the time. Another absolute requirement of mine is that the horse have a good attitude. To jump the courses being built today, you need a horse that has a good mind and is in control of it. He can't be crazy. He must go down to his fences willingly and boldly. A working hunter that can jump big jumps—that's a pretty good description of what I'm looking for.

A short-striding horse has no chance with me at all, and this is one point on which I never compromise. Today's courses are too demanding, especially the distances in the combinations such as 27 feet from oxer to oxer and 29 feet to verticals. A short-striding horse simply can't handle it. Then you have distances like 37 feet, requiring two strides; a short-striding horse has to work much too hard to do it.

On the other hand, there's practically nothing in the way of lameness that will keep me away from a good horse. I'll live with anything: bowed tendons, pin-fired ankles, horses that have been nerved. As far as I'm concerned, as long as a horse has the athletic ability for jumping, you can learn to live with the rest.

When I bring a new horse home, I test him for scope, no matter how green he is. I set up an easy gymnastic, say an X with a nice two strides to an oxer. (I don't use many verticals.) I start it low and keep building it up to 5 feet or 5 feet 6 inches to see how he handles it and if he reaches his limit there. I try to get rid of horses with limitations or weaknesses before I've spent a lot of time on them. If the horse deals with it pretty well, then I back him up and start teaching him to handle himself the way I want him to, and progress from there. I don't fool around in the Preliminary Division very long—maybe three or four horse shows. Then I go right into Intermediate and Open.

All of my schooling is done with gymnastics. Only rarely do I jump a course. During the first month, my horses do little more than trot to fences, except when I use the gymnastics: simple ones like a cross-rail with 18 feet to a little oxer and then 24 feet to another oxer, and then they'll pick up a canter on their own. I always combine different distances in my lines so that the horse learns to lengthen and shorten his stride from the very beginning. When a horse is working through a gymnastic, he's completely on his own. I just turn his head loose and let him figure things out for himself.

I hate to ride on the flat myself, but it's an essential part of the horse's training, so a couple of the boys who work for me do all that work. I don't suppose we do anything radically different from anyone else.

Basically, what we want is a horse that is well balanced no matter what he's doing. Our flat work is geared toward making him supple, light, responsive, and ambidextrous, so to speak. We do figure eights, flying changes, serpentines with changes of lead every other stride, shoulder-ins, shoulder-outs, leg-yielding, circles. Elementary dressage is what it boils down to. The final result is a horse that is able to use himself equally well in either direction, on either lead, and can automatically switch from one to the other in order to maintain his balance at all times.

All my horses go in a jointed snaffle bit with either a copper or rubber mouthpiece. The copper keeps them salivating, mouthing the bit and playing with it, which makes them a little lighter and easier to handle. I like the rubber because it's easier on the horse. We also do a lot of work on the longe line with side reins, and I think these bits are particularly good for that. Incidentally, I don't longe horses over fences very often, because I ran into a lot of problems when I did. But I jump them loose from time to time.

Draw reins and side reins are just about the only artificial aids I use, and then only on the flat. Most of my horses are really easygoing and free-moving. I try to get them feeling happy about what they're doing and let them think they're doing it all themselves. I don't want to restrict them in any way if I can help it.

Barney Ward rides Sedac. Photo: Karl Leck

I don't use much in the way of schooling devices (such as tack rails, wires, and offset) on my fences. I used to use a lot of tack rails until I found they did more harm than good. The momentary results aren't worth the possible damage, like blemishes. While I use offsets on rare occasions, mostly I build a lot of solid jumps that won't come down. I also use really deep cups for my rails, so that a horse has to hook a fence pretty hard in order to bring it down.

I never set traps. False groundlines, offset fences, triple bars in reverse and the like, are schooling methods that, in my opinion, belong to a past era. Today, if you get a horse jumping too big and airy over his fences, worrying about hitting them, he's not going to make it because the courses have become too demanding.

A horse has to be a natural athlete with a desire to jump in order to get to the top today. He has to go like a working hunter: gallop, jump, hit the ground, and move on. If he's worried about the fences all the time, he won't be able to cope with today's courses; at the very least, the distances will get him. If you have an oxer-to-oxer with a distance of 27 or 28 feet and the horse jumps the first one and hangs there a foot over the top, he's going to be going nowhere when he lands or else he's going to have to work like hell to get the next distance; it simply takes too much out of him. That's what happens when horses try to jump too clean. That's why I don't keep my horses long in the Preliminary Division. If you want to win there, you've got to be out there poling them and keeping them sharp. You may win for the time being, but if you're trying to develop a horse that can make it as a big-time jumper, you can't get him worrying like that.

One of the reasons I emphasize natural ability in the horses I buy and train is that even if they can't make it as grand prix jumpers, they'll be good enough movers and jumpers to sell as first-class junior, green, amateur hunters, or whatever. If you get them too keen, too sharp, trying too hard, then they'll be no good to anybody if they fail as open jumpers. I think this explains why you haven't seen many horses progress into the Open Division during the past several years. People were too busy trying to win in the Preliminary Division, which doesn't mean a thing in the long run.

Since speed is frequently a factor in winning a class and since running between fences increases the chances of having rails down, I prefer to gain time on the turns. I practice turns a lot, both on the ground and in the air. We set fences all over the place at odd angles and then work over them, not so much running at them as making good turns. When the horse is in the air, whether he's bending to the left or right, he'll break off on that lead with his hocks underneath him, ready to move on to the next jump with a flowing motion.

The horse's introduction to this kind of thing is over random fences 3 feet or 3 feet 6 inches high. We simply canter along and encourage the horse to jump them, catching lines of fences that are all set at angles to each other, changing direction every other time, so the horse begins to realize that as soon as there's a fence in front of him, he's expected to jump it. Once he's jumping confidently over the lower fences, we raise the fences until they're quite a lot higher and continue the same exercise.

Half the battle is making the horse believe that he can jump anything you aim him at. Usually, by the time he's reached this stage of schooling, all he really needs is experience with the various situations he may encounter in the show ring. At this point, I'm not preoccupied with jumping style, only practice and perfecting the horse's ability to use himself. This is why I test a new horse up to 5 feet right away—to see if he can handle big jumps so that when a vertical gets to be that high, for example, I don't suddenly discover that he throws his legs behind him. A lot of horses will jump a vertical at 4 feet, but lose their form when you raise it to 4 feet 6 inches. They panic, twist a little, lose their confidence and hang legs, hollow their back, dwell in the air, and more. This doesn't mean they couldn't make super hunters, equitation horses, or anything else that doesn't require jumping more than 4 feet. While there are certainly exceptional cases, I want a horse that jumps comfortably, uses both ends equally well, and follows through in a straight line. Some horses will swing their hind end a little; but generally, if a horse swings his quarters a little at 3 feet, he'll be lying on his side when the fences get to 5 feet.

If a horse stops when stopping's not his problem, I don't do a thing. Let's say you took a corner too sharply and he simply couldn't handle it from there on in. I'll make a circle, canter on, jump the fence, and continue as if the stop had never occurred. But if a horse really gets balky, then I'll get into him pretty good. I figure I spend a lot of time on him, and I expect him to give me as much as I give him.

If a horse has a wreck that shakes his confidence, then I think you have to start all over from the very beginning. I won't end a school or leave a class with a wreck if the horse is able to jump something else. Whenever possible, I rebuild the wrecked fence much lower, let him jump it, and then stop. If I can't do that, I'll jump a couple of little fences and then stop. During the next day or two, I'll just fiddle around with some little fences and then, when the horse's confidence is coming back, I'll start raising them again. If a horse continues to have crashes and never regains his confidence, or if he's a chronic stopper, then I get rid of him. If you don't really believe that your horse can do what you ask him to do, then you're bound to lose over today's courses. The horse has to believe in you and you have to believe in him totally and all the time.

There's no way to get by with a phony or cheating horse and still keep your neck and his in one piece in grand prix jumping. Fakers can't fake it at this level of competition. You might bring a horse to one grand prix and impress everyone because it's all new to him and all of a sudden he outdoes himself and jumps the courses clean. But there's no way to make a grand prix jumper overnight. Ten years ago, you could get a horse to sharpen up really well, take him to a show, and win big. But today you've got to spend more time. This is what makes jumpers so much more expensive than they used to be.

Sometimes you can take a horse with a lot of mileage in the Hunter or Junior Jumper Division and make him faster. But even this would

Wow earned his name with spectacular jumps like this. Photo: Karl Leck

take at least thirty days of testing and schooling, and a very good horse to start with.

There are exceptions to even this much shortcutting: the horse with which I won the Grand Prix at Ox Ridge is one of them. Taggard, my good horse from the year before, got hurt and I had nothing else to ride. So I flew to California and bought T.R. (short for "Taggard's replacement"), brought him home, worked with him for four days, took him to Ox Ridge, and won the Grand Prix. Then we went to Canada and he was fifth in the Grand Prix there. His mileage was extensive, although pretty much confined to the leaky-roof circuit. He'd had a lot of bad rides and was scared. When I got him, he'd been shown in both a running and a standing martingale, plus as much bridle as could be put on him. I switched him to a rubber snaffle, no martingale, and a breastplate, and that's how he still goes. By the end of August, he was the fourth-biggest money-winning grand prix horse in the country.

4

Using Cavalletti to Teach Your Horse
to Jump or to Jump Better

Practical Horseman *Magazine Staff*

Cavalletti are mechanical aids that simplify schooling for a relatively inexperienced rider and are a favorite tool of experienced trainers of jumpers. If the cavalletti are used correctly (which merely means laid on the ground in the right places) and if the rider exercises patience, then any average rider can teach the average horse to jump. In fact, among the many uses of cavalletti, teaching a green horse to jump is one of the most immediately rewarding.

Cavalletti come in all shapes and sizes. The more-elaborate store-bought version consists of a rail resting on X-shaped supports at either end; they permit stacking two or more cavalletti to make a bigger jump. For teaching a horse to jump, ordinary fence rails will do just as well.

In order to produce a successful jump, three different conditions must be met: the horse must *approach* the fence at the right speed; he must *leave the ground* at the appropriate distance from the fence; and he must make the proper set of gymnastic efforts *in the air*.

When a horse approaches a fence too fast, he tends to use momentum rather than muscular effort from his hindquarters to get over it. He'll probably stand too far back and jump in a long, flat trajectory. If he jumps from too far back, he may reach for the fence, unfolding his forelegs before he has passed the apex of the jump.

When the approach is too slow, the horse has no momentum to help him, so he tends to go right to the base of the fence before making a gigantic effort with his hindquarters, which sends him in an awkward upward trajectory. He's so close to the fence that he's afraid of bumping his knees, so he hangs them back under his stomach. To clear the fence with his hind legs, he twists them up to one side and lands with a jolt on the other side.

The alternatives are even worse. If he rushes to the fence and then runs underneath, he has an even tougher job. He has to alter all his forward momentum and redirect it upward before his front legs tangle with the fence. If his approach is too slow and he stands off too far, his hind legs may come down on the fence.

Trotting

Young horses are usually taught to trot over fences before cantering over them for several reasons. They learn not to rely on momentum as a substitute for effort; the slow approach gives a young horse more time to look at the fence and get himself organized; trotting strides are short compared to cantering strides, so they improve the chances of meeting the fence at a comfortable takeoff spot.

Place about seven rails on the ground, spaced so that your horse can trot through comfortably without stepping on them and without having to extend his natural stride. The average trotting stride is about 4 feet 6 inches. If your horse is average-sized, use that as a starting point, readjusting the distances if necessary.

At first, simply walk your horse over the rails to get him accustomed to them. If he shows alarm, continue walking until he's perfectly calm. Since they're adjusted for his trotting stride, he may knock them out of position, so it's useful to have a helper on the ground at this stage. Lay the rails in the center of the ring or riding area so that you can ride through them from both sides and turn away in both directions.

You'll probably have to walk through only two or three times before your horse is ready to trot through. Don't start to trot only two or three strides away from the first pole on the ground. Start trotting on the other side of the ring, make a smooth left turn into the cavalletti, stop posting, and maintain a jumping position while crossing the rails; then turn smoothly to the right, circle right, and approach the cavalletti again. After one or two passes, your helper should have them well adjusted to your horse's stride. It's very important to get the spacing right. If the rails are too far apart, they'll encourage rushing; if they are too close together, they'll slow your horse down and cramp his stride.

When trotting over the cavalletti poses no problem, flank the final rail with two jump standards. Leave that final rail where it was, and place

the one before it—the next-to-last rail—on the standards, making a little jump no more than 18 inches high. Now you have a trotting grid of some five rails, a double space that allows for one stride, the takeoff, and a small jump.

Continue the same routine as before, except that now, of course, you can go in only one direction. The jump always has to come at the end,

so that the trotting cavalletti regulate the approach. Don't try to do this yourself. It's the purpose of the cavalletti. If the approach is wrong, it's because the cavalletti aren't properly spaced. The horse should go through them on a loose rein or light, unrestricting contact and only a little steady leg pressure, if necessary, in order to keep him moving forward.

Don't be concerned if he simply trots over the low jump. He's smart enough to realize that a real jumping effort isn't necessary. As you raise the fence, he'll find that additional effort is required. The fence can be gradually increased in height as long as the horse remains calm, but 3 feet is probably high enough for a trotting exercise with a green horse. As the fence rises, it will have to be moved back a few feet, in order to give your horse a little more room for the takeoff. The exercise can be repeated, using different types of fences as the final jump.

When the horse is jumping calmly and in good form, you can begin to wean him from the cavalletti by removing them one by one, starting with the rail nearest the jump. The first rail or two will still get him off to a good start, but from then on, he's on his own for the last few strides before the fence. Finally, all of the rails are removed. Pace should be a habit by now. If the horse is clever, he'll adjust his stride to meet the fence at the most comfortable spot for making a good jump. If not, the trotting stride is short enough that he cannot meet it too badly.

Cantering

Jumping from a canter is more difficult for most horses. Everything happens faster, and the stride is longer. Often the horse reaches a point in his approach that is too far away for a comfortable jump but too close to fit in an extra stride. He has to learn to make preparations in advance when he is meeting a fence wrong, to shorten or lengthen gradually from several strides back, instead of throwing in one desperate short stride at the last moment. Since most horses meet a fence wrong now and then, unless they are very clever or very skillfully ridden, they must learn how to make a good jump from an awkward spot.

But first the horse has to learn to jump from a canter, and everything else should be made as simple as possible at this point. Set up four fences in a row about 18 inches high with a cantering stride between them. A good average spacing is 18 inches, suitable for a slow pace and small fences. But be sure to adjust the spacing to suit your horse's stride after a try or two.

Trot into the first fence, with the aid of trotting cavalletti if necessary, so that your horse approaches it correctly and takes off from the correct spot. Give him enough of a squeeze as he lands after the first fence for him to understand he is to canter to the next three. Don't try to control his pace with the reins. If you feel you have to, it's either because the cavalletti are not spaced correctly or because the horse isn't ready for the exercise. If the cavalletti are too far apart, they'll either encourage him to rush or, if he's lazy, sneak in an extra stride. If they're too close together, he'll land too close to the next fence and jump in poor form.

As long as he is calm and jumping well, gradually raise the fences, moving them a little farther apart as he needs more jumping room, always keeping them at a height that's easy for him; a 3-foot-6-inch fence is plenty high enough for a green horse. Next, remove the third and then the second jump so that he will be on his own for a few strides.

When his approach is steady, his jump is good, and when he's learned to shorten or lengthen his stride in order to take off from the best spot, he'll benefit from some experience with odd distances between fences.

Set up the same four fences, starting them low at first but making the distance between the second and third cavalletti a little shorter or a little longer than the other distances. After a couple of awkward jumps, your horse will begin to look for distances and adjust accordingly. Then you can combine short and long distances in one line of cavalletti. But don't make the problems so difficult that you undo all of your previous work by practically forcing the horse to jump in bad form. If he's not good at handling tight distances yet, don't give him four tight fences in a row or you'll have him twisting and hanging. If he has a tendency to rush his fences, don't spread them too far apart or he'll be flattened out by the time he reaches the last one.

Alternating short and long distances is a wonderful exercise for a horse that's ready for it. He has to open and close his body like an accordion; he has to remain mentally alert, studying every fence.

Jumping Problems

Reforming a problem jumper is always harder than schooling a green one. Old habits have to be uprooted. Cavalletti are a valuable tool. Because they control pace, they often help to cure rushing, although it can be a long process.

A horse that rushes badly may have to walk over a single cavalletti on the ground many times before he can do it calmly. Eventually, he'll walk over a series of six or eight cavalletti and then trot over them. The cavalletti are arranged at close intervals in order to slow him down to a steady pace. When a low fence is finally added at the end, it's placed close enough to the last rail to encourage the horse to bend his back and push up and off his hocks instead of flattening out. Gradually he learns how to cope with a fence from a fairly slow pace, meeting it at a close takeoff point. When it's time for the cantering stage, the cavalletti are placed fairly close together to keep the pace under control and to keep the horse bending his back and jumping off his hocks.

If a horse has a tendency to sneak in an extra stride and get too close to his fences, the cavalletti are spread—only slightly at first, but then further apart as the horse's technique improves. The distance between the last trotting cavalletti and the low fence must be long enough to force him to stand off, but not so long that he can fit in an extra stride. The cantering cavalletti start out fairly closely spaced, to discourage any tendency to slip in an extra stride; then they are gradually spread. The spacing encourages the horse to move on at a brisk pace, and he learns to use momentum to his advantage.

When the approach is good and the takeoff is good, the jump itself will probably be good. Hanging and twisting occur when the pace is too slow or when the horse takes off too close to the fence. Flattening and reaching are the result of too fast an approach and too distant a takeoff. That is why, when you regulate approach and takeoff by using cavalletti, even jumping form improves.

5

Seeing the Distance

George Morris and Judy Richter

The phrase "seeing the distance" might mean different things to different people, but to jumper riders its meaning is precise and an innate aptitude for seeing the distance is one of the most envied gifts. If you aren't born with it, can it be developed? Two expert equestrians gave their views to *Practical Horseman*: George Morris, who was then devoting his energies to developing equitation winners at Hunterdon, and Judy Richter, AHSA Horsewoman of the Year in 1974, who judges and also trains young hunter riders at Coker Farm in Bedford, New York.

George Morris

Seeing a distance or seeing a stride is the rider's ability to feel through his eyes the horse's stride in relation to where he should comfortably take off in order to negotiate a fence.

It's most important to remember that the top of the fence is the part you look at in order to see your stride. If it's a spread, such as an oxer, you'd look at the top of the nearest element. In a triple bar, it would be the top of the vertical element. In my opinion, it's wrong to look at the groundline or at the base of a fence—totally wrong. It doesn't give your eye the necessary measurement. The measurement is determined by watching the top of the fence with a concentrated focus that goes into your brain and body, which is feeling the stride coming to the fence. It is the coordination of these two factors—the horse's stride and the top of the approaching fence—that dictates when it's time to shorten or lengthen.

In seeing a stride, you have to wait for the fence and the stride to come together. One very bad and common riding fault is forcing the eye to see the stride, trying to see it too soon. Sometimes when you see a stride very early, it's accurate, and that's very nice. If you come off the corner of the Devon ring and see the fence on the diagonal at the other end and just happen to see the distance and are absolutely sure that it's a comfortable distance, that's very nice! But I don't teach my riders to try for that, because then they start pushing their eye and it becomes like anything else in life. When you try to predict something too far in advance, you're starting to guess.

The first step in seeing distances with a rider who is just starting to jump comes when he sees "something" to some fences and "nothing" to others. That's the very bottom of the ladder, so to speak. As the rider improves his eye, he'll begin to find more options available to every fence. When a rider gets to be very good, he can be picky and choosy with his eye. Take Rodney Jenkins as an example of a rider with an extraordinary and extremely versatile eye for distance. Of course, people who ride both hunters and jumpers have to have more versatility to their eye than those who ride just hunters or just jumpers. That's where Rodney is exceptional. He can discriminate with his eye. He can come off a corner and see something he likes and take it. He can come off a corner and see something he doesn't like and not take it—which means that he'll steady his horse a little, settle him a bit, and look for something else. The mark of a discriminating eye is the ability to see something and not like it and to be able to wait quietly, sitting still, not pulling up or nipping, not grabbing or fighting the horse, until some other solution appears.

Some people have that feel through their eyes very early. They are the very talented, genius-type juniors. Conrad Homfeld and Katie Monahan are two riders who, I would say, were gifted with that sense of timing at very young ages. Then you have other riders, myself included, who have to really work to develop an eye. I had a poor eye for a long time. By studying and working, experimenting and exploring, watching other riders, I developed an eye for distance that I feel is quite a bit above average. So I know it can be developed through knowledge and with help, although the riders that are born with it have a great advantage.

An exemplary jump from a perfect takeoff spot is performed by Katie Monahan Prudent and The Jones Boy, with whom she finished second to Hugo Simon of Austria in the 1979 World Cup finals.
Photo: Budd

A truly accomplished rider like Rodney can place his horse anywhere he wants, be it 2 feet or 8 feet from a given fence. Not only can he "get right" time and time again, but he can get his horse just right for what he wants to do with a particular fence in order to avoid a problem after it. If it's a steady three strides between fences, you want to jump the first one off a kind of steady stride. If it's a decidedly tight three strides, you want to meet the first fence off a very deep, dead stride. If it's a long three strides, you want to try to catch the first fence off a flowing stride. So what you want for show riding today, whether it's hunters, jumpers, or hunter seat equitation, is a flexible, adjustable eye, not just a good eye off one spot.

Total concentration on the fence is an integral part of timing, but very few riders are relaxed enough to produce it. They get distracted by what the horse is doing—cross-cantering, pulling, cutting the corner. They're concerned with the horse being ahead of the bit or behind it, and they lose sight of the top of the fence. Others are tentative and timid, afraid to go down actively to the fence and look for something. They have problems galore because the most important thing in jumping a fence is finding a distance.

The eye is what makes a rider good or bad. Take, for example, Al

Al Fiori demonstrates his highly individual but effective style. Photo: Budd

Bill Steinkraus's much-praised classic style was no less effective. Here he's riding Democrat at the Garden in 1952, a sensational year for the nineteen-year-old jumper. Ridden by Bill throughout the fall indoor circuit, Democrat won every individual class he was entered in before enjoying a well-deserved retirement. Photo: Budd

Fiore and Bill Steinkraus, who competed in the Jumper Division at the same time, both with outstanding results. The first was considered a terrible rider in everything but his timing, while the second was considered an artist in all phases of his riding, including his timing. You saw riding form from the sublime to the ridiculous competing and winning, because both of these riders had exceptional timing. In other words, if you take away everything but the eye, you're still in pretty good shape. But if you take away the eye, you have nothing.

Judy Richter

Seeing a distance is a rider's ability to arrive at a good spot in front of a fence for takeoff, with both his horse and himself in proper balance.

Since there are many spots in front of a fence from which a horse can jump and still look good and be comfortable, I think that *rhythm and balance* are extremely important in finding a distance. If you watch closely, you'll see that most riders don't always get to a really good spot, but their horses are in good balance and the rhythm is right, so the fence looks good and the horse is comfortable jumping from that spot. Without rhythm you run into problems. If you're not going *at the right pace*, the gear that best suits your horse, a good spot just won't come up.

An interesting thing about seeing a distance is that some days you can and some days you can't, which indicates to me that there's a lot more involved than eye-hand coordination, so to speak. I think there's a great deal of psychological influence. You have to be in the right frame of mind. I think this also explains why some people who ride very well at home and see most of their distances quite nicely can't find a good spot at all at a horse show.

As for creating or improving a rider's eye, I believe there must be some native talent to start with, some feel for what it's all about. But it's also true that the more horses you ride, the better your eye becomes. There are things you can do to help develop your eye, like learning where to look to start with. Sometimes people are so concerned with looking for a distance that all they see is the ground in front of the fence and the spot they want to leave from. I think this spoils the overall concept of "measuring" a fence. In order to get a true picture of what you're doing, you must look at the fence itself, usually at its highest point, and let that spot on the ground just happen.

Knowing the approximate distance between two or more given fences can tell a rider how to look for a distance to the first fence. If you know that the inside distance is on the short side, you don't want to jump in too big, so you'll look for a short spot from a controlled rhythm. If the inside distance is long, you'd want to meet it with a little more forward motion. But you have to beware of the inclination to hurry off a turn or down a line simply because you know it's long and think you have to meet it big. Here again, I believe that if you come to a longish inside distance from a good cadence and out of a workable spot, you're going to catch it right anyway. Sometimes a little change of rhythm is all that's needed to improve a bad situation.

Balance is the other important factor in seeing good distances. When dealing with hunters and hunter courses, as I do most of the time, I don't think you can talk about seeing a distance without also talking about rhythm and balance.

6

Teaching Your Horse to Jump Grand Prix Obstacles

Bernie Traurig

One of the most versatile and accomplished riders in America, Bernie Traurig has been equally successful in Hunter classes and grand prix events—and, more recently, in the dressage arena.

Multiple-Oxer Combination

The great jumper trainer Ben O'Meara used to employ the multiple-oxer gymnastic on all his jumpers. Consisting of a series of low, wide oxers, it teaches a horse to be fast off the ground with his front end, yet to wait, to take a quick but short stride between elements, to round over each fence, and to be careful behind.

Although the courses Ben rode weren't as forward and flowing as courses are today, this exercise remains an excellent tool for improving performances over tight combinations of wide fences. It's also a good corrective exercise for a horse that tends to be quick to his fences. But it's not an easy exercise, and it's not appropriate for all horses: I reserve it for horses that are at Preliminary level at least. I've had the best results with horses that have a lot of scope but need to learn to cope with short distances and to arc more over the center of the jump than beyond it. I'm very careful about how wide I make the oxers and how tight the distances, keeping the distances short but comfortable for the horse's first three or four sessions and then shortening them a little more.

Trot quietly to the crossrail so that your horse doesn't land too far inside the first distance.

He'll have room for one short cantering stride.

The width of the oxers will encourage him to snap up his front and keep it up.

The need to shorten stride in every distance will teach him to stay round in the air.

And he'll learn to be careful with his hind end too. Photos: *Practical Horseman*

Step 1: Crossrail to Oxer. Place a crossrail 16 feet in front of an oxer. Set the oxer 2 feet high and 3 feet wide. The exercise will be more effective if you use oxers that are parallel rather than ramped.

Don't use groundrails. By taking away this clue to the takeoff, you'll force your horse to study the fence carefully and develop his own eye. Trot to the crossrail very quietly so that he will jump in softly and have room to fit in one short cantering stride before the oxer. This part of the exercise accustoms your horse to jumping without a groundrail. The fences are so low that he shouldn't have any difficulty with it.

Step 2: A Second Oxer. The second oxer should be the same size as the first and 20 feet beyond it. Approach the crossrail in a slow trot. Through the oxer, say "whoa," but leave your horse on his own.

Step 3: Another Oxer. Add this one 20 feet out from the second. Raise all the oxers to between 2 feet 6 inches and 3 feet; they should still be 3 feet wide. Say "whoa" as he jumps through, but leave your reins loose. Don't progress until he's really confident.

Step 4: Widen and Tighten. Very gradually build the fences wider from both sides, which will also have the effect of shortening the distances. I've used this gymnastic with 18-foot distances between oxers that were 4 feet 3 inches high and 6 feet 6 inches wide, but 5-foot-wide oxers are sufficient for your horse at this stage of his training.

As the fences widen, your horse will learn to hold his form longer; and as the distances shorten, he'll become more adept at backing himself up. Don't shorten the distances too much at first though, or your horse may try to bounce them and land in a lot of trouble.

Step 5: More Oxers. Add a fourth oxer and later a fifth, making them the same size and setting them at the same distance as the others. When your horse understands the gymnastic and performs it confidently, take away the crossrail and canter slowly to the first oxer.

If you find that he drifts to one side, use guide poles to hold him straight. Lean two jump poles on the top rail to form a chute. Start with the poles out at the ends of the jump, near the standards, and move them in gradually as your horse gets used to them.

Natural Obstacles

Introduce your horse to each natural obstacle in the simplest possible form. To familiarize him with water, for example, start with a narrow obstacle and don't even use real water: simulate it with a painted board. Make your first ditch small and shallow. When you introduce a bank, begin with a gradual slope that your horse can navigate confidently. On our grand prix course at Brumath, even the biggest bank—the one that's a copy of the Hickstead bank—has a more gentle slope than Hickstead's, in order to build our horses' confidence.

Photo: *Practical Horseman*

Most horses don't like water, so start out with a dry liverpool. You can make one out of a 4-foot-wide plywood board with a 1-inch edge all around. Paint the board blue so that it looks like water and paint the strip white to give the "water" a clearly defined boundary. Walk your horse around it, and if he seems frightened let him sniff it.

Build a vertical over the middle of the board. Ride with a lot of pace the first couple of times and jump from one side only. This will encourage your horse to make a good jumping effort and discourage him from stopping. After a couple of schools, add another rail to make a more substantial fence and then approach from the other direction. When your horse is confident, raise the vertical gradually to 4 feet.

Move the vertical to the edge of the board and drop it back to 3 feet 6 inches. Jumped from the board side, as an open-face water, your liverpool rides like a triple bar, with the edge of the water establishing a nice takeoff for the back rail. Ride to a deep spot, close to the water, with as much pace as the height and width of the obstacle requires. Since your horse will shoot out on the landing, just as he would over a ramped triple bar, be prepared to shorten stride on landing when you meet this type of obstacle in a line.

When your horse jumps the open face boldly, put water in the tray. Walk him around it until he's relaxed, but don't let him sniff it. The water will ripple and spook him. If you think the water is going to make a difference to your horse, drop your fence back to the lower height and jump several times in both directions before you pick up where you left off.

Next, build an oxer right over the water; make it between 3 feet 6 inches and 4 feet high and about 4 feet wide. The fence itself is nothing your horse can't handle easily, but the presence of the water underneath tempts him to look down and makes this a more difficult obstacle. If he's like most horses, he may fail to concentrate on the front rail, and you'll have to help him focus his attention on it by bringing him to a short-to-comfortable takeoff spot.

When your horse is experienced with water, you can add another increment of difficulty by making the oxer wider. Bring the front rail forward 6 to 9 inches so that the front edge of the water is recessed behind it, making a false groundline. Now your horse must ignore the water and focus entirely on the fence. This is an excellent sharpener if your horse is lazy about square oxers, or right before a class with a difficult liverpool.

Liverpools

Photos: *Practical Horseman*

Wide Water Jumps

The last thing you want is to have your horse put his foot in the water, as he'll quickly lose respect for it. So start with your liverpool tray, which will be easy for him to clear.

Fill the tray with water, put a brush box across the front edge to make sure the horse jumps up in the air, and put a 2-foot-high rail across the middle of the tray to be sure he stays in the air. Canter down with enough pace so that even if he's wrong in the takeoff, he can make it comfortably to the other side. He's familiar with the tray, so this obstacle shouldn't be a problem. Then move the brush boxes away from the water so that the overall dimension is about 6 feet and school until your horse is stabilized.

Progress to a real open-water obstacle about 9 feet wide. Set the brush box right at the edge and put the single 2-foot rail over the center. Let your horse walk around all sides until he's not afraid, and then come with enough pace for you to actually override the jump a bit the first three or four times to make sure that your horse has the confidence to jump out over it.

Add another rail toward the far edge of the water. This gives the jump a triple-bar effect and puts the horse's arc further out over the water. When he's confident, remove the rails and jump the open water with a lot of pace so that he'll clear it easily.

Put back the center rail or build a sloped oxer over the water, gradually widening the entire obstacle to 12 feet by pulling out the brush. When the horse is comfortable with the greater width, take away the rails and practice a couple of times over the widened water alone, approaching with plenty of pace. But don't drill once your horse is confident. A few schools a year are normally sufficient. If you overschool, your horse may lose respect for the water. When you school, use a 12-foot water with the brush boxes pulled out about a foot in front. (This is the dimension of the obstacle you're most likely to meet in competition.) Put one rail over the middle and another toward the far edge. Jump two or three

Photos: *Practical Horseman*

Photos: *Practical Horseman*

times and leave it at that. When your horse gets into the ring, he'll still be thinking "up and out."

Ditches

Start with a grass or dry ditch deep enough to catch your horse's attention but not so deep that it is likely to spook him. First jump the ditch with a 2-foot vertical over the center; then follow the same steps as you did for the liverpool, gradually increasing the difficulty.

Photo: *Practical Horseman*

Banks

When they encounter their first banks, a lot of horses jump off with a huge leap and land on all fours at the bottom. To counteract that tendency, start with a low, easy bank and a quiet approach.

This little bank of mine slopes up to the drop-off, which makes it easier to steady the approach. Ride quietly to the edge and encourage your horse to drop off without making a big jump out.

Once he comes off the bank quietly, turn around and teach him to hop back up. Come with an easy pace to a normal spot, and be sure to let him use his head and neck freely. Once he's confident, add a rail 1 foot high at the edge of the bank and introduce your horse to jumping on and off a bank over a rail.

A table is a bank with several cantering strides (usually three) between the "up" and "down" jumps. Mine, a copy of the one at Hickstead, is 3 feet above the level of my grand prix field, but I left out the ditches that are at each end of the Hickstead table to make it easier on the confidence of a green horse.

My table calls for three steady strides across the top . . .

. . . and an easy hop down at the other end. Once your horse is handling the table comfortably, build 1-foot-6-inch verticals at each end so that the jump onto the table and the drop off at the far end are both 4 feet 6 inches. If your horse is competing in an advanced competition like the American Jumping Derby, replace the vertical at the "up" edge with a 2–3-foot-wide oxer. Since your horse will have a tendency to forget about the back rail of the oxer as he concentrates on the bank, let him negotiate it a few times, and then widen it in order to remind him that he has to be tight with his hind legs. Because some speed classes call for a 90-degree turn on top of the table, practice jumping up and then jumping off one side.

A derby bank is a high bank with a steep face on the down side. In competition, your horse will have to canter up the slope and walk or slide down the other side. It's important that he keep his hind feet planted firmly under him so that he's ready to negotiate the next obstacle. There could be a little fence right at the bottom of the downhill slope, or a full-sized obstacle one stride away. There might be a fence at the base of the uphill or on top of the bank, or any combination of these.

A bank with a variety of gradients is ideal for training. Accustom your horse to gentle slopes before moving on to steep ones. Start by walking; then trot and canter up while you're still walking down.

Place a small fence at the foot of the slope. Practice jumping up onto the bank over the fence and then turn around and hip down off the bank over the fence. Once your horse has done this well, two or three times from the steep slope, there's no need to keep on practicing it. Photos: *Practical Horseman*

The Grab

This is a triple combination with one stride between elements situated in a V-shaped depression with a fence over a ditch at the low point of the V. You travel downhill from the first element to the second (the one over the ditch), and uphill to the third.

Make sure your horse is confident over ditches before you introduce the grab, and then start out with just the middle element set as a vertical. Next, add the out vertical; and when your horse is handling the two obstacles confidently, add the in.

The first fence is usually the most difficult element of the combination. In the big derbies, when the fences get high, your horse will be inclined to look down the slope to the ditch and pull the top rail down with him. Before a derby, I make sure my horse is concentrating on the "in" by making it very big.

The middle element will seem small because it sits at the bottom of the V below the level of the takeoff and landing.

The final vertical, an easy one-stride away, shouldn't give your horse any problems. Photos: *Practical Horseman*

295

7

From Equitation to Open Jumpers

Armand Leone with Stephen D. Price

Armand is the eldest of the three Leone brothers, who are something of a phenomenon in the contemporary show-jumping world. All of them have achieved excellence as jumper riders; all are not only amateur but also part-time horsemen. Armand, like his parents, is a radiologist; Peter is a stockbroker. Mark, who has a college degree in political science, manages the family stable while envisaging a career in real estate.

The Leone brothers formed a family Nations' Cup team at Lucerne in 1982, and (with Will Simpson) won the first AGA Team Jumping Championship at Tampa in 1985. But they are most often seen as friendly rivals on the grand prix circuit.

I'd been showing in junior equitation classes, and as my eighteenth birthday loomed ahead, I was faced with a choice. I could have gone the Amateur Owner route, but instead I went into the Open Jumper Division.

When I made that decision, I knew I was taking on a major commitment both in terms of the amount of time I'd have to devote to the sport and the amount of money. To succeed at the top level, I'd need to have access to one or more grand prix-caliber jumpers. And then the burden would be on me to produce the best possible performances.

The equitation I'd learned from George Morris in my junior days is

Armand Leone with Jonker in the 1985 World Cup finals in Berlin. Photo: Courtesy of USET

simply the art and science of using the human body in harmony with the horse's movements. A balanced seat, as it's understood in hunt seat equitation, with the rider's weight in his knees, lower leg, and heel, provides the best base of support and stability from which to influence a horse most effectively, whatever the level of competition.

However, as the fences I was jumping increased in size, I began to modify my hunt equitation style. I found that I had to tilt my upper body back a little, closer to the vertical. A horse generates his thrust from the hind end. If some of his own weight and his rider's weight can be shifted toward the source of power, the effort becomes easier for him. I haven't discarded the forward seat, but I use it mostly for galloping long distances between fences.

Along with the more vertical posture goes what George Morris would call "a following hand." Whereas hunt seat equitation riders carry their

"When I began riding jumpers, I learned to raise my hands from their equitation position so as to maintain a straight line from the bit through my hand to my elbow. This direct relationship from elbow to bit enables me to compress my horse into a springier frame just by pulling back slightly on the reins; and to lengthen his frame by moving my arms forward a little. It's a push-pull feeling with the horse moving his chin in and out along the line that connects his mouth with my hands."

hands low and close to the withers, jumper riders follow their horse's mouth to minimize the risk of interference. Throughout my junior days, I used the crest release. But when I worked with Bert de Némethy at Gladstone, he instructed me to take my hands off the horse's neck so that they would reach directly toward his mouth. This frees the horse's neck and back so that it can round its body over a fence. At the top of the jump, his neck is actually between the rider's arms. More than once I've held myself off a horse's back over a large oxer by squeezing my forearms against its neck. I still use the conventional crest release, with my hands pressed down on the horse's neck, to retard a jumper over a straight vertical. I've learned which release is right for each situation, not to please an equitation judge but to help my horse.

As the courses grew tougher and the margin for error diminished, I didn't forsake the basic skills I'd learned as a junior rider, but I found that I had to refine them. An equitation rider with an eye to a USET medal learns basic dressage: shoulder-ins, voltes, and changes of lead. Jumper riders do more advanced work on the flat, but always for its

"When your hunter's head goes up in the air, you keep your hands low and work it down by giving and taking or with bending exercises. But when my jumper comes out of his push-pull frame, my hands follow him up, maintaining the unbroken line. With my hands and legs I keep a steady contact, opposing his tension with equal tension of my own, until his head returns to a lower frame. Then I relax the pressure on his mouth and sides." Photos: *Practical Horseman*

practical value in the show ring. Bending exercises prepare the horse for sharp turns it will need in speed classes. Transitions from the full gallop (equitation riders only do extended canter) to the collected canter are important over long, galloping grand prix courses. Two-tracking at all gaits creates the suppleness you need in order to find lines between fences.

"This springy frame gives me a number of options as I approach a fence. Pulling back slightly on the rein compresses Sombre into the 'ready' position. With his hind end underneath him, head up, and front end light, he's prepared to jump a big vertical."

"If I have to gallop between fences in a speed class, I move my hands forward, and as he accelerates, his whole frame lengthens, his head following my hands as if I were pushing his head forward. From this position he's easy to recompress as we reach the fence." Photos: *Practical Horseman*

"As I approach a turn, I maintain an equal feel with both reins, but I raise my outside hand just a hair above the inside one to keep my horse's head straight in relation to his body. I move my outside leg back a little to prevent the haunches from swinging out and I squeeze my inside leg just behind the girth to bend my horse around the turn."

Bert de Némethy's theory that a rider relates to his horse through a system of resistances and rewards is not very different from the theories I learned as a psychology major in college. You use your hands, legs, and seat to resist your horse's undesirable impulses and movements. When the horse is in the proper frame, when he's going at the speed and in the direction you wish, you withdraw your aids as a reward.

For example, I might ask my horse to move forward in a straight line at a working trot. If he pulls ahead and swings his haunches off the track, my hands and seat resist the speed while my legs correct the lateral deviation. But as soon as the horse is trotting properly, I ease up and reward him with relative freedom.

"This picture demonstrates what USET coach Bert de Némethy calls 'riding from your inside to your outside.' Using your inside leg, you push your horse up into your outside hand, which controls the degree of bend and prevents him from bulging out through his shoulder."

"As an equitation rider, my position in the saddle looked something like this. I only moved my upper body a few inches to make subtle changes in my horse's stride. As we left the ground, I'd sit passively, letting the horse close all the angles."

"Now it's an active process. I move into a very forward position over the fence to lighten the load on my horse's back. But when I gallop to a fence, I use my upper body as a brake, as in this photo, to help me re-collect my horse before the takeoff. I sit down in the saddle with my upper body slightly behind the vertical. This has a slowing effect on my horse, so that I don't have to rely entirely on my hands to bring him back. Approaching a water jump or a wide oxer that we may not have enough impulsion to clear, I take hold of the horse's head and sit in the back of the saddle, as I'm doing here. This 'closes the back door,' preventing a refusal. When I see my takeoff spot, I drive my horse forward with my seat and, if necessary, my spurs." Photos: *Practical Horseman*

Bert also stresses that the horse really wants to be in harmony with its rider. This is why a very slight, subtle rider movement can be effective. If you sit properly, you can make your horse move to the left or right by the slightest shift in the weight of your seat.

You can test this principle on yourself. Stand with your arms out to the sides and have a friend stand behind you and place his hand on your right shoulder. First you'll lean to the right, and then you'll step to the right in order to place yourself more comfortably under the added weight. In the same way, when you shift your weight onto your right seatbone, your horse naturally moves in that direction to support you more comfortably. Of course, if he feels that your other leg is insecure, he may prefer to duck to the left and dump you. That is why sophisticated aids must be coordinated with sound basic equitation.

When I'm working on the flat at home, I lengthen my stirrup leathers so that I'm sitting deeper in the saddle. This modified dressage seat gives me a little extra sensitivity as I practice exercises to improve my lines of communication with the horse.

Variety is very important in flat work, as well as in schooling over fences. I plan long-range so that my horses reach competition with the fewest possible number of schooling jumps but the greatest possible variety of experience. One day, my ring may contain only a simple line of fences made of poles. Another day, I'll set up bend-related distances instead of straight lines, and use filled-in fences such as brush boxes and walls. Although changing the order of fences may seem like no big deal, it keeps a horse thinking and prevents staleness. I can teach my horses all they need to know over fences that seldom rise above 4 feet 6 inches.

If a horse is to have three schools within ten days of a show, I might set up three combinations like these: (1) an oxer to a vertical, to another oxer; (2) an oxer to an oxer to a vertical; (3) a vertical to a vertical, to an oxer.

First I encourage the horse to jump forward through the two oxers, and then the pair of verticals sharpens him up. As a jumper rider, I want to rev my horse up to attack a course. Equitation and hunter riders try to calm their horses down.

Hunter-class course designers create pretty straightforward routes, emphasizing distances between fences and such problem obstacles as a jump at one end of the ring or a fence coming off a turn. Open and grand prix courses are much more demanding. Strides matter less than the size and width of the fences. Jumper course designers often have quirks, favorite patterns they use again and again. I try to remember course patterns I've competed over and rebuild them at home, duplicating the lines and combinations but keeping the fences small. In this way, I can correct a problem before I encounter it another time.

Thoroughbreds used as open jumpers, selected for their courage, are more easily stirred up than those used as equitation mounts. Little details startle and upset them. I teach my horses to have confidence in my commands, not only in the ring and over fences but all over the show grounds. In stadium grand prix competitions, there are often long concrete walks between the schooling area and the field, as well as arches and tunnels. I seek opportunities at home to teach my horses to cope with all kinds of distractions. For example, I never avoid moving past a candy wrapper or a sheet of newspaper on the road, a new pile of jumps next to the ring, or a puddle. I'm careful to pick only those fights I know I can win. Finally, my horses learn to handle most horse-show distractions.

Equitation riders compete a lot, often weekly, especially when they need blue ribbons to qualify for Medal or Maclay finals. Not so with jumpers. I find myself planning in terms of a year, not of days or weeks.

Like many other jumper riders, I divide the year into two segments. February through June (Florida through Ox Ridge) is a spring training period for exposure and experience. Then, for the balance of the year (Lake Placid through New York or Toronto), I push a little harder. I single out from three to six competitions in which my horses will be asked for peak performances, consulting coach, veterinarian, and black-

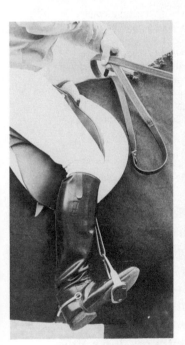  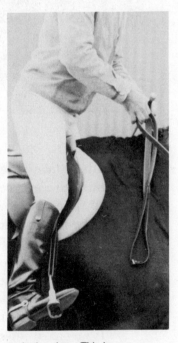

"I still use the four different stirrup lengths George Morris taught me in my equitation days. This is what George calls 'flat-test' length. It sits you fairly deep in the saddle, important for sitting trot in Medal and Maclay competition. I use it when I'm combining work on the flat with schooling over small fences. If you stand in your stirrups, your crotch won't quite clear the saddle."

"One hole down from flat-test length, where my foot is now, is my dressage schooling position. It puts my leg closer to my horse's sides and gives my seat a little extra influence in the saddle."

"One hole shorter than flat-test length is useful for jumping medium fences, from 4 to 5 feet. It's the length I used in equitation competition over fences and now I use it in schooling. Standing in your stirrups, you should just clear the pommel of the saddle. For grand prix fences, I take my stirrups up one more hole. It helps me keep my body out of the saddle and off my horse's back in the air."

"In equitation competition, I used a crest release, planting my hands near the mane to help support my upper body in the air. Now, shoot my hands forward to give my horse plenty of freedom while maintaining the straight line from hand to mouth. If I think I'm going to get left behind or fall back in the saddle, I clamp my hands against the side of the neck. Sometimes I even hook one under the neck."

smith. It takes a team of experts to set a schedule for each horse that is competitive and realistic.

In spite of expert help and careful preparation, I found that going to Europe the first time and competing against such international superstars as Nelson Pessoa of Brazil or Eric Woutters of Belgium was quite a culture shock! Over there, speed classes mean speed. You don't just pick up the pace at the end of the course; you gallop from start to finish. The rails are set in deeper cups, so you ride at the fences without worrying too much about having a rail down if your horse rubs.

It was hard for me to see my distances, because the fences don't often have groundlines. I learned to balance around the turns, relax to the takeoff spot, and then make small adjustments at the last minute. None of the "forward fives" and "steady sixes" of my junior equitation days!

Back in the United States, jumping against champions like Rodney Jenkins, Bernie Traurig, and Melanie Smith was mind-boggling and not a little terrifying. But you have to think of it as a challenge. You're

"Entering a grand prix arena, especially on a little horse, I like to know we have enough impulsion for those big fences. Here I send him into an extended trot to make sure he isn't scared to go forward; if I'm really concerned about his scope, I'll move him up into an extended canter. Once I know we have enough gas, I compress again before the first fence. In equitation competition, everything was smooth and subtle. You'd never make an obvious transition." Photos: Karl Leck

comparing yourself to the country's best riders. It's a way to gain recognition of your ability. And believe me, when you've only recently graduated from the Equitation ranks, to produce a clean round over an Open Jumper course is a milestone!

8

From Pony Club to Grand Prix

Melanie Smith

Since riding her first pony at the age of three on the family farm in Germantown, Tennessee, Melanie Smith has devoted her life to horses, and in particular to show jumping. Her extraordinary talent and persistence led her from one success to another to become one of the most consistent winners in the show-jumping world, one of the most popular, one of those most laden with honors.

A few highlights of her impressive career, are her first appearance on a winning U.S. Nations Cup team at the 1975 Washington, D.C., International, the first of many; a gold team medal in the 1979 Pan-American Games; a bronze medal at the 1980 "alternate Olympics" in Rotterdam; a superb record in the annual FEI World Cup finals, being champion in 1982, third in 1983 (both times with Calypso), and second in 1980 (with Val de Loir); female Athlete of the Year in 1982 of the U.S. Olympic Committee; Rider of the Year of the American Grand Prix Association in 1982; winner of the Show-jumping Triple Crown; and member of the gold-medal-winning U.S. team in the 1984 Olympics at Los Angeles.

Interrupting her riding career while at the top, Melanie now shares her expertise with young riders in lessons and clinics.

This is her story of how it all began. It was written when she was a promising young show rider and not yet the international star she was to become.

I learned to ride by riding. And I've ridden hundreds of different horses. That's the way you learn to be a good rider: by getting on as many different horses as possible.

My grandfather, who raised Shetland ponies for nearly seventy years at his Sunny Crest Farm near Fort Dodge, Iowa, gave me and my sister our first ponies. Both of them produced foals, so we were in the pony business. Gradually the business developed into a boarding and training stable.

Around our area there are some five major stables. It's pretty difficult to sneak up on a promising horse. But we have contacts in New Mexico, Oklahoma, Texas, Nebraska, and Kansas. The cowboys don't like big horses because they do a lot of getting on and off. They call them "tall" horses. When they find big horses, they gather a little group together, call my mother, and we go out and take a look. You never know where you're going to find a good big horse.

We buy two types of horses: two- and three-year-old Thoroughbreds that I train from scratch; and older horses (usually Thoroughbred–quarter-horse crosses) that have been used for ranch work. The quarter-horse cross gives you a sturdy horse with a quiet disposition. Since they're usually broken and much easier to start over fences, they're our quick-sale horses. We can bring them on in a couple of months and make money on them faster.

Generally, we may go out and buy eight horses, and if two turn out, we're lucky. We're always looking for the horse that might make a jumper, but there are so many slots in between, such as pony clubs, local shows, and so on, that we're looking for all kinds of horses. You never really know what's going to make a show horse. The most expensive Thoroughbred colt isn't always the one that makes it.

Bootlegger was the first hunter I was really successful with on the A circuit in the East, although I'd won a lot of local championships with several junior hunters. The first year we showed Bootlegger, he was Amateur-Owner Hunter Champion at Madison Square Garden, and he finished the year in fourth place in the national standings. We'd bought him from a man up in the Ozarks. He called and said he had a horse that was going to be my conformation hunter. He brought him by our house for us to look at, along with a second horse. Well, I didn't like the first one at all. He was pretty, but he was stiff. He had a long neck, and his head just hung out at the end of it.

The other horse was Bootlegger. He was stringy and scrawny. He had a long winter coat and was really quite ugly. But my mother liked him right away. She said, "That's the horse I want." So I got on him and

Melanie Smith and her home-trained hunter Bootlegger, winner of the Amateur-Owner Hunter Championship at the Natonal Horse Show in 1971. Photo: Budd

hacked him around. He'd just been broken, but I jumped him over a couple of little rails and he had so much spring, so much bounce, that I knew he'd make a good jumper. At the same time, I was a little wary because he was a horse that was always on the muscle, not tense but just good-feeling. I was a little worried that he might not settle down, but he had so much talent that I decided to take the chance. Another thing in his favor was that he was inexpensive. We'll pay from $500 to $1,500 and sell anywhere from $2,500 to $25,000. We're working on an average, so we can afford to make a few mistakes.

What qualities make a horse a good risk? Horses are all built differently, but you look at each one to see whether he fits together. He either looks like an athlete or he doesn't. We look for a horse that stands square, a basically sound horse, and we like a goose rump. It's a good jumping hind end. We also look for a big strong horse—the bigger, the better—because they're more salable and can usually jump the big fences. My mother can really pick a horse; it's a gift some people have.

Training

When it comes to schooling the horses we buy, I have no set pattern. I get to know a horse's personality well and do what I feel like doing with him from day to day. When I start work, I already have an idea of what I'm going to do, but I don't necessarily follow my plan exactly. I might quit early or work a little longer. I might be planning to jump, but if, after working on the flat, I feel the horse isn't in the mood to jump, I might just trot over a couple of fences and put him away. That's the advantage of not always being in a hurry.

I always start by getting our horses broken on the flat. I don't mean dressage training. Just getting them ridable, taking them out on hacks so that you can guide them and so they learn to balance themselves. I don't think a two- or three-year-old horse is physically or mentally ready for flexion, collection, or that type of dressage work. I just like to get them quiet and confident and going forward. They also learn their leads, learn to circle; as you keep riding and working, they gradually learn to balance themselves better. Some horses are naturally more athletic and can start over fences right away. With others, you have to wait until they're a little older and have learned to carry themselves better.

I start out with poles on the ground, then very low fences, and lots of trotting. I trot slowly to the fence so that they have plenty of time to think about it. You're less likely to meet a fence wrong when you trot to it, and you can control the approach better because the horse is going slowly and quietly. I try to keep a horse out of trouble until he's balanced enough to cope with it. I just try to keep him quiet and confident and make him think of jumping as a pleasant experience.

Of course, he'll make mistakes; that's how horses learn. If you control the approach so that when the horse gets there he's paying attention, then even if he gets to a bad spot he'll be able to take care of it.

Every horse has his own natural jumping style that can't be changed much, but I think a horse can learn bad form if he has to avoid hurting himself. If a young horse is permitted to run underneath fences, run deep, then he doesn't have time to get his legs up properly in order to avoid hitting himself. So he'll learn to twist, hang his knees, or throw his legs to the side.

I don't believe in longeing a horse over big fences, but I sometimes longe young horses over low fences at a trot. It teaches them to set themselves and think a little on their own. Still, I prefer to ride them most of the time. Occasionally we put a new horse in the Hitchcock pen and jump him free, just to see what natural talent he has, to see if he's worth working with or if it's better to sell him and make a small profit right away.

Sometimes you can be fooled. I had one horse that jumped like a deer in the pen. I've never had another horse that leaped in the air the way he did. But when I started to train him, he had a weird style. He didn't use his back at all when there was a rider on him. We sold him as a pleasure horse.

I don't do a lot of gymnastics and combinations at the beginning. I just get the horses confident over many individual fences with good groundlines. A groundline gives the horse time to get his knees up so that he starts using himself properly from the very start.

We want a horse to bring up both front and hind legs correctly and evenly; but at first I'm more concerned with the way he uses his front end than his back end. If a horse is really good with his front end, he can get by in the hunter classes, even if he's not as good with his back end. If he's even and tight with his front end, his hind end can get away with being a little uneven or strung out. But if a horse hangs his front legs, he's not going to be a success as a show hunter, even if he's wonderful behind.

After a week or so, when the horse feels as if he knows what he's doing at the trot, when he's balancing himself well enough so that I can adjust his stride at the canter, then he's ready to start cantering low fences.

When I start cantering I don't always put the horse in the ideal spot because he has to learn to jump from deep distances and long distances as well. He has to learn to adjust himself and to think about what he's doing. But I always try to put him in a spot from where I know he's capable of jumping. If he's confident that his rider is going to get him to the fences well, he'll learn to jump in good form and learn to want to jump. That's why I bring my horses along very slowly and carefully and try never to overwhelm them.

Showing

How long does it take to get a horse ready to show? It all depends on the individual horse, and most of all on his temperament. I've had older horses who thought nothing of going around a course and took to jumping at once. I could start them over fences and be showing by the end of the week.

Melanie and Radnor II, winner of the 1976 American Gold Cup. Photo: Karl Leck

But a good young prospect might need several months to a year. It isn't the height of the fence that matters to the horse. Almost any horse, if he has any talent at all, is capable of jumping 3 feet 6 inches. It's the step up from 3 feet 6 inches to 4 feet that makes the big difference. I always school over low fences, changing the fences and gradually building up to combinations. I think you get a horse stale if you practice jumping him over the height he's going to show over. I'd rather keep him fresh so that he'll jump better at the shows.

Besides, I think a horse learns more from jumping different types of fences, from increasingly difficult distances and from different spots, than from jumping high. As he becomes better balanced and develops confidence, I'll make him get deep to some fences, make him stand off at some, do some fences at angles. I'll build different types of fences, jump him up and down hills, do little one-stride and two-stride combinations, get him so he thinks nothing of doing whatever I ask him to do. If he makes a mistake, he won't be in much trouble, because the fences are low.

After several months of this, the horse needs to go to a show. I start most of my green horses in Florida. I usually sell three or four young horses there. By the end of the circuit, they're pretty salable and I know which ones are good jumper prospects. I love to work with young horses. But once I get a horse to his first-year green stage, I like either to train him as a jumper or start a new one.

Riding

I'm more of a natural rider than a mechanical rider because I learned to ride by the seat of my pants. George Morris always used to tell me that I'd skipped grammar school because I didn't know basic equitation and dressage-type work. When I went with George, I didn't know anything about counting strides or distances either. I just went in there and rode it by sight.

I met George at a clinic in Knoxville, Tennessee, when I was eighteen. I wanted to get some help in starting to ride. It was very hard for us, because we lived in an area where there was no link to the East and the A shows. We drove 800 miles to get to that clinic.

I asked George if I could go to Florida with him. He told me I was too old. I was out of the Junior Division and my horse wasn't good enough, there was no place for me, and, besides, it would be a waste of money. But I was so determined that I went back to the clinic the following year, told him that I was going to Florida anyway, and wanted to meet him there.

I groomed and braided and worked for everything I got, because I couldn't afford to pay for lessons. But things really worked out. I showed The Irishman. He was Amateur Jumper Champion of the Florida circuit and finally National Amateur Jumper Champion, after winning the championship or reserve at every show but one that year.

When I first started riding with George, I was so in awe! I couldn't believe there were so many things to think about. Then I realized that I was doing it all anyway. Things had worked out for me the same as they did for other people; I just didn't know the fancy names.

Natural ability is the most important thing; you can always learn the technical part. Ideally, of course, you should have both ability and technical knowledge. There are natural riders who haven't a clue as to what they're doing, and there are robot riders who follow a set pattern and don't deviate one inch from it. If the trainer says the distance is five steady strides but the robot rider happens to jump in really big or really tight, he won't think of making an adjustment; he'll just ride as he's been told to do and he won't meet the fence right. The natural rider, on the other hand, won't think of what the distance might be; he'll just leave out a stride or do what his eye tells him to do.

Melanie up on Val de Loir. Photo: Budd

At any top show, you'll find riders in all three categories. But the rider who has both the natural ability and a knowledge of distances and strides will make the adjustment between the two fences and meet both fences well. He'll come out ahead of the other two.

Show Jumping

When you ride Equitation, you think about position. But in jumping you have to think about your horse and his problems.

The Irishman, for example, was a great horse. He always tried hard, and we made a good combination. Jumping big verticals and wide oxers was never easy for him, so in the schooling area before each class, I'd start him off over small verticals and then small oxers, gradually making them wider, trying to stretch him out a little. I'd end up over a wide low oxer, because I was trying to get him stretched out and didn't want him

Melanie and Calypso, one of her most successful international jumpers. In 1980 they won the individual bronze medal at the Rotterdam alternate Olympics. Four years later, they made the team again and took home a team gold medal from the Los Angeles Olympic Games.

to worry about height; and then over a big vertical, because he was never really good with his front end unless I kept hold of him. I'd always let him jump a big vertical confidently before going into the ring, to show him that he could jump it well.

Watching other horses go helps me as much as, or more than, walking the course. I watch the first few horses and plan my strategy. The Irishman could handle short or long distances, but in the first round I'd be conservative and fit in the extra stride, because he was more careful if I didn't get long with him. I never wanted to be long to a wide oxer. I'd plan to get to a really good spot. In the jump-offs, I could leave out strides to make time. He was very competitive and I could take all sorts of chances with him, leaving out strides, jumping off tight turns. And he could make up time galloping between fences.

I prefer a quiet, sensitive horse with a good mouth to a strong horse that pulls, but it really doesn't matter. I've ridden all types and I can cope with them.

I'd rather ride a jumper than a hunter because it's more of a challenge and more exciting. But I've been fortunate to have good horses. Bad jumpers are what frighten people. The sport is not all that dangerous if you have a good horse and ride him well.

But people shouldn't ride jumpers until they've had experience and are sure of themselves. You don't put pony riders on jumpers. A rider has to go through stages of learning just as the horse does.

9

Training an Olympic Jumper

Dennis Murphy

**Dennis Murphy is so busy training young riders and young
horses that he seldom travels as far afield from his Alabama
home as he did a decade ago. Then, as member of the USET,
he competed in nine Nations Cups, and rode on the fourth-
placed U.S. Olympic Team in Montreal and on the gold-medal
U.S. team in the 1975 Pan-American Games.**

My method of training a jumper may be different from, and take much
longer than, the training methods of many professional horsemen. I am
not a professional. My training goal is to produce a horse that will be
competitive at the Olympic level. You can't afford shortcuts when you're
training a horse for international competition.

My approach to schooling jumpers is based on the belief that training,
not innate ability, is the deciding factor in obtaining the maximum
performance from any horse. Sensitive, step-by-step schooling tailored
to the needs and progress of each individual horse will move a fair horse
up to good and could make a good horse great. Time and again, you
see an educated horse with less inherent jumping ability perform better,
more consistently, and over a longer period of time than a horse that
has spectacular native talent but lacks good basic training.

Under normal conditions and in his own environment, I believe that
almost any horse is capable of jumping between 3 feet 6 inches and 4
feet. I suppose there is a small percentage that couldn't jump that height
under any circumstance, but that also means there must be an equal

Dennis Murphy with Do Right, perhaps the most outstanding jumper he has trained and ridden.
Photo: Courtesy of USET

number of horses that are athletic superstars. This very small percentage (I'd say about 2 percent of the horses in the world) is what every horseman looks for. Finding and recognizing horses of this caliber is virtually impossible, mainly because it is training and accomplishment that bring out the ability. By the time such superior talent becomes evident, the horse's price has usually escalated beyond reason and the reach of most people's pocketbooks.

I don't think anybody can recognize this type of talent in an untried horse, so you have to settle for selecting horses that seem to be the right type. Of course, a great deal depends on the horse's level of training. One person may ask me to look at a horse that has never been ridden, and the next person may say, "Here's a super horse. Ride him." In the first case, I could only evaluate the horse on the basis of his conformation, way of going, coordination, and whether or not he appears to be a real athlete, but I could ask nothing of the horse himself. The other one could be tested to the ultimate and asked to perform over the most challenging courses I could devise.

Understanding the horse's level of training and what you can expect of him is an important part of looking for a good jumper. You have to be a pretty good horseman to be able to determine how much of the horse's performance is due to training, how much to natural ability, and how much more progress you can expect the horse to make. Nobody can just look at a horse or watch it jump a few fences and say, "This horse is a super athlete. Let's start training him." If there were such a person, he'd be a millionaire because all he'd have to do would be to go around pointing them out. The most you can do is say, "This horse meets all of my requirements for a good jumper. Let's start working him and see."

We all have personal preferences. The most difficult horse for me to work with is a short-coupled, stiff-going horse that is very compact, with very short fetlock joints and a short neck, an overall blocky, close-built horse. The horse I like for myself is longer and leaner; he moves with elegance and grace; his stride is fluid and long. I guess I simply feel instinctively that such a horse has more potential athletic ability than any other type.

Some people just get on a horse and start jumping. Horses that make progress from such an abrupt beginning are exceptions. The sound way to train a horse is to start with flat work, proceed to cavalletti, and then go to gymnastics. When the horse has mastered all the basic procedures and takes the step into the Open Division, you'll find that he is well trained, easy to ride, and already familiar with the problems that confront him on a jumping course.

The horse that started jumping right away because he had lots of ability is bound to run into problems during competition sooner or later, and he won't know how to handle them. You'll probably say to yourself, "I know my horse can jump a lot bigger than this. Why am I having trouble?" The answer is simple. The horse lacks basic training. Personally, I think it's much harder to retrain a horse than to educate him from the very beginning—like one that has already jumped a lot but doesn't know how to trot a fence or to shorten his stride.

One of the advantages of bringing a horse along slowly and carefully from the start is that he learns how to use his ability without wasting energy by overjumping his fences. He also becomes familiar and adept at utilizing various jumping techniques in different situations. A horse that knows just how high he has to jump to clear a certain fence is able to approach it with confidence and will jump it much better than one that is unsure of himself.

I don't think the average person can make a horse ready to compete in the Jumper Division in less than two years. An exceptional horse and rider might do it faster, but two years is a fair estimate of the time required to produce a horse that is well broken on the flat and confident to his fences. This horse must ride well, turn well, stop when you ask, go forward when you ask, slow down or accelerate when you ask, feel comfortable over fences, without ever a doubt in his mind. If a young horse is overfaced or frightened about jumping, you don't back up just a day or two—you *run* backward.

The horse's education is an unending process, of course. What you try to do in those first two years is to give him enough knowledge and experience over the types of fences and courses he'll meet in competition so that he'll be able to cope with any problem confronting him.

I love a horse that wants to work things out for himself. Lots of times I'll just give a horse his head and let him add a stride or leave out a stride, without trying to make him do one or the other. There's nothing better than riding a horse who knows what he's doing. I'll help a horse when I'm riding him, but I don't want to dominate him. For instance,

An Olympic jumper, like Dennis Murphy's Do Right, must be able to clear long courses comprising such difficult obstacles as these parallel bars—and do it twice. Photo: Courtesy of USET

during a gymnastic I want him to be thinking, "What do I do now?" and "What shall I do now?"

If you're trying as hard as you can to solve the problems, and the horse is thinking and trying as hard as he can, then you're bound to get more answers and more problems solved than if only one of you were working on it. What I try to do is give the horse the tools with which he can solve his problems at each level of training. Then I expect him to employ these tools as he gains experience, so that he's pretty much working on his own.

When I start with a young horse, the first thing I do is work on the longe line. I want him to be able to walk, trot, and canter on the line and to learn voice commands before I ever ride him, so that there is already some basis for communication and control. If you just snatch a horse out of the paddock, slap the tack on, and jump on him, he doesn't know what's happening. He'll probably resent the pull on his mouth and the weight on his back; his instinctive reaction will be to resist or fight. But if you start him on the longe, teach him voice commands, and drive him a little, he'll learn that "whoa" means stop, "trot" means trot, and already you will have established some elementary controls. Then, when you get on him, he'll already be familiar with the sound of your voice and the feel of your hands on the reins. I like to use relatively loose side reins with the longe line so that the horse will begin to find his own balance and start to bring his hocks in under him.

I expect to spend approximately six months on flat work. My initial goals are relatively simple. I want the horse to be able to do a collected, ordinary, and extended walk, trot, and canter. Once he can do all that and go forward and back, I include a little shoulder-in, turn on the forehand, turn on the haunches, and perhaps two-tracking over short distances. These basic maneuvers are also exercises in control and discipline.

Another part of his basic flat education is the simple change of lead at the canter. I don't want the horse to anticipate his next move. Sometimes I'll canter, then ask for a trot for four or five steps, and then ask for the opposite lead canter. Other times I might ask for an ordinary trot and then a collected trot before breaking into the canter again so that the horse has to listen and wait before completing his change of lead. Flying changes are the last thing I teach a young horse, because the horse might anticipate it when we're showing. Besides, I think that a well-balanced, well-broken horse will change his lead naturally when the need arises.

After about six months of flat work, the horse should be ready to start jumping. Some horses may reach that point sooner than others, and I may already have included some cavalletti work and little gymnastics in the program of a horse that seems to be losing interest on the flat. But generally speaking, only when my horse is thoroughly responsive, well balanced, and fairly confident on the flat do I proceed to jumping.

I begin with cavalletti on the ground. When the horse handles that easily, I put a fence at one end that almost locks in a distance so that the horse can't stand back too far or get in too close. This more or less "mechanical" distance of the cavalletti is made to measure for each individual horse. I want him to trot to the cavalletti, put his four feet down, and stand up on his hocks at just the right spot for clearing the fence. I always space everything to make it easy for the horse to jump almost naturally. I certainly don't want him to get confused and either rush to his fences or stand way back from them. I want him to understand from the start that this is the distance he should be from this size fence so that he'll learn to handle it that way whenever he faces it.

I go from cavalletti to a single set (or placement) fence going in, and after that I begin working on single fences. I trot all of my fences up to about 2 feet or 2 feet 6 inches, after which I start to canter. I don't like to jump a horse very big in the beginning. Some horses have more talent than others and require a slightly bigger fence to make them work, but you always want to keep them relaxed and comfortable. The horse should approach the fence thinking, "I know I can jump that!" so that he can concentrate on learning the technique of how to jump it, how to pick up both leads on landing at the other side, how to jump across it at a little angle. Later, when I know the horse's ability and know that he has learned how to use himself and the techniques he's been taught, I can build bigger fences and create problems, certain that the horse will know how to solve them.

Sometimes a horse may seem to be getting bored or sloppy because he's hitting a lot of fences. That doesn't bother me during the early stages of training. It may take the horse quite a while to find out just how much energy he must expend to jump even a small fence, and when he's not yet sure, he can have rubs and even rails down. I check to make certain he's not simply bored by changing things a little, such as substituting different colored poles, perhaps putting a cross-rail under an oxer, or changing the components of a fence. If boredom is the problem, you don't have to make too much of a change to impress the horse; he'll brighten up immediately.

When the horse is comfortable with small single fences, he can be introduced to combinations, gymnastics, and the problem of making simple adjustments to meet measured distances. After about six months of work over fences (one year from the start of training), the horse should be ready to make his debut in the Hunter Division.

He'll need a year learning about horse shows, courses, and experiencing as much as possible each time he goes away from home, before he's ready to take a crack at the Jumper divisions. It's a good idea to take advantage of the structure of the Open Jumping Division, which permits a horse to start in the Preliminary Division and win himself out and up the ladder.

By following this schooling program, you'll seldom encounter any serious problems with a horse. If he's confident and comfortable at each level of training before proceeding to the next, there's virtually no reason or inclination on his part to be disobedient. Of course, any horse can come up to a fence so wrong that he knows he can't possibly negotiate it without a crash, and so he'll stop. But such occasions are few and far between.

I don't like to use a stick very often. If a horse does something that I think is deliberately contrary to what I want, then I'll go after him. But the entire incident should not last more than three or four seconds, and the correction must be immediate or he won't know what he's being punished for.

I'm also not much in favor of using "equipment," such as martingales, draw reins, side reins (except on the bitting rig at the very beginning, to help set the horse's head), "chambons," and the like. I feel strongly that if a horse is brought along slowly, he won't need the support of any of these devices.

I'm convinced that a horse trained "overnight" is short-lived in comparison to one that is trained slowly and thoroughly. You'll find the well-trained horse competing over a much longer period of time than the "quickies." I think this is due partly to the fact that a well-educated horse makes fewer mistakes and seldom tangles with the problems that tend to discourage or damage less well trained horses.

Even if he should have a disaster (and when you're showing in the Open Division they're bound to occur now and then), the educated horse is more level-headed, more apt to make another try at the same fence or combination willingly, than is the horse that was rushed along. The educated horse is a thinking horse that even seems to understand that every now and then something happens that must be chalked up as a mistake and then forgotten.

10

What My Horses Have Taught Me

Rodney Jenkins

Few riders have so marked their era as has this famous redhead from Virginia. Considering the total number of victories (including more than sixty-eight grand prix events), the amount of prize money won, the number of different winning horses, and his consistency during more than twenty years of competition, Rodney Jenkins' accomplishments must make him the most successful rider in North American show-jumping history—quite possibly in the history of the world.

As a professional horseman, he'd never been eligible for an Olympic team, although he competed with notable success as a member of the USET in the World Championship and on the fall circuit. But a change of rules permitted him to regain his amateur status in time to win the individual silver medal in the 1987 Pan-American Games. And who knows? Perhaps he will one day add an Olympic medal to his incomparable record of show-jumping achievements.

In twenty years of riding hunters and jumpers, I've never had what most people would regard as a training program. I don't train horses; horses train me. It was that principle which made possible my early success with stars like Nanticoke and Idle Dice and most recently with The Natural.

Listening to, and understanding, my horses, instead of trying to cram them into my own mold, has helped me weather two decades of radical change in the sport. It's made me better able to adapt to the rise of grand prix jumping in the United States, the evolution of tighter, bigger, more technical courses, and the trend to the new sport horse that excels on those courses.

Just as I've never had a set training program, so I've never had a formal riding lesson. But I had something better: my father, Ennis Jenkins, was a genuine horseman. Horses were an important part of my life from the beginning, and as soon as I was old enough, I helped my father in his work as huntsman for Manley Carter in Virginia. In the process, I absorbed his attitude: always put the horse first and take whatever time is necessary to do the job right. In this case, the job was getting twenty hunters ready to go out in the morning and then cleaning them up again and putting them away when the hunt came back at 4 or 5 P.M. It all had to be finished and the hounds fed before my brothers, Larry and Dale, and I got anything to eat.

My first riding was done out on those hunts. I loved it. But more than riding out I liked to go to shows and watch my father take field hunters into the ring. Even though I was drawn to showing, I didn't have a chance to do it myself for years, so I practiced jumping on my own at home instead. Down in the woods near the barn, I built a lot of little jumps like those I'd seen at shows. When I had time, I took a horse down there and practiced. I'd jump maybe a hundred fences, trying to get to a variety of spots, sometimes taking the horse in close and sometimes standing off. I had no idea what I was doing. I was just trying to duplicate what I'd seen in the show ring.

The hunting I'd done stood me in good stead while I was learning to jump by feel this way. Out in the hunt field, I'd always had to think of what was coming ahead, actually think for the horse because he didn't know where we were going next. Hunting was also a great way to learn about balance over different kinds of terrain and jumps. In my homemade practice ring, I found that I'd developed an eye in the process: I could see the distances, and I had an instinct for knowing when the horse was going to leave the ground.

When I was twelve years old, I had my first chance to show, riding an old hunter mare named Whirly, which I took into a warm-up class of about a hundred horses at a schooling show in Orange, Virginia. It was exciting because all the big professionals of the day like Bobby Burke and Raymond Burr were there, and Whirly and I came fourth. That was the beginning of several years of showing in Junior Hunter classes.

I didn't get my first jumper until I was seventeen and went to work for Gene Mische (now chairman of the American Grand Prix Association)

Rodney started his show riding career in the Hunter Division. Here he's riding New Hope at the 1975 Ox Ridge Horse Show in a first-year Hunter class. Photo: Budd

Rodney riding Mrs. A. C. Randolph's memorable Quiet Flite to the Conformation Hunter Championship of the North Shore Horse Show in 1976. Photo: Budd

in Florida. Gene showed mostly hunters, but there were also a few jumpers in his barn. For the next three years, I rode a lot of different horses for him, and since many of them were bought through my dad, that helped business at home too. But one of the most important things that happened to me then was meeting Ben O'Meara, trainer of the great jumper Untouchable, which Kathy Kusner was riding. His horses were stabled next to Gene's at the old Palm Beach Polo Grounds during the Florida circuit. When Benny saw me riding, he put me on a few of his horses and gave me my first pointers on how to ride the jumpers of that era.

Ben was the kind of old-time great horseman who could succeed in any age. But his approach to training jumpers would seem peculiar today because the sport is so different from what it was in the early 1960s. There were no time limits in jumper classes then; you could do anything as long as you kept moving forward, and it was common practice to trot around the ends of the ring if you wanted to. Courses were designed so that you could just go around and jump the jumps one at a time. Jump-offs were rare; most classes were knock-down-and-out.

Benny O'Meara had developed a style that worked well in that situation. He never cared what his horses did with their legs as long as they kept a balanced canter on the approach to the jump and had their hocks under them and their heads up. He didn't achieve this by flat work the way we do today; nobody did flat work then. When we brought the jumpers out to school, we trotted around a little, and then the ground crew started setting up jumps.

Ben believed in tight standing martingales for jumpers, not to bring the head down but to help the horse balance. He never rode with his hands. From riding his jumpers I learned the feel of a horse that's been trained to respond to shifts in the rider's weight instead of pressure on the reins. Shifting the weight of my seat well back in the saddle kept the horse coming forward under me, and as his hocks came under, his head went up. Ben's horses were also trained to respond to the angle of the rider's upper body, speeding up if you leaned forward and slowing if you sat more upright; they changed direction if you put more weight in one stirrup than in the other. And although the rider's leg was driving these horses forward, his seat was not. The horses didn't go well with weight pressing directly into their backs; it made them tense.

The technique of riding with my breeches just grazing the leather, which I developed with the help of Ben's jumpers, also helped to relax the hunters I was riding for Gene Mische. But hunters had to look smoother than jumpers, so I couldn't strap them down in tight martingales to balance them. This was a "no flat work" era for hunters too. I used to work over fences to back them off the bridle and soften them. By trotting hunters to a lot of deep spots, I taught them what use of the hocks was all about. If I wanted a longer stride in a line, I learned to meet the first fence long so that my horse would land already going forward.

After three years of working for Gene and riding some of Benny's horses on the side, I returned home to help my father run Hilltop Stables, a farm he'd bought in Gordonsville, Virginia.

Nanticoke

The skills I'd picked up were soon put to the test when we got a horse named Nanticoke to show as a jumper. He was the first really good jumper I ever showed. He was also the first of a long string of talented problem horses that nobody else could, or wanted, to do anything with.

A Nasrullah son, he was a talented steeplechaser that got ruled off the track after going berserk in the paddock at Belmont one day. His owner's place wasn't too far from Hilltop, and my father and I somehow managed to load him in a trailer and bring him to our farm. Then Dad, who was a very gutsy rider, began by taking the horse to the local cattle market and riding him in the calf pen with all the livestock bumping into him until he learned to tolerate it.

After that, I took the horse to a lot of local one-day shows, but I always had to bring somebody from the stable along to help me mount. If I made Nanticoke stand still while I got on, he froze and then flipped over. So the other guy would jog him as I ran alongside until I could catch the horse in stride and swing into the saddle. Once up, I stayed on him all day long, just sitting on him between classes. At the end of the day when he was tired, I dismounted and then got on and off some thirty times before I took the tack off.

Nanticoke reinforced a lesson I'd already started to learn from other horses: never try to muscle your way with a horse. There may or may not be an ideal way of doing things; but in the horse world you have to be realistic, willing to try different solutions to a problem until you find one that works for both you and the horse. Letting Nanticoke jog along while I mounted wasn't ideal, but it was good horsemanship because we started the ride relaxed instead of with a fight.

Once we got past his problems, Nanticoke proved his talent: he took me to one of my first grand prix wins—at Oakbrook, Illinois. We sold him later on to Harry Gill, the owner for whom I rode Gustavus and shortly later a big black horse named Idle Dice.

Idle Dice

Idle Dice was a five-year-old Thoroughbred whose racing career had begun and ended with his first race (in which he finished last). We first saw him when Bernie Traurig was showing him as a hunter. His conformation didn't seem to me ideal for that because he had a very short neck and big shoulder. But he also carried his hind leg up under him (which I love) and he had a short strong back and the high wide hips that cry "jumper" loud and clear. At 17.1 hands, with gaskin muscles like a quarter horse's, he was a real weightlifter. My father, who could

Rodney is inseparably identified with the phenomenal, lengthy jumping career of Idle Dice. Photo: Karl Leck

live with any horse to a certain extent, seldom committed himself to one and was always quick to burst my balloon if I got too excited about a prospect. Idle Dice was the exception. Dad looked him over, watched him trot a 6-foot fence, and said, "This one will make it."

As everybody knows, Idle Dice made it in a big way. But first I had to let him teach me a few things. I was still going along with the old system of standing martingales for jumpers, so before our first jumper class I automatically tied his head down, as I did with all the others. He never finished the course. Partway round, he simply stopped. I couldn't understand it at first. Then I remembered that his style coming off the ground was to keep his head up instead of putting it down and over. The martingale was grabbing him at every fence. I took it off after the show, and from then on he seemed to win everywhere I took him.

Idle Dice was a rare natural equine athlete. In spite of his high head carriage, he wasn't stiff. He always carried himself "with the poll bent," as horsemen say; even when he was simply trotting around the paddock, he had his hocks under him. He was so supple that when we turned him out, he used to reach around and grab his own tail at the gallop. You could tack him up and walk him straight from the stable to a 6-foot fence. But talent isn't everything. I've had plenty of talented horses that lacked the essential quality: the desire to win. Idle Dice had that too. I'd feel him puff up with that will to win every time we walked into a ring. If he rubbed one fence at a show, it upset him so much that he might not touch another one during the next month.

When I started showing Idle Dice in the early 1970s, I was still somewhat oriented toward the old style of riding. For example, I'd yet to hear discussions about teaching a horse to switch canter leads on course, and I don't remember teaching Idle Dice to do it. That didn't prevent him from being one of the best turning horses I've ever had. In fact, it was almost as if once we were on a course, he took charge and whatever he told me to do, I did. I didn't have to school him over fences at home. I concentrated on keeping him fresh, letting the horse shows teach him, and letting him teach me.

There was plenty for him to learn and pass on, too, because those were eventful times in the horse-show world. Grand prix jumping was introduced in the United States during the late 1960s, and there were already several permanent grand prix courses. Some of the older riders had difficulty adapting to the new rules, especially the idea of time limits. They'd jump clean and then be amazed to find they hadn't done as well as they'd thought, because of time penalties. At the same time, oxers were getting wider and distances more technical; new obstacles like water jumps were making an appearance.

In this changing horse-show scene, I observed the people who were winning. Mary and Frank Chapot, for instance, used a riding style that kept the leg in contact with the horse while the seat stayed out of the saddle. Their leg position was different from the kickup style I'd admired in John Bell, a leading rider during my early years. I could see that the horses meeting the new challenges successfully were also different. Jumpers that could jump high but had no adjustability were fading from the scene. The winning jumper was now more likely to be a breeder horse: a Thoroughbred like Nanticoke or Blue Plum (which I showed for Bert Firestone) . . . or Idle Dice. Scope was all-important (although we didn't have a word for it yet). The horses that won could gallop to the jumps and float over the wider oxers; they could leave out strides on a line to win against the clock.

Some aspects of my riding changed almost without my being aware of it; others stayed the same. I kept my stirrup leathers a couple of holes shorter than many riders did in order to feel my leg securely enough anchored to let me use my upper body; I continued to put the weight of my seat a little further back than usual in order to keep the horse coming forward under me without driving by pressing directly on his back.

While I was mostly concerned with keeping my horses happy, I also learned from observing other riders' mistakes. I was beginning to think a lot about hip and shoulder angles: why correct with the hands when a horse drifted left or right over jumps? If I had a horse that drifted left, I brought him into the jump with his hip angled left and his head angled right, and then let him jump the way he wanted to. His natural drift to the left straightened out the angle, so that he came down centered, less bothered than if I'd tried to straighten him with my hands.

Once I'd figured out what qualities a horse needed to succeed over the new jumper courses, I didn't have to look far to find one that fit the bill. Idle Dice had been ahead of his time when we bought him; with his power and flexibility, he was now in his element. He made the transition with me. He taught me to jump the new courses. I've never had another jumper with his ability to win a speed class today, a grand prix tomorrow, and a puissance the next day.

Although I was doing a little more gymnastic work with my other jumpers by now (things like cantering X's to oxers to get them there in the right frame), I never needed to do that with Idle Dice. He got all the schooling he needed in the show ring, and that was where I worked on any little things I wanted him to do. I supplemented his uncanny turning ability, for example, by teaching him to turn in the air over a jump, pressing him with one leg or the other so that he curved around it as he landed. I also must have taught him to switch leads at some point, but I couldn't say when. It simply happened.

The long-running success of Idle Dice is one of the reasons why I've been fortunate in riding a high average of outstanding jumpers and hunters. It also gave me and my family the confidence and money to invest in our first expensive jumper, a horse named Balbuco, which was being sold by the Argentine Olympic team.

Balbuco

I'd been watching Balbuco for several weeks during the indoor circuit and had finalized arrangements for his purchase at Harrisburg, although he couldn't be released until after the Toronto show. I noticed that he had a tendency to stop on course between jumps, but he appealed to me all the same because he met so many of my criteria for a good jumper. The first thing I look for is a beautiful hind end that's always kicking off after a jump, almost giving the horse an extra thrust forward. It doesn't bother me if a horse hangs his front legs; if the hind end is good, I can eventually control the front. That's why I don't get as excited as some people do about horses that snap their knees up. The next thing is scope. Not many horses have super scope; but if a horse has little or none, I know it's going to cause a problem sooner or later because he's got nothing in reserve. I also like a thin horse that doesn't make me sit with my legs stuck out; and I like a deep shoulder and a short cannon bone. My dad always told me to look for a short back in a jumper, but I've come to like horses with a slightly long back because this gives extra length in the muscle running through the hips to the hock.

Balbuco didn't fill all of these requirements any more than any living horse could, but I was impressed by his hind end and his scope. When I brought him home from Toronto, I figured he'd had a hard season. I turned him out for a month and a half before preparing him for the Florida circuit.

The day I finally rode Balbuco for the first time, I thought I'd thrown away the family savings. He simply couldn't canter. When I tried to slow him down from his usual gallop, he broke into a very fast trot. And he wouldn't take a step backward. I spent a couple of weeks trying to pacify him into slowing down and backing up, but nothing happened except

Rodney and Balbuco. Photo: Alix Coleman

that the Florida circuit got closer. Finally, I woke up one morning determined that this would be the day on which Balbuco would back up.

It was. But it took eight hours. In the process, he jumped halfway out of a barn window, got himself back in, and then knocked me through a stall with a front foot. When I eventually got him to take a single step backward, it was by using long lines from the ground.

While Idle Dice was teaching me new techniques in show jumping, Balbuco was a refresher course in why the old pragmatic solutions are sometimes still necessary. For example, I finally slowed his gallop to a canter with that old standby, a tight martingale. I discovered that Balbuco would go in it, but if I touched his mouth, he'd just fall over. I was grateful that other horses had taught me to ride off my leg and my weight. At first, the only thing Balbuco wanted to do in the noseband and martingale was trot. I rode him over lots of three-foot fences that way, keeping my leg on him but my weight off his back, and throwing the reins at him. All of a sudden he got off that noseband, came back at the canter, and started going around the jumps. "Well," I thought, "I've got him at home now, but I wonder what he's going to do at a show."

He did fine. During the Florida season he progressed to a fat snaffle and a martingale with a regular noseband while I tried to figure out how I was going to show him in the Gold Cup (then in Florida), my goal for the circuit, where he wouldn't be permitted to wear a standing martingale, although running martingales are allowed. One day I had a brainstorm. I sewed stoppers the legal 5 inches down from the bit on a pair of reins, passed the reins through the rings of a running martingale, and then sewed another set of stoppers on the other side of the rings. In effect, I had a standing martingale.

We won the Gold Cup in that getup. Although someone tried to have me disqualified, it was ruled legal. Balbuco's performance in the Gold Cup after a good record throughout the circuit made a success out of what had looked like financial disaster the first time I rode him. We sold him for a good price soon afterward. I kept on riding him for a while and eventually got him happy in a running martingale with no extras. He had a body as long as a manure spreader, and I think that's one reason why he needed that steady pressure to keep his canter balanced.

Sloopy

Sloopy came my way during the period when I was working with Balbuco. I saw him during a visit to Bernie Traurig's barn, where he caught my eye by jumping a big vertical on his own while he was loose in the paddock. When I offered to buy him, they warned me that he wouldn't load; but I got him into the van with a twitch and never had any problem loading him after that.

Sloopy wasn't a pleasant horse. He was big, with a little pig eye set over on the side of his head, and he'd come after you if he felt like it. He also got stubborn and sulky—walking up a loading ramp, for instance, or from the barn to the paddock. He was the type of horse who'd get behind the in-gate and refuse to enter the ring. Previous owners seemed to overlook the fact that these problems, aggravating as they were, had nothing to do with his jumping ability, which was enormous. Once he was in the ring, there was no problem at all. Once he was convinced that I was determined to ride him, his performance caused me no problems. Unlike Balbuco, who wanted to stay behind the bit and away from my hand, Sloopy went better if I used more leg to drive him up to the bit and rode him more with my hand. In my experience, this livens a horse up and makes him more tense. But Sloopy needed it to keep him ahead of me and to keep him directed. When he got sullen away from the

Rodney turned over Balbuco's reins to Conrad Homfeld, who won the 1980 World Cup finals with him. Photo: Karl Leck

ring, I didn't nag him. He was like a bad kid. If I needed to correct him, I made sure it left an impression.

After about six weeks, the two of us got things ironed out, and I showed him once, winning the Grand Prix at Oakbrook—after which he was sold to Patrick Butler. He continued true to form: he had to be shipped to Europe when he refused to board the airplane.

Mr. Demeanor

Although I didn't realize it at the time, I was approaching a turning point in my career. I was gradually adapting to changes in the sport—but first I had to deal with Mr. Demeanor.

I acquired this jumper in desperation when I was temporarily without a top horse to ride and had been invited to some competitions in Mexico following the Florida circuit. He was jumping grand prix in Florida with terrible results: 32 faults in one round and 17 in another. In normal circumstances, I'd never in my wildest nightmare have got involved with a horse like him. As it turned out though, he taught me some important lessons.

Mr. Demeanor had a jumping style that I hated more than that of any horse I'd ever ridden. He arrived in front of a fence inverted, his head stuck up in the air and his belly sagging. The only thing that saved him was his hind end, which flowed out behind; he had a very scopey feel off the ground, even though he always hit his fences. Because he went with his head high, he could work only in a running martingale, but he also wore a gag bit because you couldn't turn him to the left by any other means.

My first school on Mr. Demeanor took place in Mexico the day before our first grand prix. I found out right away how unbalanced he was: in addition to the bending problem, he didn't have a right canter lead. He was a very lean horse with a weak back. I had no trouble keeping my weight off his back, but it added to everything already going against

Rodney and Mr. Demeanor, "one of the last problem horses whose difficulties I tried to solve with jumping rather than with work on the flat." Photo: Karl Leck

him. I took him over a few fences. He met them rigidly, hitting every one. The absolute opposite of what I liked in a horse! As a rule, I'd never consider one that went out and hit three or four jumps in a row. It seemed as if he wasn't trying. But for the moment, Mr. Demeanor and I were stuck with each other. I had to figure out which were his strong points that I could leave alone, which were the weak ones I couldn't change, and which were those that I could do something to improve.

His best feature was scope: he managed somehow to flow over the fence, even though he dragged his belly across. His worst trait was rubbing almost every jump, because of the way he was made. I figured that I might be able to change the way he hit the jump: if he was quick and tense, he'd hit it hard and knock it down, but if I got him to open up his gallop, it might stay up. I must have taken Mr. Demeanor over sixty jumps during that first school. He never cleared one, front or back, but I pressed on until he eventually got so tired that he relaxed. Over the last fence (which he hit solidly) I felt him give in and soften to me. I said to myself, "That's enough," and quit right there. The next morning I brought him out and warmed up for the class riding him very soft and supple, exactly as we'd left off at the end of the school. He came third in the grand prix. We won the next one.

If Mr. Demeanor did so well in Mexico, it was because I learned to adjust to his jumping style instead of trying to transform him into my ideal jumper. With our very first class, I learned that it was best to bring him into the ring about 25 percent tired. Later on, I learned to tell when he was too fresh: if I hadn't taken off enough of the edge during the warm-up, his right hip would shoot off toward the middle of the ring when he landed after a fence.

Back home again, I worked with him not on the flat but over lots of small jumps, trying to get him to turn better. Once again I was thinking about hip angles, using my right leg and an indirect right rein to try to control that right hip. Eventually I got him more or less trained, even to the point where I could bend him a little to the left on the flat. After a year of work, he was something I would have normally considered buying in the first place!

Mr. Demeanor was one of the last problem horses whose difficulties I tried to solve with jumping rather than with work on the flat. I finally handed him on to Terry Rudd, and he went better for her than he had for me. She won the American Invitational on him and tied with me and Number One Spy for the President's Cup.

Second Balcony

By now I'd become aware of the extra dimension that flat work for jumpers and hunters was bringing to the sport. I was still watching other riders who were doing well at shows, people like George Morris and Bill

Rodney up on Second Balcony. Photo: Karl Leck

Steinkraus, whose horses were sometimes able to jump beyond their natural talent because they were so broken and supple. But I was accustomed to learning from horses more than from people. I needed a jumper that could teach me the moves to make horses supple on the flat—and that's just what I got in Second Balcony.

He was a former combined-training horse who left Eventing in the late 1970s to try to make a go at the Jumper Division. But he hadn't got very far when he came to me in 1979 because he had a stopping problem.

I found the key the second time I rode him—his hip angle. Second Balcony tended to arrive at the fence with his hips angled to the left, which made him feel unbalanced in the takeoff because he wanted to push off from his left hind leg. Using a stick didn't help because he didn't feel ready to jump. Instead, on the approach I touched him with my left spur to move his hip to the right so that he could get the push from his left hind leg; I then supported him with an indirect left rein.

He never stopped with me again. But during the brief time it took to work out his difficulty, he turned my training ideas right around.

On Second Balcony, I found myself riding a horse that had been given lots of work on the flat. "This feels great!" I thought, as he gave to my hand, bent at the poll, balanced himself, and responded smoothly to changes in hand and leg pressure. His well-trained responses made me realize the possibility of getting my hunters and jumpers around the courses without having to ride as aggressively as I'd been doing. He showed me that a horse well schooled on the flat is easier to keep under me on turns. For example, he'd respond to my indirect outside rein by keeping his hip angle straight instead of falling to the outside. As I rode Second Balcony, I worked back through his supple responsiveness to discover which aids I could use to create it. I wanted to make all my hunters and jumpers like him. My knack for riding by feel, sensitive to what made the horse happy, helped me to find them.

Third Man

I should have remembered that a rider doesn't fit horses into a program; he fits the program to them. Third Man came along to remind me of this.

He was a jumper that couldn't canter—like Balbuco. I'd cranked Balbuco's headlong gallop back to a manageable canter in the old-fashioned way, by using a short martingale and a tight noseband. But I thought Third Man was a perfect candidate for reschooling. He had a

Third Man, with Rodney in the saddle. Photo: Karl Leck

soft mouth, never jumped flat, and was quick off the ground with his front end. Unfortunately, I had to abandon my ambitious plans when I realized that his try was bigger than his scope. If I brought him back from his customary gallop on course, he couldn't get across the oxers. He needed the revs. I could spin him around the turns, keep him right under me with an indirect rein, but I had to do it at a full gallop. At home, I avoided tight combinations of fences that might have backed him off the pace; instead, I opened the gymnastics out, always encouraging him to lengthen his stride.

I had to make allowances for Third Man in other ways as well. My father always said that while a good rider can last through changes in horses and riding styles, the mark of a true horseman is to make his horses last. Third Man was a challenge in that respect because he was basically unsound. I nursed him from one competition to another, gauging when he was up to showing and when he wasn't. I never gave him "Bute" (Phenylbutazone) before a show. I don't do that with any of my horses because it deadens their mouths. But I'd medicate him for a couple of days afterward to relieve any soreness he'd developed. Then

I'd take him off it in order to deal with any new problems the drug had masked. My conservative approach led to disagreement with his owner, and Third Man eventually left my barn for a brilliant one-year career with another trainer—before the soles dropped out of his feet.

Coastline

Third Man was still with me in 1979 when Sally Donner, a friend from Pennsylvania, recommended that I take a look at a six-year-old in Bucky Reynolds' Virginia barn that was showing in the Preliminary Jumper Division. His name was Coastline. Since I was on the road at the time, I sent my business associate, Larry Aspen, to check him out.

When Larry tries out a new jumper, the first thing he does is take the groundlines away from the schooling fences to see what the horse does with his front end. This one hung a front leg so badly even over 3-foot-6-inch jumps that Larry said in disgust, "How come you're trying to sell us this thing?" And that was that.

Later that winter, when I was showing Third Man and Dr. Smalley, I noticed a little horse in the Preliminary Division, less than 16 hands, but

with such a long stride that he seemed to bound down the lines. He didn't seem to have had much schooling, but he had a naturally soft canter and that extra kick from behind over fences that I like in a jumper: it's the sign of a horse who's really trying not to hit the jumps. The bad news about this little horse was that while his back end showed him to be a trier, his front end showed complete lack of confidence. Once he took off, he dropped his shoulder and hung a foreleg as if he were feeling for the ground.

In spite of his problem, I liked him. I found myself analyzing his jumping the way I'd analyze a horse in a riding clinic I was giving. I noticed that he stiffened his neck and jaw on the approach, grabbed for the bit, and hollowed his back. All of this, I felt, was due to lack of confidence. If I could make him relaxed enough to accept my guidance, I was sure that I could teach him to get over the fences. As I arranged to buy him, I was already thinking about the techniques I'd learned from Second Balcony that might help.

Only when I brought Coastline home did I learn he was the same jumper that Larry had turned down at Bucky's place not long before. "What have you done to us?" Larry exclaimed when he recognized the horse. But I was convinced that while Coastline wasn't a great natural jumper, he had the potential to do the job and the receptive mind that would enable him to learn how to do it.

I started his retraining program right away. I had no idea how long it would take, but I was pretty sure it wouldn't be a short-term project. That might ruin him. Instead, I started at square one with basic flat work. I used a lot of dressage principles, but without too much emphasis on getting him right on the bit. I was more interested in getting him to carry and balance himself without much rein pressure, because I like to ride my jumpers and hunters with as little hand as possible. I worked him a lot at the walk, which not only reduces pounding on the legs but also slows things down to where I can control every stride. During a typical session, we'd walk 100 yards on a loose rein and then I'd pick up a contact by pushing him into the bit with my leg while keeping my seat light so that he wouldn't be inclined to hollow his back. I wanted to get his hips really working on cue, so I used left leg and left rein, then right leg and right rein. As soon as I felt his jaw soften, I'd drop the contact, keeping my leg on as I gave with my hand. He'd hold the frame for a few strides, and when he lost it, I'd pick up the contact again.

As Coastline got comfortable with the bit, I went on to more advanced suppling work. He was naturally flexible and could walk forward with his head drawn back to either hip. When he stayed relaxed doing that for a couple of minutes, we'd go on to the same kind of bending at trot and canter. I gradually added basic exercises such as figure eights, circles, and counter-canter. Work over fences was also part of his program, though very low-key. I lowered the jumps to 3 feet, a height at which even Coastline felt comfortable; I rolled the groundlines out to an easy distance from the jump. I didn't try to make him stand off or do anything but feel happy about the whole idea. For that reason, I didn't alter the jumps for days at a time. To keep him from getting bored with the work at home, I continued showing him in the Preliminary Division, riding in rub classes. After a few weeks of going quietly around the show courses, I took him home again, tightened up the gymnastics a little, and raised the jumps a bit. I never advanced a stage until he'd stopped hanging a leg over the fences he was already jumping.

In order to make the most of Coastline, I couldn't simply adjust my own style to suit his way of going, which I'd done successfully with many other horses. Only by letting me change him was he going to be able to jump at all. As he gradually accepted the bit, I was able to do just that.

One of the training aids I used to accomplish this was draw reins. They're effective in suppling some horses, but in the wrong hands they can teach a horse to kink up his neck in an evasion. That's why I never recommend them for young riders who haven't the experience to use them properly. I attached Coastline's draw reins to the ring on a hunting breastplate in the center of his chest so that the influence was front-to-back rather than lateral. As I used my weight and legs to push his hocks up under him on the flat, the draw reins kept his topline rounded. They also enabled me to use stronger aids. When I pressed the weight of my seat forward along the saddle to encourage him to engage his quarters (but never driving my seat down into his back), he couldn't evade by hollowing his back and neck. The draw reins also helped me balance him over fences. Because of his old nervousness, Coastline tended to fade right or left when I started to collect him for takeoff; in draw reins, he was obliged to remain straight. This gave him the half second he needed to gather himself, and once I felt I had him in the right spot with his hocks under him, I let his mouth go. My leg still pushed him forward, but since I wasn't bothering his face, his hind end had complete control.

Coastline's jumping confidence developed gradually as he went over bigger fences and more challenging distances. By the time we'd reached the point where I could remove the draw reins, I'd developed a three-stage takeoff for him: slowing up in front of the fence, backing off a little to get his front end out of the way, and then kicking off with his rear end. During that half second, I softened my leg. When he felt that, he trusted me: I was giving him his turn. When I felt both shoulders come up evenly, I put my leg back to push him forward, up, and out across the fence. My own position during this sequence never got ahead of his motion, which would have caused him to drop his shoulder. I rode to the fence a little upright and waiting, then leaned to a more forward angle as his shoulder cleared the rail; but my seat always stayed back.

At this stage of his training, Coastline stopped grabbing for the bit as he left the ground, because he knew I'd give it to him anyway. If I felt a shoulder starting to drop, I'd pick up the rein on that side and barely touch his mouth to remind him to soften and correct himself. Once he'd become confident over fences, his natural suppleness made him one of the best turning jumpers I've ever had, a real threat in speed classes. He could twist his body four hundred different ways to change direction in the air.

It took three years of schooling every spare minute at home, riding in Preliminary rub classes; but one day Coastline suddenly started thinking of himself as a big shot. When I believed he was ready, I took him out of Preliminary straight into the Open Division. Our first show at that level was the 1981 Grand Prix at Southampton, where he finished third. After that he was such a success that the owner who had purchased him from Larry and me for $50,000 turned down a $300,000 offer for him.

The Natural

Now that Coastline was a made jumper and although I was busy showing Arbitrage, Second Balcony, and Sugar Ray, I missed having a special horse to work with. I began looking for another prospect. While hoping it wouldn't be one with a major problem this time, I wanted a horse that was ready to move right along but hadn't started to as yet. I've never been interested in taking on a horse that was already a big success.

I was still looking in June 1984 when I went to the Upperville Horse Show, where I saw Katie Monahan ride a seven-year-old Hanoverian named The Natural in the Intermediate Division. As I watched him go around the course, he seemed to overjump each fence by about two feet. At the liverpool, he looked at the obstacle, spooked, jumped way up instead of over, and landed in the middle. I was curious to see how Katie was schooling to get that kind of a jump out of a horse that barely topped 16 hands, so I hung around the practice area before the next

Rodney and The Natural. Photo: Karl Leck

class. When she came out to ride The Natural, there was no heavy-duty schooling over big fences; she seemed to be just playing with him. I noticed that he had such a stride that he looked 17 hands or more when you stood back from him; and he liked to canter on his forehand with his head held low.

The next time I saw The Natural was in Detroit. The fences were lowered because the footing was bad after a heavy rain. Again, he leaped over everything as if the jumps were 6 feet instead of 4 feet and he never jumped flat. I thought he was one of the most promising young horses I'd seen since Idle Dice.

Coastline left my barn at about this time, which meant that while I had plenty of horses to ride, I was without a top jumper. Then I heard that The Natural was for sale. He was stabled at Mike Cohen's barn in New Hope, Pennsylvania, and I went to look at him as soon as I could.

However exciting The Natural was to watch in the ring, when I saw him up close I found he had his little flaws like any other horse. His front pasterns were straight, which reduces shock-absorbing capacity. Some jumpers with straight pasterns eventually become reluctant to face the impact of landing after a fence and compensate by hurrying their hind end over the jump or by landing as short as possible, since this jars them less. Along with those straight pasterns, The Natural had small feet. Typical of his breed, they don't take the pounding as well as bigger feet do. He also had big splints. On the positive side, he was the small, light type of horse I've always liked to work with. A full hand shorter than Idle Dice, he had the same kind of muscular development, with gaskins like a quarter horse. He was a bit long in the back (which I also like), and I liked his high hips. It's the type of build that gives a horse more push behind when he rolls back to spring over the jumps.

I got on him and, after a few minutes, asked for a canter. The low head carriage with the balance on his forehand made him feel as if he was pulling even when he wasn't; while his gallop on course had looked smooth when I'd seen Katie ride him at Upperville, this schooling canter felt almost stiff-legged. When I asked for lead changes, he was nice and soft-going to the right, but I couldn't get him to bend on the left lead. His mouth felt dead on the left side, he leaned to the inside with his left shoulder and hip, and he kept his head cocked to the right. When I put my left leg on him, he moved away from it but wouldn't bend around it. Then I tried him over a few jumps. After the first crossrail, I knew I'd somehow have to find the money to buy him. I'd never felt such power in a small package. I still had some reservations about getting him to turn well to the left when he wouldn't bend to that side, but if I could solve the problem through flat work I'd have a super talent on my hands.

I found a buyer to go in with me. As soon as I got The Natural home, I started to work on softening his left side. I set him in a bitting rig with side reins, the left shorter than the right, and turned him out in the paddock for thirty or forty minutes at a time. This might have bothered a hotter horse, but I knew his quiet, sensible warm-blood temperament could take it. Next, I began to longe him in the same rig so that he would have to follow the curve of the circle with his body.

I continued this program in ridden flat work, putting him in draw reins set up to give lateral leverage. I worked mostly to the left, leaving plenty of slack in the right rein, concentrating on left leg and left rein until he accepted them. He had a very good mind. It was almost as if he recognized that he had a problem and wanted to help me correct it.

Over fences, however, I soon learned that he lost his scope in draw reins. They interfered with his naturally low head carriage; he felt inhibited. Since that was the last thing I wanted, I removed the draw reins for jumping and carried over the left-bending flat work by jumping a lot of small fences and turning left when we landed. The ironic part of all this was that I myself have always been weaker on the left side than the right. While working on The Natural's left side, I was also struggling with my own.

When I got The Natural in the fall of 1984, he already had the scope and power to jump open and grand prix courses. My first impulse was to start showing him at that level. But then I thought of his future. A horse that needs to jump out of long galloping strides, as The Natural did at that time, stays round out of caution as long as everything in the ring is new to him. But sooner or later he gets ringwise and then starts to jump flat. If he isn't schooled so the rider can get him close in to the deep spot that makes him jump round, there's no way to protect him: he begins to knock down jumps. But if the horse is broken and you can put him in that deep spot, you don't need any other tricks.

My co-owner was new to big-time jumping. In planning The Natural's program, I had to demonstrate the horse's potential to the owner and, at the same time, give the horse time to learn what he needed to know. We started in the Gold Cup, in Intermediate rather than Open classes; we then went on to the fall indoor circuit. Since I was still teaching him his canter, we had time faults everywhere.

"Rodney," my wife, Vicki, would say when I came out of a class, "this horse cannot canter so slow."

And I'd reply, "If I'm going to keep him nice for more than a year, he's got to."

After Baltimore and Washington, D.C., I entered him in the grand prix at New York just to show what he could do. I didn't push him, and we missed winning the class by a tenth of a second. I settled for that because The Natural wasn't yet ready for the extra pressure required to win such an event. And he still hadn't learned to canter properly. I figured it would take six months to turn him into a super horse who would stay super, so I decided not to spend that time on the Florida circuit, where the fences, crowds, and pressure are tremendous. Instead, I took him with a group of young horses to the Arizona winter circuit, where I hoped to pick up mileage and some ribbons.

It was one of the smartest moves I've ever made. I entered The Natural in big classes, usually showing on Wednesday and Friday in preparation for the Saturday Grand Prix, and he took some seconds and thirds. I wasn't really looking for wins; I was schooling him. I taught him to canter more slowly right on course by adding extra strides on the lines, making him jump out of a short canter stride instead of half a gallop stride. The worst score he had was four faults. But often he jumped clean when I considered it a bad round. I knew he could be a bit of a spook, and he got lost a few times from staring at things in the ring instead of moving smoothly from jump to jump. When that happened, or when he started hawking over everything by a 2-foot margin, I'd enter him in a couple of extra classes. Then I'd switch from his regular D-ring snaffle to a big fat one and try to carry him a little more forward, encouraging him to go back to his natural low head carriage just in case all the bending and low canter work was causing him to raise it.

As the season progressed, he was going more fluently, cantering slower. But I knew he'd never have the rocking-horse canter that is really comfortable. Even though he moved forward from the shoulder and laid that leg out there, sitting his canter was like riding a pogo stick. On the other hand, I'd learned that the ride I got on the flat was not the ride I was going to get in the ring. The extra schooling really showed up on course. So I let up on the long, tedious, left-bending sessions and saved his legs between classes by doing no more than hacking, while continuing longeing in side reins. As he improved, I weaned him off the three classes a week and concentrated on the big events.

Sold to Paul Greenwood for $1 million, The Natural was ridden by Katharine Burdsall (in the saddle here) to a stunning victory in the World Cup finals in 1987, by which time some thought him not only the most valuable but perhaps the very best jumper in the world. Photo: Karl Leck

When we came home from Arizona in the spring of 1985, I figured he was all set for a grand prix win. After a month's rest, I entered him in the $25,000 Dominion Grand Prix at Culpepper, Virginia, and he won it easily. We then settled into a routine. If he showed in a Sunday grand prix, we were usually home on Monday and I turned him out. Tuesday, he might wear his rig for half an hour during turnout, and if the weather and footing were good, I'd hack him on the race track. If we had a show scheduled the following weekend, we'd often go there on Wednesday and I'd ride him quietly around the grounds. We'd have one class on Thursday, just to loosen up, and then the grand prix. During the summer we scored a second place and then a seventh, third, and thirteenth. Our worst show was at Upperville in June, where he recognized the liverpool he'd knocked down with Katie the year before. I knew he wouldn't run out on a straight approach, so we just went for it—and he knocked it down again.

Box Car Willie eventually passed from Rodney's expert hands to those of Canadian team rider Mario Deslauriers, who'd won the 1984 World Cup finals with Aramis. In 1986, he finished second behind teammate Ian Millar and his great Big Ben in the Grand Prix of New York at the National Horse Show, and also contributed to Canada's victory in the Nations Cup there. Photo: James Leslie Parker

In the fall we won the Mercedes American Gold Cup at Devon, where we'd gone Intermediate the year before. As the ribbons were being passed out, I thought how different it would have been if this horse had come my way ten years earlier. I'd have taken him straight into grand prix as soon as I'd bought him. But horses like Coastline had taught me to wait.

I knew that with The Natural I had my best chance for a spot on the World Cup team since I'd gone to Gothenburg for the finals with Idle Dice in the 1970s. We won the Grand Prix at Culpepper in late September, took second place in the President's Cup at Washington, and were leading by eight points with three qualifying events left before the selection, when the horse was sold to Old Salem Farm for $1 million. While I was personally a bit disappointed about the World Cup, it was for myself rather than for The Natural. By then, everyone knew what a winner he was.

VI

Showing a Jumper

1

Year-by-Year Goals

—

George Morris

Three-year-old: Start in the spring, maybe one or two schooling shows in the late summer or fall.

Four-year-old: Light showing in Pre-Green Hunter or Schooling Jumper Division.

A collector's item, this early photograph shows George Morris riding his parents' Triplicate to the Green Hunter Championship of the North Shore Horse Show in 1965. Photo: Budd

George Morris schooling on the flat. Photo: *Practical Horseman*

Five-year-old: First-year Green Hunter or Preliminary Jumper.

Six-year-old: Second-year Green Hunter or Preliminary Jumper.

Seven-year-old: Working Hunter or Intermediate Jumper, advancing to Open, perhaps some grand prix.

Eight-year-old and above: Maintenance for the hunter and grand prix for the talented jumper.

2

Warming Up a Jumper

Buddy Brown

Buddy Brown was one of the youngest members ever on the USET, but he started early: at the age of five, he used to accompany his father to a New York City rental stable and sit in front of him in the saddle. Later riding lessons came from Pat Heuckeroth and her father, Otto; Wayne Carroll; Bob Freels; and George Morris, under whose tutelage he won the Medal finals. The very next year he was invited to go to Europe with the USET, still riding his equitation horse Sandsablaze (now an open jumper). Buddy and Sandsablaze climaxed that trip by winning the Dublin Grand Prix. Quite an accomplishment for a rookie!

In 1975 the same pair won the individual silver medal at the Pan-American Games and clinched the team gold. Buddy brought home a second team gold medal from the Pan-American Games in 1979. Within the next few years he scored another signal achievement: having already won the Devon Gold Cup (with Felton) and the American Invitational at Tampa, his 1982 victory in the American Jumping Derby (with Charles Fox) made him one of only two riders—the other being Melanie Smith—to have won the Show-Jumping Triple Crown. And he added a second Derby win with Charles Fox in 1983. Since 1986 his top grand prix mount has been Aramis, the 1985 World Cup winner, and Tolad, a French-bred stallion owned by Acres Wild Farm.

No longer a child prodigy but a popular star of the grand prix circuit as well as a top hunter rider, Buddy is still the idol of many a young rider who dreams of making the team one day.

When I anticipate three big rounds in a grand prix competition, I don't want to use any more of my horse's energy than I have to right before the class. Instead, I take my jumpers out in the morning for thirty minutes or so of flat work. During that half hour, I remind my horse of the basics, doing simple dressage movements, such as leg-yielding and shoulder-in, to make him supple and adjustable for the important class in the afternoon. If he has a special problem, this is the time to work on it. Afterward, he'll have a few hours in which to recoup his strength and relax a little before the competition.

In the afternoon, I get on him when there are about ten horses ahead of me in the jumping order. Since I've worked the horse in the morning, I spend only about five minutes on the flat, just to loosen him up. I don't ask for very much during this brief flat work because some jumpers are a little hot. The more you try to bend them or collect them, the

Buddy Brown rides Aries at the 1975 Farmington show. Photo: Barrows

Buddy Brown and Sandsablaze, his equitation horse whose progress matched his own, to culminate in silver and gold medals in the Pan-American Games, and a sensational winning streak on the indoor fall circuit in 1977. Photo: Courtesy of USET

more nervous you make them. I'm careful not to stress the horse's weaknesses in my afternoon warm-up, because it's important to keep him relaxed and concentrating. I don't want to make him mad.

With about seven horses left to go, I begin jumping. I trot ten or fifteen jumps, starting with a cross-rail or a very small vertical of about 2 feet. After loosening the jumping muscles, I begin to raise the jumps, continuing to trot up to about 4 feet. At that point I may canter the vertical a few times or move right to the oxer, depending on the horse. With an older horse, I want to keep his attention and make sure that he jumps clean. I do most of that at the oxer. Once he's jumped the vertical up to about 4 feet or 4 feet 6 inches, I start the oxer at about 3 feet 6 inches, keeping it square. As I raise it, I also move it out so that the horse has to reach a little for the back rail. This keeps his mind on what he's doing. I gradually build up the oxer to about 4 feet 9 inches and spread it about 5 feet 6 inches wide. If the horse is jumping well and

Buddy Brown and A Little Bit clear the water in a Grand Prix course. Photo: USET

trying hard, I don't try to get a rub every time, or it won't work when I really need it.

I like to conclude my warm-up routine with the same kind of fence that is on the first part of the course. If there are many verticals and a lot of collected striding, I'll end up with a fairly big vertical. If the first fence of the course is an oxer followed by a galloping distance, I'll end up with an oxer.

I like to finish warming up with two or three horses still in front of me so that I have time to get off, reset my saddle, and let the horse catch his breath. Before I go into the ring, I usually return to the schooling area and jump one fence at about 4 feet, just to get my horse's motor running again.

I try to jump as few big jumps as possible in the schooling area, especially if the class consists of two rounds and perhaps a jump-off. I spend more time on low jumps to get the horse's muscles loosened up and then use the few big fences to get his attention. I've seen a lot of people take forty or fifty jumps in the schooling area, where the horse performs fabulously. By the time they get to the ring, the horse is winded, his muscles are sore, and he's tired. While he may get around the first time, by the second round he's totally exhausted.

3

Grand Prix Glossary

Donald Cheska

Grand prix jumping has a language all its own, and Donald Cheska is fluent in it.

Reared in Minnesota in a hunting, riding family, Donald and his two brothers (one of them a twin) learned to ride as soon as they learned to walk, and as soon as they'd learned to ride they began competing in horse shows, working their way up through the divisions until they reached the top: international grand prix jumping. A few of Donald's major achievements to date: second place in the 1982 World Cup finals in Birmingham (with the 1976 Olympics veteran South-side), winner of the 1982 International Jumping Derby in Newport (with Eadenvale), and member of the USET's gold-medal team in the 1983 Pan-American Games.

An eavesdropper to a conversation among grand prix riders at the outgate might be mystified by some of the expressions they'd hear unless they had read Donald's glossary.

Grand Prix Glossary

DEEPER	"I got there much deeper than I'd anticipated."	Closer to the fence
BOTTOM	"I went near the bottom of the class."	The end of the class

OFF YOUR EYE	"It had to be ridden pretty much off the eye."	As seemed best at the time rather than according to a predetermined number of strides
EARLY LINE	"I noticed a lot of people adding a stride in the early line."	The first line of jumps on the course
DEEP, SOFT RIDE	"I concentrated on giving Southside the deep, soft ride he responds well to."	Riding to the fence with a minimum of hand and leg, taking off from the base
ADD A STRIDE EARLY IN THE LINE	"Wherever you decided to add a stride, you had to do it very early in the line."	Make the adjustment immediately after landing from the fence before
REGROUP WHEREVER THERE WAS A LONG LINE	"If the other courses were designed in the same way, it would pay to regroup wherever there was a long line."	Relax and rebalance where the space between the fences allowed
CANTERED IT	"But if I'd cantered it like the usual kind of jump . . ."	Ridden to it on the horse's normal long stride
KEEP A NICE, STEADY DISTANCE	"I had to ride to it carefully and keep a nice, steady distance."	Meet the fence at the ideal takeoff spot
BUILD	"Build a little for the next oxer."	Add impulsion
EARLY	"That I'd have to get to early . . ."	Have to add strides early in the approach to a jump
SLEPT IT	"If I slept it and got there long in five, I'd have trouble."	Neglected to make the adjustment at the beginning of the line

Donald Cheska and Southside, partners in many show jumping adventures, including second place in the 1982 World Cup finals and a team gold medal in the 1983 Pan-American Games. Southside was retired at the age of eighteen in 1985. Photo: Karl Leck

SLOW BUT TO A GOOD DISTANCE	". . . an oxer-vertical-oxer requiring an approach that was slow but to a good distance."	Requiring a slow approach but a long takeoff
SCOPEY BUT TOO SNUG TO REALLY RUN AT	"Although this combination was scopey, it was too snug to really run at."	Big, but with no room for the long stride that would make the easiest approach

4

Analyzing Grand Prix Jumper Courses

Neal Shapiro

"Jumper courses aren't like the old days," say horsemen and spectators alike. "They're better." For the spectator, they are more colorful, more beautiful, more impressive; they lead to competitions that are more spectacular, unpredictable, more thrilling. For the riders and horses, they are more demanding but also more interesting.

The change is due to the evolution of rules along international lines, as well as the skill of the present generation of course designers, many of whom were trained or influenced by the great USET coach Bertalan de Némethy. One of these is Neal Shapiro.

Now a noted harness racing trainer based in Florida and Saratoga, Neal is a former USET member, a medal-winning U.S. Olympic Team rider (individual bronze at Munich in 1972 with Sloopy), and winner of the Grand Prix of Aachen with Jacks or Better. Here he talks about grand prix jumper courses from the dual point of view of the course designer and the rider, two roles he has filled with distinction.

By the time a horse and rider reach grand prix level, there isn't much new for either one to see or experience in the line of obstacles. If an oxer, a colored plank, or a fancy gate with flowerpots is going to faze them, they don't belong in grand prix competition.

A course designer must find other ways to challenge horses and riders.

Neal Shapiro and Trick Track, with whom he won the Puissance at the 1968 Washington International. Photo: Budd

Depending on the caliber of the competition, he'll choose from a variety of problems. He may build a course with lots of turns, running room, and places for a clever horse to take shortcuts, where the winner will be the horse that navigates the fastest. He may not necessarily be a powerful horse that can jump tremendous fences, but he'll be very handy. On the other hand, he may ask a horse to demonstrate sheer power by building a course of huge fences all the way. Or he might combine the two and build a course that tests the skill of both horse and rider by intermingling long and short distances between fences and combinations. He might present several fences designed to put the horse in a long frame and then, suddenly, some very tight distances and fences that are difficult to jump when a horse is strung out. Problems like this are created to see how quickly the rider can get his mind together and say, "Whoa! Come back here!"

Here are examples of some of the tools which a course designer might use:

Two vertical fences, 5 feet high. If these two fences are spaced 25 or 26 feet apart, they'll probably be quite easy to negotiate. The horse will be able to meet the first fence at a comfortable distance, take one comfortable stride, and jump out. But if the inside distance is shortened to 23 feet or 23 feet 6 inches, you have a problem. The horse must meet the first part on a comfortable or short stride, take a short stride, roll back on the hocks, and jump the second. On the other hand, if the inside distance is lengthened to 27 feet, for instance, the horse might get a little strung out, jump a little flatter, and have the second part down.

Two oxers, 4 feet 9 inches high and 5 feet 6 inches wide. A distance of 24 feet 6 inches or 25 feet ought to ride comfortably. The horse should not stand a long way off from the first element, because he'll flatten and tend to lose impulsion. But he can't be buried to the first fence either, because he won't be able to clear its furthest element, much less the one stride and then the second fence.

If the inside distance is shortened to 23 feet, it creates a problem. The horse needs a little momentum to get across the width of the first fence and will therefore need a little extra space for his stride to the second. If the distance between the farthest element of the first fence and the nearest element of the second fence is too tight, the horse will probably wind up right against the second fence, with no room to fold his legs or leave the ground. But if the inside distance is lengthened to 27 feet, remembering that the fences are 5 feet 6 inches wide, the last element of the second fence is quite far away and the horse has a good chance of knocking it down.

The problems presented by either of these combinations are complicated if the horse is to meet the first element off a long or short stride or off a turn. The course designer can set you up in any way he likes. He might give you four fences to start with and then throw the curve on the fifth. For example:

First fence: small oxer
Second fence: rampy vertical (a lot of brush, flowers, etc., in front of the fence)
Third fence: triple bar
Fourth fence: another oxer set at a good galloping distance from the third fence

Then, when the horse is all strung out and galloping, fences 5 and 6 are two verticals set at 24 feet, which means that you must get your horse collected—fast!

It could work as well in reverse: beginning with neat, tight distances requiring the horse to stay collected and just rock back and jump off his hocks, and then suddenly two big, wide oxers.

There are also a few specialty fences which you should be prepared to encounter, if only occasionally:

Water. A water jump can be a big factor when planning or riding a course, mainly because you can really set somebody up by the use of the fence before or after it. In itself, the water jump isn't difficult. But it requires the horse to get long and flat and take off at the base. It's easiest to jump when placed after a combination requiring a long stride; it's difficult when preceded or followed by a very tight combination.

Banks. At the beginning of grand prix jumping in the United States, the bank was included for spectator appeal. In reality, it is a nothing fence. How many horses knock down a bank? It's simply a big mound of dirt to jump up on. Once atop the bank, the horse is supposed to put his front feet over the edge, slide about halfway down, and then push off. There are very few banks anywhere nowadays, except for a couple of European classics.

The Devil's Dike. This is a triple combination frequently found in Europe, mostly in speed classes, consisting of a rail of some sort, usually followed by a little water jump with rails over it and a third fence identical to the first. The trick is that you leave off level ground for fence 1, land on a decline for one or two strides before fence 2 (the water), and jump uphill the same distance for one or two strides to fence 3. The tendency is for the horse to get a little flat to fence 3 on the upgrade, because he has to jump higher to clear an uphill fence. Without sufficient impulsion, he might take it down behind or put in an extra stride and meet it chest-high.

There are certain unwritten rules that our course designers tend to follow more or less subconsciously. Horses of grand prix caliber are seldom stoppers. While they may commit faults and have rails down, they don't fall much either. If a number of horses crash on a course, the designer has not built a course suitable for the level of competition or for the existing conditions. For example, you don't want to put two tremendous square oxers consecutive with some unbelievable distance between them. Either the horse takes two strides to meet the second fence chest-high and deep, or, if he tries to make it in one stride, he's too far off fence 2 to get out—so he crashes. Most of all, course designers want to guard against putting up lousy distances. Testing, yes. Demanding, yes. Dangerous, no!

When a rider has the opportunity to walk a course, he's meeting the course designer's first test. How well he defines and interprets the problems he encounters determines how prepared he'll be to ride the course. Some people go out on a course not knowing what they're doing, just because everyone else is walking it. Others go out there with a real purpose.

Ten years ago, when time was seldom a factor, a rider could wander around a course in haphazard fashion, finding the best possible line to every fence. But now almost every class has a time limit. Although the limit is not so tight as to disallow some sort of breather somewhere on the course, there's no time for pirouettes, circles, and serpentines between fences. Of course, you may not always want to gallop straight down to every fence, but it's the course designer who decides whether or not you'll have a choice to make. He may give you room in which to drift out or make you hold your horse to the corners. These are the things you try to discover when walking the course.

Before you ever set foot on the course you know what type of competition it is (a speed class, grand prix, a one or two jump-off class, and so on) and whether you're going to jump the original course on the first round and then a different course, comprised of some of the same fences, on the second round. You also know your horse and his ability, his strengths and weaknesses, which is especially important as you walk the distances between connecting fences and combinations. You don't need to walk a distance of ten or fifteen strides. There's plenty of room in there to make changes, so that if it walks ten strides, it doesn't have to ride ten strides. Outdoors, the terrain becomes a factor. Not all outdoor rings are perfectly flat. You should take into account the ups and downs as you walk the course.

I measure my strides by figuring that each of my steps is approximately 3 feet long. Considering that the average horse's stride is 12 feet, it takes four of my steps to equal one of his strides. Then, regardless of whether it's uphill or downhill, long or short, my stride never changes. For example, if I'm going downhill and the distance walks out to be a very nice four strides (or would be if it were level), I know that because it's downhill, it will ride four pretty tight strides or three pretty long ones, since the horse's hindquarters are carried well under him going downhill and permit him to lengthen his stride. If it's the same distance going uphill, I know it will ride four very long strides or possibly five short ones, because the hindquarters are not under the horse but strung out behind him, obliging him to work harder to move forward.

You also have to take into consideration the characteristics of related fences. The way in which you meet fence A and the type of fence it is will greatly influence the way you arrive at fence B and are prepared to meet it. Vertical to vertical, vertical to spread, spread to spread, and spread to vertical are all slightly different and require adjustments tailored to your particular horse. Because of the way the fences relate to each other, you might want to get a little deep to fence A or perhaps stand off from it and just keep running to fence B. Or you might have to choke your horse a bit and just slide over fence A in order to get to fence B. These are the things you keep in mind while walking a course, always planning ahead for options too. You know from walking the course that if you get to this point and are not just right, you may have to put in another stride or leave one out, so neither eventuality will come as a shock. You also know where you have no choice at all.

When a rider walks a course knowing the order of fences for the jump-off course, he first walks the original course and then the jump-off, looking for where he can cut inside of a fence, where he can turn. When you see Frank Chapot leave from some "impossible" spot in a jump-off, you can be pretty sure that it's a calculated move: that's just where he planned to be. When he walks the course, he might see that the wing of one fence is in the way of the perfect line for the shortest route between two fences, but he also knows that in order to win the class, that's where he wants to go; and he'll take that route, even though the less than ideal approach means risking a fault.

A lot of things happen when you ride a course that are different from when you walk it. It doesn't always work out the way it walks for a lot of reasons: terrain that you didn't take into account, footing (deep or hard) that could alter the horse's stride, peculiar lighting. It helps to watch several riders ahead of you go.

At first, walking courses may not be very meaningful. However, the more courses you walk and then ride, and the better you understand the tools the course designer has at his disposal, the more you'll find you're able to learn from walking. After a while, a walk around a course is almost as instructive as riding it.

5

Jumping Grand Prix Fences

Anthony d'Ambrosio, Jr., Rodney Jenkins, Michael Matz

*Sequence photos by Karl Leck
taken on the American Gold Cup course,
with comments by the riders*

The horse: Sympatico, owned by Alligator Farms
The rider: Anthony d'Ambrosio, Jr., former member of the
USET, former holder of the U.S. indoor puissance record—7
feet, 4 inches—noted for his superior riding style and strategy.

2

3

4

5

6

7

8

Sympatico just eats up a triple bar, and judging from these pictures, he jumped the hell out of this one.

He's a funny horse. By nature he's very quiet, but certain things upset him. He's at his best in natural surroundings. He likes Cleveland, with the great big grass field, and he likes big grass stadiums. You can clearly feel the difference in him. At country fairs, for instance, he's not relaxed. And any athlete has to be in a good frame of mind in order to put his body to work for the job.

I can never tell what he's going to be like till I get on him. Then I can feel whether he's ready to win, or if it's going to be really tough.

But I don't think I've ever had a triple bar down with him, so my approach to this fence was pretty cut-and-dried: get to the fence forward and deep. With a horse that's as scopey across an oxer as "Tico," you don't have much else to worry about. In photo 3 you can see that he doesn't just jump across the fence: he makes a definite effort to form an arc. In number 4 I like the way he's really drawn his hind legs up so that they're perfectly square. I'd say he's jumping in perfect form.

The horse: Idle Dice, owned by Harry Gill
The rider: Rodney Jenkins, grand prix rider par excellence.

Idle Dice gets pretty uptight over a big course, but he always jumps well. When you have four or five classes over the same course in a

regular horse show, it gives the horse a chance to warm up to it. I like this type of competition, with one class over the course. It really takes a nice horse.

Idle Dice is meeting this fence very well. In photos 1 and 2 you can see him setting himself on his hocks. In number 1 his head might be a little high, although I like a jumper's head to be up slightly. As long as his nose is down and he's flexed right, he's easier to balance with his head maybe 6 inches to a foot above his shoulder blades.

His knees are really good in number 3; but in number 4 he's getting a little flat in back. When he jumps high, he has a tendency to get his belly down in order to bring his legs up. See how in number 5 he has his hind end pulled up under him. This is Idle Dice's worst fault. From this position, if he rubs he'll carry the rail with him. If he'd throw his hind legs out behind, there'd be less chance of his pulling the rail up out of the cup.

He's landing very well. I love his head and neck. See how he's reaching for the next stride in numbers 6 and 7. His head didn't jump up, which would have shortened his stride. He's really going forward for the next fence. An unusual thing about this horse is his hip. It's so long and so high. Look where it is in number 5. I love high-hipped horses. Most of them can really jump.

5

6

7

The horse: Grande, owned by F. Eugene Dixon

The rider: Michael Matz, one of America's most admired riders, now also trainer of a lucky few. Since first riding on the USET in 1973, he has won three gold, one individual gold, and three individual bronze medals in three Pan-American Games, the team and individual bronze in the 1978 World Championship, and the FEI World Cup in 1981 and 1984. He is also the AGA's leading career prize-money winner.

This was a particularly difficult class for Grande because he'd just arrived in this country from Germany. I'd ridden him only four or five days at home and was competing on him for the first time. We had to find the ins and outs of him very quickly.

I was afraid of this combination because we were unfamiliar with the horse. What I feared did in fact happen. He looked down into the water at the liverpool and as a result didn't land as far from the ditch as I'd hoped. He had even more ground to make up at the oxer. He's an extremely talented horse and the best came out in him then, because he was certainly in trouble. But he got out of it.

He's jumping well. You can see in photo 2 how he jumps with tremendous strength. His left front leg might be up higher. It's not behind, but it's not up where it should be. This will happen when a horse is a little insecure. Here he was with a strange rider, big fences, and deep going. In this situation the rider has to ride very strongly and confidently in order to communicate his confidence to the horse.

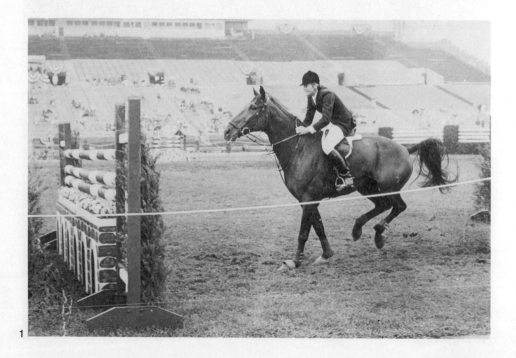

1

2

3

4

5

6

7

6

To the Top with Fred

Lisa Jacquin

Lisa Jacquin

Raised in Tucson, Arizona, Lisa Jacquin came out of the West to become a leading member of the younger generation of America's international jumping stars.

One week after the Invitational that Lisa writes about here, she was on her way to Paris for the 1987 World Cup finals, where she'd set herself the goal of finishing among the top ten riders. After a clear first round, she and For the Moment (alias Fred) clinched third place with four faults in a hotly contested jump-off. They then won a place on the 1987 U.S. team for the Pan-American Games and brought home a silver medal. In 1988, after a brilliant season, Lisa and Fred made the Olympic team and helped win the Team Jumping Silver Medal in Seoul.

For me and my jumper Fred—a Thoroughbred better known to grand prix fans as For the Moment—1987 was the year when everything came together. I can't say it happened because he made me a star or I made him a star. The way we helped each other to the top may not be a program that would work for every other rider and horse; in fact, some people might think we did certain things backward. Intuition, teamwork, and trust sometimes took the place of training by the book.

Fred came into my life at exactly the right time. It was December 1981 and I was almost twenty years old. After riding with a number of trainers

Lisa Jacquin and For the Moment in the 1987 World Cup finals in Paris, where they placed third in a close race to the finish. Photo: Courtesy of USET

during my junior years, I'd taken a job at Fairfield Hunt Club in Westport, Connecticut, and was looking for a young jumper prospect that I could afford. One day our veterinarian's assistant brought over her backyard horse for rider Leslie Burr (now Lenehan) to look at. The eight-year-old Thoroughbred gelding had a hard-luck story as a $5,000 claimer. His latest owner had never shown him, but she thought he might have potential as a children's hunter. He wasn't especially big, about 16.1 hands, and he was so scrawny that he looked even smaller.

Since Fred had never been jumped, Leslie rode him over some tiny crossrails to see how he'd react. While he seemed to enjoy going to the jumps, I couldn't ignore his high, stiff head carriage and the way he hung his legs. Leslie next substituted some small fences for the X's, and in an ungainly pogo-stick fashion he jumped every one without so much as a tick.

His owner brought him back another day, and I rode him while Leslie watched. She continued to praise him, saying he had a lot of spring and power behind. But Christmas was only a couple of weeks away, and I was intent on getting home to Arizona for the holidays. I left Fairfield without giving Fred another thought.

I'd been home for only a few days when Leslie surprised me with a phone call suggesting that I buy Fred. She and Fairfield's owner, Bruce Burr, had continued trying him over fences up to 3 feet 6 inches and 4 feet, as well as combinations, and he looked better and better. At the least, she felt, we could school him into a junior jumper prospect whose sale would enable me to look for something more expensive. At last I agreed, convinced more by her enthusiasm than by any sympathy for him, but once the check was in the mail I felt excited. I hurried back to greet the first jumper I'd ever owned—and he greeted me with his rump. Ears pinned back, he refused to turn around even to eat the carrot I'd brought for him.

During the next few weeks, in addition to riding Leslie's jumpers on the flat, I spent as much time as possible with Fred, trying to get to know him. He was a complicated mixture of bravery and aversion to situations that made him uncomfortable. He was very powerful, and if conditions were right he'd jump anything, often with a kangaroo leap; but his courage evaporated if something upset him. And the list of things that sent him into a tizzy was a long one!

Fortunately, I had some background in dealing with sensitive Thoroughbreds, thanks to several years of junior training with Kaye Love back home in Arizona. At age eleven, I was a bit rough when I started with her, and she'd taught me to be quieter with my hands and body, a skill that helped me with Fred, who needed the quietest possible ride. Later in my junior career, Kaye and I took her jumper Sterling Image, which I was showing for her, to work with Conrad Homfeld in Virginia. I was reminded of those weeks in Virginia as I tried to come to an understanding with Fred in 1982, but applying earlier lessons to my new horses turned out to be quite a challenge. He wasn't only stiff and tense, he was also out of control. While he jumped anything and everything if he was feeling comfortable, he wouldn't listen to me between fences. He refused to change leads in the corners. I couldn't turn him, and it took a lot of room to stop him. When I put pressure on the bridle, he just threw his head in the air and kept going.

At first we tried a standing martingale, but the moment Fred felt it he reared. After he'd broken three of them in a single day, we tried a slightly stronger bit to see if he'd respond better on the turns; but at the first touch of my hands, his head shot straight up in the air. Eventually, I decided that flat work rather than tack changes was my best hope of getting him more ridable, and went back to the D-ring snaffle he was wearing when I bought him.

Leslie wasn't bothered by Fred's unusual jumping form. She believes in letting a horse go in the way that's best for him; while flat work is an important part of her program, so is getting out on course and jumping. She thought I should begin competing Fred while I was getting him broken on the flat. So after a few weeks in Fairfield, we took him to Florida and started him off over fences at 3 feet, 5 inches in schooling jumper classes at Palm Beach. I still could hardly turn him, but showing him was fun because he overjumped everything by about 2 feet. Within a few weeks, we'd moved him up into high Preliminary classes, where he consistently took sevenths and eighths. Although our turns cost us time in the jump-offs, he usually had clean rounds.

In Florida I had a chance to discuss Fred with George Morris. While coaching me during part of my last two junior years, George had taught me a lot about exactness in riding. He watched us for a while and then said that Fred was a very strung-out horse who needed a huge amount of flat work, especially in counter-canter, before I could shorten his frame and balance him. I incorporated his advice in my flat program, even though flat work was like a required course in school that neither Fred nor I could feel excited about. The subject that interested us was jumping.

Fred hated having rails down. If we fetched up at an awkward distance because I couldn't adjust his stride, he'd stop rather than attempt the jump with the possibility of hitting it. I didn't want stopping to become a habit, but as classes got bigger and jump-offs harder, the likelihood of his stopping increased. The odds of a crash were increasing too, and considering Fred's sensitive nature, I felt that a real crash would be devastating to his confidence.

My problem was to design a show schedule for Fred that was also a training program, a schedule that wouldn't frighten or discourage him while his turning and stride adjustment improved. At the start of the outdoor season, I looked for classes in big fields with long galloping lines and generous turns, which he loved, and avoided classes held in cramped rings. He also hated muddy or slippery going, so I tried to improve his confidence by competing him only on good footing.

By the summer of 1982, Fred seemed so comfortable in the high Preliminary classes that Leslie thought he was ready for the Intermediate Division at Lake Placid. It seemed like a big step, but the courses there were laid out on a wide, grassy field that felt good underfoot. After hundreds of hours of flat work and because he'd finally consented to wear a (very long) standing martingale, he was now easier to turn and stop. The decision worked out well. He won three or four classes.

After Lake Placid, we thought it was time for him to slow down a bit. I didn't show Fred again in 1982. At the end of the year I took him back with me to Arizona, while I was laid up after corrective surgery on my knees. He had a six-month vacation at a local stable, with nothing to do but eat and enjoy his daily turnout.

When I was ready to ride again in mid-1983, Fred looked better than ever. He'd put on needed weight and seemed more relaxed. But he had been rested for so long and had competed in Intermediate so briefly that I didn't think he could pick up showing at the same point where he'd stopped. He'd already won his way out of the Preliminary Division, but out west there is a Modified Division that is a transitional stage between Preliminary and Intermediate. Most of these classes are held in fields or big outdoor rings with fences about 4 feet 3 inches and fairly open galloping courses. This level was my goal as we started work again.

I continued my previous year's approach of coping with things that bothered Fred by sidestepping them. Still using the D-ring snaffle, I followed George's advice and worked him daily on the flat, especially in canter and counter-canter. In jumping schools, I concentrated on getting his attitude more relaxed. We worked in a small area over low jumps, even over poles on the ground where there was no room and no need to build up speed. I often stopped or even backed him up after a fence.

When Fred and I began competing in the Modified Division, he was soon winning a class or two at every show. Meanwhile, I was continually learning more about how to keep him happy.

Fred liked his warm-up to go a certain way. I learned to start with a 3-foot vertical and work up to 4-foot-3-inch fences by easy stages, making sure the groundlines were rolled out properly. Fred hated trotting fences; even over the lowest practice jumps, he simply stopped. Instead of fighting over it, I started the warm-up at a canter after a few suppling exercises. I never considered letting him hit a warm-up fence so that he'd go more carefully in the ring. He was already so careful that if he bumped himself over one of the final practice fences, he became flustered enough to stop at the first fence on the course! I was also alert to footing. If his class was on a grass field that seemed slippery, I'd put caulks in his shoes and school him on similar footing.

By the end of the summer of 1983, I'd moved Fred up into Modified Open classes. The bigger fences weren't a problem as long as we stayed with open fields where all we had to do was gallop. When we did have a difficulty, it was usually at tall, isolated verticals. Fred liked to stand off and jump out of stride. If the distance didn't feel right when he got there, he stopped. Combinations were less of a worry: once he cleared the first element, his aversion to touching a fence took over and he bounded across the remaining components with his kangaroo leaps.

Lisa and For the Moment also qualified for the World Cup finals at Gothenburg, in 1984. Photo: Courtesy of USET

At the Griffith Park show in Los Angeles that September, Fred went so well in the Modified Division that I entered the regular Open and won. Several riders and trainers I knew encouraged me to take him in the Mercedes International Grand Prix, the climax of the weekend. I was a bit worried about moving him up to a World Cup qualifier class with a huge course, but Fred seemed confident after his two wins. In retrospect, my decision to enter the Grand Prix was rather like my decision to take him Intermediate at Lake Placid, perhaps because the result was the same: we won. Afterward, I felt once more that I'd pushed him enough for a while and decided to stop competing him in 1983 while we were ahead.

In early 1984, I took a group from Bill Herring's barn to the Arizona circuit, as I began what I expected would be Fred's first full year in the open division. Then I learned that he had qualified for the World Cup finals in Sweden. I should have declined because my horse just wasn't ready, but I was too inexperienced to realize it.

The trip to Gothenburg was a disaster. We managed a fifth over the lower jumps of the initial warm-up class, but everything fell apart after that. The jumps were so big and came up so fast, especially in the jump-offs, that we never got around without a stop. My only comfort was that stops were better than a crash, which would have destroyed Fred's confidence.

Setbacks continued when we returned from Sweden. I'd entered Fred in an Open class at the Del Mar, California, show as a prelude to getting back into grand prix, but I hadn't considered the fact that these classes would be held at night under lights. Lights were new to Fred. Confronted by the unfamiliar glare and shadows on the course, he stopped three or four times. I added evening classes to my list of things to watch out for.

In mid-1984, I realized that I needed professional help if I were to progress further and arranged to work with Judy Martin, a California hunter-jumper trainer I'd met at the shows. After Del Mar, Fred went to Judy's barn in Rolling Hills Estates, while I went back to Arizona for more knee surgery. This time, postsurgical complications prevented me from riding Fred more than a week or two at a time until the end of the summer. But even those short periods of work with Judy proved that I'd been getting sloppy. Judy told me I was getting ahead of Fred's stride and needed to sit behind him a bit more to stay in balance with him. I was carrying my hands too high and using too little right leg—a problem for me because it was my right leg that had suffered the complications.

Judy takes a tougher line with her horses than I do. Although she likes Fred, in her view his little quirks were those of a spoiled brat whose owner-rider had let him get away with murder. Our goal during this period was to teach Fred to take more responsibility for organizing himself. He didn't like me to ride very much with my hands, but in order to be more competitive in bigger classes, he needed to compress his frame and shorten his stride. As I was gradually able to work with him for longer periods during the fall of 1984, Judy spent hours with me on exercises like a pole on the ground followed by a small vertical and another pole on the ground. The pole, rather than my hands, forced Fred to adjust his stride, so that he got to the vertical in a shorter frame. Judy's next step was to set up tight lines with small jumps so that Fred wouldn't be intimidated into stopping if he arrived at an awkward distance but might realize that he was more comfortable when he shortened his frame. Then she told me which striding she wanted between the fences, and she made us do it correctly even if I had to stop and back Fred several times.

When we started the 1985 season on the Arizona circuit, Fred was beginning to feel broken on the flat. His stride was more adjustable and I often had the option of adding strides in a line instead of always having to press forward and leave strides out. On the approaches to single verticals, he felt more comfortable about shifting his weight back over his quarters and pushing them from his hind end. We took a third at the Kachina Grand Prix and fifth or sixth in a couple of others. The most significant riding problem was still turning, especially to the right. All our ribbons came in classes where the jump-offs happened to be designed with galloping lines rather than tight bends. We still wouldn't be able to win in a small ring or indoors. My next goal was to be able to turn Fred well enough to be competitive at any show I chose.

Our Arizona season once more qualified us for the World Cup finals, held in Berlin that year. I decided to go again. The results may not sound like much of an improvement over our disastrous 1984 effort (we finished below twentieth again), but I noticed a big difference. This time Fred had no stops; his more adjustable stride enabled him to extend and compress in response to the big technical courses. Considering that we'd come to this indoor competition without any opportunity to practice indoors, I thought we did very well.

Back home, the summer and fall season seemed to bear out this promise. In August we took a third at the Seattle Grand Prix. In October I entered Fred in the grand prix at Flintridge, held in a much smaller ring than we were used to. The course, designed by Conrad Homfeld, was difficult: big jumps and tricky distances. Only two horses went clean in the first round, Robert Ridland's Benoit and Fred. We were first to go in the jump-off. Because I wasn't sure how effectively I'd be able to turn Fred in the small ring, I chose a careful clear round over a very fast one. Robert tried to go faster and had the first fence down.

By the end of 1985, Judy and I began to discuss the game plan for Fred in 1986. I thought it might be possible to qualify him for the indoor fall shows back east, although I knew what we were up against: Harrisburg takes the forty Open jumpers that have earned the most money, Washington takes the top twenty-five, and New York the top fifteen. But the tally of earnings dates from the previous September, and Fred and I had had a good autumn in 1985.

We weren't far into our first show of the year on the Arizona circuit before I wondered if we'd aimed too high. After withdrawing from our first grand prix because the ring was deep in mud, I had a nasty fall when Fred stopped for no apparent reason at a skinny gate in an Open class. After this upset, he reverted to his old habit of hollowing his back and running at the jumps. The same skinny gate was included in the grand prix course, and he stopped there again. I recognized the pattern: the stops and my fall had panicked him a bit and he was upset. But I still couldn't figure out what had triggered that first refusal.

In Tucson the pattern continued. Fred stopped twice at verticals in open classes and picked up eight faults in the grand prix. At Goodyear, Arizona, I got him so deep to a big vertical that he stopped again. While this was my mistake, I still suspected there was some other reason for his series of refusals. I had him reshod, and the farrier discovered a bad bruise on one sole.

Soon after Tucson I learned that we had qualified for the World Cup again, but I decided not to go. Even if Fred's mysterious stopping problem was solved, I needed to stay home and keep showing if we were to have any chance indoors. So Judy and I went to Del Mar, where Fred was third in the grand prix—under lights.

Now that he was placing regularly in big classes, I was even more careful to keep his warm-up calm and consistent. On the morning of a class, I'd ride him through his regular flat program and then put him away until the afternoon. With ten or fifteen horses left to go ahead of us, I'd supple him with backing up and bending. I'd set the first jumps at about 3 feet and build in careful stages to an oxer comparable to what he'd face in the ring, although I never schooled over a vertical higher than 4 feet 6 inches. Single verticals were still his least favorite, most worrisome jump. If he bumped himself late in the warm-up, I'd jump a few more fences to efface the memory when he got on course. I'd try to watch a few rounds to see how various options were working out for previous riders. But I invariably stuck to the plan I made after walking the course. I've learned the hard way that I know intuitively what works best for my horse.

At Houston, our next show, the ring was muddy, but I decided to attempt a class anyway as a warm-up for the grand prix. After struggling miserably over the first two jumps, Fred faked me out at a triple bar with one of his worst stops ever. I kept going into the fence, bruising two ribs. There were so many complaints about the footing that the show management improved it, and Fred and I (with ribs taped) tried for the grand prix after a long school to convince him that the footing was now trustworthy. He took a fifth, and a third the following weekend.

We were entered in three grand prix at Griffith Park in California. Fred won the first two and then came fourth in the World Cup qualifier that followed. After a good ribbon at Flintridge a few weeks later, we had qualified for all three indoor shows (squeaking into New York in fourteenth place).

Judy and I decided that I'd need more turning leverage than the D-ring snaffle provided for the cramped rings at these shows, so we wrapped tape around a gag bit until it felt like a fat snaffle in Fred's mouth. He accepted this and it gave me a little more control, although I thought he jumped slightly better in his old bit. At least we didn't disgrace ourselves. Fred placed third in the Harrisburg Grand Prix and second in the President's Cup in Washington. The climax of the year was an invitation to compete at the Royal Winter Fair in Toronto with the USET. By now I felt that Fred and I had a reasonable chance of winning whenever we went into the ring, not only when everything was going his way.

Back at Judy's, I gave him a couple of weeks off and made plans for 1987. I wanted to start on the Arizona circuit again, as it was my family's only chance to see me ride. From there I'd go to Florida in time for the Tampa Invitational. I hoped to qualify for the World Cup finals again, perhaps even have a chance to ride in the Pan-American Games. Judy and I discussed the jumping problems involved and prepared Fred for them. For example, I'd heard from riders in previous Invitationals of a jump consisting of a liverpool between two verticals. So we built a simulation and practiced over it until Fred thought it was old hat.

When we arrived in Florida in late March 1987, Fred had already won two Arizona Grand Prix. He was warmed up and confident after six weeks of showing. I was glad of that because the Tampa setup wasn't the best for us: no chance to school in the arena and no chance to watch other rounds, since we were scheduled to go third. Walking Bert de Némethy's course, I found that the jumps, though not of maximum size, posed some tough riding problems: a tight three-stride distance between fences 5 and 6; a single vertical on a downhill slope at 7; a triple combination at 9, like the jump we'd practiced at home, except that the liverpool was twice as wide; a maximum-width water jump around a right turn at fence 11; and two jumps later, a line consisting of a skinny black gate positioned three forward or four steady strides before an oxer-oxer combination at fence 14.

Two years earlier, I would have had trouble opening and closing Fred's stride around this course. But after our usual meticulous warm-up, I followed my plan from start to finish. At the end of the first round, Fred and I had one of only five clears in a class of thirty-five. The other finalists were Jeffrey Welles, Joe Fargis, Greg Best, and Rodney Jenkins. Pretty heady company! The jump-off course of six fences, requiring accurate turns and an adjustable stride, might have been designed to test all of Fred's earlier problem areas.

Jeffrey went before me and knocked down a couple of fences. But

With For the Moment, Lisa again won great praise for their smooth, apparently effortless style during the 1987 World Cup finals in Paris. Photo: Courtesy of USET

with those top riders behind me, I knew that a safe clear round wouldn't be enough to win; I'd have to try for speed. As I cantered into the ring, I looked at the easier option for the first right turn and wondered if I should take it. "No," I decided as I galloped to the first fence, "I didn't come here to be third or fourth." Fred balanced himself to pivot around the turn and as we made the corner, I saw the distance and realized we were going to be all right.

After that the course flew by. I saved time by leaving out a stride on the line across the center to the single vertical so that I could let up a little on the hairpin turn back to an oxer. We were able to really gallop again back across the center to the oxer that was the fifth jump. Now we had to double back again to the two final elements of the first round's triple to finish the course. I thought the left-hand route was slower, and I'd decided to take the right. Not only that, but I cut inside the adjacent Swedish oxer (fence 3) to get a better line—a bit of bravado I'd never have dared attempt a year before.

When we finished with a clear round, I knew that Fred and I had just put in the best effort of our career. It was so hard to watch the rest of the jump-off that I went back to the barn area. One by one, the others had rails down, until only Rodney remained. Moments after he started his round, I heard a groan rise from the crowd as his horse hit the second fence. When the results were official, not only had Fred jumped the only clear second round, but his time was two seconds faster than the second-placed horse, Joe Fargis' Olympic gold medalist Touch of Class.

7

Handling a Champion Problem Horse:
Abdullah

Conrad Homfeld

A native of Houston, Texas, Conrad Homfeld's riding talent was spotted by George Morris, who offered to work with him. Two years later, Conrad was one of the few riders to win both the Maclay and the AHSA Medal finals, and an exemplary show riding career was born.

In 1978 Conrad and Joe Fargis, with whom he'd shared riding assignments at Frances Rowe's barn (as well as management responsibilities for a while), decided to set up a training and teaching establishment of their own. Sandron, as they called it, was successful from the start. Conrad was a frequent member of the USET jumping squad. When he and Abdullah were selected for the 1984 U.S. Olympic Team, he'd already ridden in twelve Nations Cups—six of them winners.

Los Angeles was a triumph: a gold medal for the team, an individual gold for Joe and Touch of Class, a silver for Conrad and Abdullah. In 1985, Conrad won the World Cup finals for a second time, the only rider to have done so. At the end of the year, he was named Equestrian Athlete of the Year by the U.S. Olympic Committee, a tribute to his teaching as well as to his riding achievements. In the 1986 World Championships at Aachen, Conrad and Abdullah helped the United States win the team title and Conrad was runner-up to Canadian Gail Greenough in the individual competition.

What is the secret of his success?

"I've always been surrounded by the best," he says. "I've worked hard, but I've also been fortunate to have associated with some really top people. From them and from my own experience, I've learned that being truly successful isn't a one-dimensional thing. There's a lot more involved than just knowing how to ride."

My performance with Abdullah in the April 1984 World Cup finals in Sweden was so abysmal that I'd have been thrilled with four eight-fault rounds at the next year's World Cup in Berlin. He stopped with me three times on the second day and actually threw me to the ground. We didn't even finish the competition. After that, we won team gold and individual silver medals at the Los Angeles Olympics—but the Olympics were outdoors, the World Cup is indoors, and indoor arenas seemed to magnify Abdullah's problems.

Our 1984 World Cup disaster occurred just three months after Sue

After many trials, Conrad Homfeld and Abdullah came through in a blaze of glory at the crucial moment: the 1984 Olympic Games in Los Angeles. Photo: Courtesy of USET

and Terry Williams asked me to ride Abdullah. His previous rider, Debbie Shaffner, had already worked through the worst of his problems, but remnants lingered, the most severe of them being an honesty problem. As former Olympic rider Kathy Kusner says, "I want a horse to assess each jump with a positive attitude: *How* am I going to jump this? Not *am* I going to jump this?" But Abdullah sometimes seemed to have second thoughts. He was particularly negative about jumps placed close to the end of the ring; he seemed afraid of landing in the seats. To overcome his lack of bravery, Debbie often left out strides, using pace to drive him over the jumps. The tactic was appropriate at the time, but in grand prix courses involving highly technical distance problems, Abdullah had to be capable of adding strides confidently without pace.

While I knew about his problem, I may have been a little lax in preparing for Sweden. He'd gone well for me in Florida during the first few months of our partnership, and I thought I could handle an indoor, problem should one arise. I paid a heavy penalty for my optimistic attitude!

Because Abdullah is a breeding stallion, he goes home to the Williams's farm in Middleport, New York, between shows. Sue works him on the flat and rides him cross-country to keep him fit enough for the long grand prix courses, and he joins me a few days before each show. After the Swedish experience, I knew I'd have to use our brief times together to try to solve the problems we'd encountered.

Whenever Abdullah arrived for his preshow preparation, I'd spend a good deal of time working on the flat, trying to make his stride more adjustable. The first day I'd ask him to work in a long, low frame—nothing difficult, but very forward. Each day I'd add more collection, trying to get the transitions as extreme as possible by the time grand prix day arrived. He has a great canter for jumping, although it's hard to compress into smaller steps. His stride is naturally so elevated that you can ride him at a jump without having to hold him off it. I used this natural ability to develop his flat work and then worked backward to his trot and walk, which were weak. After a session in the canter, I always found the other gaits improved.

Abdullah is also much softer to the right rein and leg than to the left, so I focused on his stiffer side a good deal of the time. Flat work consisted of basic movements: two-track, shoulder-in, leg-yielding, turn on the haunches, and a lot of counter-canter. A horse that's trained to do flying changes would much rather swap leads than deal with the unbalancing imposed by the counter-lead. He has to be athletic and listening to the rider's leg in order to hold the counter-lead gracefully.

On the flat I rode him in a full-cheek twisted snaffle with a figure-eight noseband, substituting a regular cavesson with a drop attachment and standing martingale for jumping schools. For showing, I used a wing-twisted-snaffle gag. The gag has a little pulley that lets it slide more efficiently than the type that runs through the bit. I didn't need the gag's elevation function; I needed it for control.

Once in a while we'd hit a rough spot in our flat work and Abdullah would have a temper tantrum. His mind would quit, just as it did when he faced a jumping situation he found frightening. I'd have to work through the problem step by step. That might be a white-lather day. But the next day, when the dust had settled, he'd usually be very good. I don't view horses sentimentally, but I do try to see things from their point of view. "How would I respond to what I'm asking?" I say to myself. "Is there only one door open, or am I opening so many doors that he doesn't know which one to go through?"

Part of the fun of working with horses is that each one is unique, an individual personality and talent. I never try to make a horse conform to a pattern. I take him as he is, decide what can be improved and what

Conrad Homfeld scored many wins with Balbuco, who was not the easiest horse in the world to ride either. Photo: Courtesy of USET

I must accept. Abdullah was already thirteen, with proven jumping ability. The more I worked with him, the more I realized how easygoing he was—a far cry from my previous World Cup mount, Balbuco. With him, the day might be spoiled if I simply sat down too abruptly when I mounted. He was always looking back at what was going on behind him; he was suspicious of my mildest movement. Abdullah's quitting, I realized, was not a sign of a complex temperament; it was concern for self-preservation.

The rest of the spring shows were indoors, and he showed no sign of stopping. I'd thought that our performance in Sweden had ruined any Olympic chances, but we placed in every trial and won Old Salem. We were selected for the team because of our consistency in the trials. The Olympics are usually a once-in-a-lifetime opportunity, and I wasn't going to be unprepared this time! The arena at Santa Anita was outdoors, but it was very long and relatively narrow. I thought that Bert de Némethy, the course designer, would probably place jumps, even lines, in combinations going across the short sides into the grandstands—just the sort of thing Abdullah found so frightening indoors. So for one of my schools in Los Angeles, I built a course to challenge his courage, a triple combination down the middle of the schooling area—a wall to a liverpool, to a vertical. To the right and left of this triple, I placed lines that could be ridden either very steady or very forward, both headed diagonally into the track railing. I also had several individual jumps headed directly into the railing. The fences weren't big, but the situation invited a stop or hesitation.

I walked Abdullah from the barn to the schooling area, picked up the canter, and went right to the combination. He spooked at the liverpool; I hit him with the whip behind my leg and he didn't stop. I continued with the outside lines and individual fences, adding strides and leaving them out, using my whip behind my leg when he hesitated to jump toward the railing. I followed up this school a few days later with one that got him round again. A few days after that, he competed successfully in the main arena.

After the Olympics, Sue, Terry, and I decided that our next long-term goal would be to solve the indoor problem and then qualify and compete in the 1985 World Cup finals in Berlin. It wouldn't be easy, because four of the qualifying competitions are indoors. I preferred not to depend on these for accumulating points and aimed at two early qualifying classes held outdoors: the Hampton Classic on Labor Day weekend and the American Gold Cup at Devon in September. If he did well there, the indoor shows would not be so crucial, and I'd still have the outdoor Florida shows in February and March to pick up some more points and, I hoped, make the cut. During the indoor shows, I wanted to be able to concentrate on Abdullah, not have to worry about winning points.

As it turned out, I found the early momentum and kept it throughout the indoor shows. We were second at the Hampton Classic and tied for first in the Devon qualifier. At the first indoor show in Baltimore, Abdullah showed no sign of stopping, and we were second in the qualifier. Since all was going well, I scratched from Harrisburg, the next indoor show, to give him a break before riding on the USET in Washington and New York. Although he didn't place in the Washington qualifier, he jumped well; he was second in New York. Our position was pretty solid. Unless a lot of other riders finished up with really great years, we'd be qualified for the World Cup finals.

By now I thought the indoor problem had been solved. Abdullah didn't jump as boldly indoors as out, but he seemed to have accepted indoor shows as a fact of life. Some horses are better in one environment than another, but I've never known a horse that would perform only indoors or only outdoors.

In late January, Sue brought Abdullah down to join me in Florida. My plan was to start slowly, with one class at the third Palm Beach show, and then work up to the Invitational, the biggest and final grand prix of the Florida circuit. You have to save your horse for the occasions when you've got a chance to win something very important. I wanted to take a good swing at the Invitational and, in the long term, do well in the World Cup finals in Berlin.

Sue rode Abdullah on the days I didn't school him. The first week, while other riders were warming up for their class, I caught some of their first jumps, maybe ten in all, no more than 3 feet high. I did the same thing later in the week, going up with them a couple of raises to maybe four feet. The following week, I did a trotting gymnastic one day and cantered a combination later on. In the third week, I rode in a low class in place of a school. When we moved to Tampa, I showed Abdullah twice a week—one unimportant class to get the cobwebs out of the machinery and then the grand prix. Of the two grand prix held at Tampa Fairgrounds, Abdullah had four faults in the first and won the second. Next was the Invitational, held downtown in Tampa Stadium. Abdullah was clean in the first round. In the jump-off, I made a turn and met an impossible distance. He stopped. In a less important class, I'd have beaten him for it, but we still had a chance to place better than those who had four faults from the first round. So I opted for a good kick and continued. We finished fifth.

After Tampa, Abdullah went home to cover mares for two weeks and then joined me at the USET's Gladstone headquarters a little less than a week before we were to leave for Berlin. The AHSA makes all travel arrangements for the American qualifiers, and Frank Chapot was *chef d'équipe*. Since the World Cup is an individual competition, each rider followed his own program at Gladstone. I decided to repeat my school from Los Angeles as close to the departure day as possible, concentrating on jumping into the ends of the ring. I put 3-foot-high crossrails in each corner so that Abdullah would have to jump and turn at the same time to avoid hitting the wall. I also placed some narrow jumps without wings in the ring, inviting a run-out that would give me an opportunity to punish him. My only goal was to tune his attitude.

I brought him directly from the barn to the indoor ring, walked in, picked up the canter, and aimed at the crossrail in the corner. After that, I incorporated the other jumps at different speeds and angles to invite a stop. Abdullah passed the test. This school gave me confidence, but I still wouldn't have been surprised if he'd stopped in Berlin.

We arrived in Berlin early Monday morning. Among the Americans were my partner, Joe Fargis, with Touch of Class, his Olympic gold-medal-winning mount, and two of our students, Louis Jacobs on a new horse, Janus de Ver, and Christian Currey with Manuel. In all there were forty-five finalists: sixteen Americans, four Canadians, and twenty-five competitors from the European and Pacific leagues.

The World Cup finals involved a possible six rounds spread over three days (Thursday, Friday, and Sunday), with some optional warm-up classes scheduled on Wednesday. Using a rather complicated system, placings from the first two competitions would be converted into faults that would determine standings and order of go for the final day, the pair with the fewest faults going last.

My first impressions included two major pluses: the ring was big and wide; and Olaf Petersen, a brilliant German course designer, was building the courses. From what I'd seen of his work, I expected his courses to lean toward Bert's style, maybe a little bigger but still technical.

While Abdullah had Monday off to recover from the trip, Sue hand-walked him a couple of times to let him stretch his legs. On Tuesday I rode him on the flat in the main arena. I started by putting him on the bit in a long, low frame. Each morning I'd continue building toward the compressed frame I'd ultimately want. By Thursday, I hoped to have a completely soft, adjustable horse.

The ring was just wide enough for the course designer to place a single jump, or possibly a double combination, across the short side. So besides riding all over the ring on Tuesday morning, I spent a good deal of time doing flat work in the ends. These went very nicely. Abdullah was walking along, low and relaxed. We stopped at the end of thirty minutes.

On Wednesday we had a choice of warm-up classes: our foursome decided on the class with lower jumps. If Abdullah dug his toes in, I wanted to be able to discipline him without having lumber falling all around us. It's hard to discipline a horse over big jumps and still have him understand the meaning of it; with a smaller fence that doesn't test his jumping ability, he's freer to absorb the purpose of the discipline. As it happened, he gave me a clean round.

On Thursday morning, we worked on the flat. Again, Abdullah was very good. It was encouraging. This time I asked for bigger transitions because I wanted him to ride perfectly for the first leg of the final that evening, a Table C, seconds-added speed class. The course would be big enough to screen out speed horses that lacked scope and prevent riders from getting by with a lucky round. For every rail down, seconds would

Conrad and Abdullah during their victorious final round in the 1985 World Cup finals in Berlin (repeating his 1980 victory on Balbuco). Photo: Courtesy of USET

be added to each rider's time; the lowest time would win. Because of the scoring system, strategy was already critical: you had to do pretty well on Thursday to be in contention on Sunday. If you went early and misjudged the class, you could finish too low to be within reach of the leaders in the final leg.

Fortunately, I was in the middle of the draw. Since I didn't want to repeat the previous year's performance, my goal was simply a neat and tidy round, nothing crazy. The course was big and tough, but we jumped a clean and reasonably fast round, finishing in fifth place. It had gone better than I'd expected.

The other ribbon winners were Michael Whitaker of Great Britain, with 55.88, in first place; Hugo Simon of Austria second, with 56.71; and then two Americans, Hap Hansen third, with 57.81, and Armand Leone fourth, with 58.30. Nick Skelton of Great Britain finished sixth in 59.33, proving that speed could match conservatism and showing what a great competitor he is: he crashed through the oxer but raced around the rest of the course clean.

The second leg on Friday had a timed second jump-off that might entail three big rounds, with another two-round competition still to come on Sunday. I kept Abdullah's Friday morning flat session short in order to save his energy. I just wanted to check his soundness and get his mouth and back soft again. Like most horses after a speed class, he'd lost his roundness. I no longer considered stopping a major problem, but there's also the matter of having the horse sharp enough so that he doesn't want to hit the jumps. There are various methods for doing this, legal and illegal. Some horse lovers find these methods abusive. I consider them tools that, properly applied, are simply a fact of successful competitive life. Abdullah would be sharp.

I kept my warm-up for Friday's class short but effective. Without using many jumping efforts, I wanted to invite Abdullah to rub a jump. So I deliberately started right out with a 3-foot-6-inch oxer with a 4-foot spread, hoping he'd be a little sleepy and hit it either in front or behind. I didn't want a crash, just a solid crack. His placid temperament will tolerate this strategy. I jumped the oxer once. Then Terry and Gretchen, Abdullah's groom, raised and widened it. To get a hind rub, I intentionally rode to a deep spot with minimal impulsion, not one rev more than necessary for clearing the jump. The next time, I jumped from the same deep spot but with too much impulsion and pace, so that he'd slap the pole coming up if he wasn't quick in front. I repeated these two approaches about three times and then moved to the vertical. Since Abdullah is weaker at verticals, I wanted only two or three confident efforts.

While speed had been used to weed out horses the previous night, the focus on Friday evening was on size and awkward distances. The course impressed me as *big*. A double liverpool combination early in the course, with a wide oxer coming out; another big oxer across the end of the ring; and a long oxer-oxer combination were particularly tough spots I thought would catch a lot of competitors.

There were already a number of clear rounds when my turn came. Abdullah jumped well, but we also were lucky: he whacked the back rail of the oxer across the end of the ring so hard that it bounced in the air—and landed back in the cups. That close call probably helped us go clean over the rest of the course.

There were sixteen clear rounds, including Abdullah's, more than the course designer or the riders expected. The first jump-off reduced the field to ten, and we were still clear. The final jump-off consisted of seven jumps. Nick Skelton, who went a couple ahead of me, was clear and very fast. Frank Chapot, who'd been in the stands to provide our riders with information on the progress of the class, told me that if Nick won, he'd be on top of the heap for Sunday's final; I had nothing to lose by going all out and trying to move ahead of him.

The best laid plans don't always work out. We were fast but had four faults, and so finished seventh. Nick stayed on top, with his fellow Britisher Malcolm Pyrah second, France's Pierre Durand third, and Peter Luther of Germany fourth. An American rookie, twenty-one-year-old Lisa Tarnapol, finished fifth. When all the conversions were done, Nick would go into Sunday's finals in the top spot with a zero score. Malcolm Pyrah was second with 1.5; Hugo Simon third with 2.0; and I was fourth with 3.0. I realized how critical the first speed class had been. If I'd finished a place or two lower, my score would now have converted into 4.0 or 4.5, more than a rail away from the leaders, possibly too far away to catch them. A converted score of 3.0 or under was less than a knockdown, so the top four entered the final round almost equal. If Nick had one fence down and any of the rest of us left them all up, we had a chance to win.

Since Abdullah is a very sound horse (so far), we weren't terribly concerned about the effect of four big rounds. I stayed off his back on Saturday, the "free" day, but Sue took him for a light hack outdoors.

On Sunday morning, I rode in the main arena with the others in preparation for the afternoon final, the toughest test of all. A world title was at stake. I wanted Abdullah not only to be sharp; I wanted him to go through the roof! And there in the ring was the perfect tool: a dressage-ring railing. I used it as part of my flat work, as if it were a single pole on the ground. Since it couldn't be knocked over and was higher than a pole, Abdullah had to be very careful stepping over it to avoid an unpleasant crack. I did this exercise mostly at the walk and trot on a circle, varying the diameter and speed. By the end of the session, he was very aware of stepping accurately over the railing.

I'd expected a big course, and that was what we got: bigger than Bert's Olympic courses but still with emphasis on the technical side. One of the jumps was a replica of the Charlottenburg Palace in West Berlin. The principal trouble spots were a triple that came early in the course going away from the gate, a line with awkward distances down the center; and the last fence, a very large oxer made of narrow white rails.

I wanted to do a minimum warm-up for this class—four or five jumps of moderate height and width. When a horse is sharpened, it only lasts for a certain number of jumps, so you've got to make them competitive ones.

We jumped in reverse order of our standings, placing me thirtieth among the thirty-three finalists. By the time my turn came, there had been nine clear rounds, with Hap Hansen, Joe Fargis, and Anne Kursinski among them. I, too, was clear. Hugo Simon had four faults, moving him back to sixth place and putting me in second. Malcolm Pyrah also had four faults, slipping to fifth. Nick Skelton was clear with St. James, holding onto his lead. Pierre Durand was also clear, putting him in a tie for third with Hap Hansen.

While the course was being changed for the second round, I tried not to be overwhelmed by my position. I'd arrived in Berlin prepared to be satisfied if I finished twentieth! Instead, I concentrated my thoughts on giving Abdullah the best ride I could, making sure that he, too, would furnish his best effort.

Throughout the entire competition I had the feeling that Nick Skelton could and would win. He's a great rider and competitor, especially on St. James; I've always been in awe of his brilliance indoors. I knew I was a strong contender, but in the script I'd imagined, Nick was a worthy World Cup champion (as a professional, he was ineligible for Olympic honors).

The second course was a work of genius: very difficult but also very fair. Fourteen jumps, including a quadruple combination across one diagonal, two big oxers off a short turn with a forward one-stride distance between them, followed by a tight two-stride distance to two tall verticals with a tight one-stride distance between them. This line was a killer. And it was followed by a line of three jumps with awkward striding, which I felt had to be done in a very steady way. I thought my major trouble spots would be the two verticals in the quadruple and the steady three line, because they asked Abdullah to jump a vertical with maximum impulsion and a vertical with minimal impulsion. The course finished with a narrow vertical-oxer combination made of solid white rails. Since it would fall very easily, your horse had to be still sufficiently interested after so many efforts to be careful.

I watched the first few riders go. Hap had two fences down and finished sixth. Pierre, who'd been tied with him, had four faults, which gave him third place. Abdullah and I were next and scored the second clear round over the course, the other being that of Stefan Schewe of Germany. Nick rode next. If he had three faults, we were tied; if he had one fence down, I'd win.

He got through the forward part of the quadruple combination and the rest of the course suited his horse. I thought the title was his. But horses can make liars out of you. St. James picked off the vertical in the middle of the awkward line. For a few minutes, I couldn't believe it really happened.

Conrad and Abdullah perfectly negotiate a liverpool on Bert de Némethy's demanding 1984 Olympic jumping course. Photo: Courtesy of USET

At the press conference afterward, Nick shrugged off his disappointment like a seasoned veteran, saying, "That's show jumping." He was right. Luck plays a big part. You also make your own luck, and I know he'd done his homework in preparing for this event as many others of us had.

The only superstition or magic in my act is a dollar bill that Bill Steinkraus gave me and the others at the Olympics to tuck in the browbands of our bridles. He'd had one in his bridle for his individual win on Snowbound in the 1968 games. I'm almost ashamed to admit it, because I don't believe in that kind of thing. But that dollar bill was with me and Abdullah in the Olympics and in Berlin for the World Cup finals.

8

Riding a Timed Jump-off

Mark Laskin

Mark Laskin first made a name for himself on the international grand prix circuit and then as a member of the Canadian Olympic Team, in partnership with Damuraz, an ex-racehorse with an unorthodox but effective jumping style. He took home a silver medal from the 1976 Olympics, and his "double clear" with Damuraz in the 1980 "alternate Olympics" in Rotterdam clinched the gold for Canada.

Mark has been voted Canada's Equestrian of the Year four times, which is indeed an honor when there are such accomplished riders north of the border as his teammates Ian Millar (who, with Big Ben, formed one of the all-time great show jumping partnerships), Mario Deslauriers (1984 World Cup winner with Aramis), Gail Greenough (World Cup winner in 1986), and Jim Elder (veteran of seven Olympic Games with two gold medals to his credit).

I wasn't chosen for the Canadian team on the fall indoor circuit in 1979, so I competed as an individual. I'd almost forgotten my ambition to win a place on the Olympic team. I just wanted to compete, beat the courses, and keep my horse jumping confidently. My horse was Damuraz.

The key to Damuraz, I'd learned, was to keep him happy and comfortable. He was thoroughly cooperative during the Toronto show and jumped himself into an eight-horse jump-off in the big-money class, the Rothman's Grand Prix.

Dennis Murphy was first to go, and when Dennis goes fast, no one

Mark Laskin and Damuraz. Photo: Budd

goes any faster. I was second in the jumping order and so could watch
only three or four of his fences, just enough to get an idea of his pace
and watch some of his turns to decide if I could move my horse inside
them. I didn't need to see more to know that he'd laid down a patented
Dennis Murphy round. As I mounted Damuraz, I heard the crowd go
wild and saw a group of excited admirers running to meet him at the
out-gate.

I had to beat Dennis by only one-hundredth of a second in order to
win the class. I knew exactly how I'd have to ride. Dennis had decided
it for me. Damuraz and I had to go in the ring and give it everything
we had.

Before an important class, I ride the course maybe twenty times in
my head with every horse I'm taking around, picturing the way I want
them to jump and turn. I make mental notes of every place on the
course where the horses might have a look and back off so that I can

plan where to make up the lost time. Then I forget the whole thing and ride into the ring with a clear mind. I suppose I file my decisions in the subconscious. When I'm on course, I'm free to react to the way my horse is going, rather than riding numbly to a plan. I've watched some very polished American riders kill themselves to put in five strides because that's what they've planned. But everything that happens to me in the ring is unexpected.

When I went in to try to shave that fraction of a second off Dennis's score, everything I tried worked. I turned tight to the first combination, and jumped the oxer and the vertical in and out; then I left out a stride going down the next line. We turned neatly and came out of the corner at a dead gallop that carried us to the triple bar; then we left out another stride going to the wall. By this time, I knew that Damuraz's time was faster. When we turned into the last line for the difficult triple combination, I could afford to use a second to re-balance him. Even though we'd been galloping over the whole course, leaving out strides all over the place, Damuraz responded to the check immediately. He knew this was something important I was asking him to do. He left from the right spot and bounced accurately through the triple.

We won a very prestigious class, $10,000 in prize money, and—most important of all to me—a place on the team representing Canada at the alternative Olympics in Rotterdam.

9

Jumping Safely at Speed

Rodney Jenkins

One of America's all-time great riders gives practical advice on a crucial subject of which he is a past master.

In a timed jump-off, speed over a fence is not always what makes the difference.

You want to make time on turns. But if you have to turn after a jump, galloping into the fence may carry you too far beyond it to let you make a tight corner. What you want to do then is to bring the horse in so that you can turn him in the air and cut distance on the corner. The shortest distance is always the fastest. That's what makes the difference in timed classes.

You know the times of the horses that have jumped before you. Try to predict the times of the horses that will follow you (experience helps a lot here). Unless one of them puts in an unexpected performance, you should have a pretty good idea of what you have to do to win the class.

The first time around a course, try to plan for the eventual jump-off. Figure out where you should be pulling to the inside of the fence to save ground, where you should go to the outside. This will help a lot when you get to the timed rounds.

For a rider just starting out, I'd advise him to take it fairly easy at first. Speed is a dangerous thing. If you lose control over big fences, you can get hurt. An inexperienced rider is also more likely to freeze in a

Rodney Jenkins on Idle Dice in the process of winning the first American Gold Cup in 1973—at such a speed that Rodney's lost his cap. Photo: Karl Leck

tight situation. I'd say, work on speed in one particular part of a course, and if everything goes all right, then build on that experience in the next class. It won't take you too long to build up your competence, and if you take it gradually, you'll do it with far fewer wrecks.

10

How Do You Keep Your Nerve
in a Hazardous Sport?

Jim Day, Mary Mairs Chapot, and Steve Stephens

Jim Day, a former member of Canada's national teams in Three-Day Eventing as well as show jumping (helping to win the Olympic gold medal in 1968 with his great Canadian Club), has since become a leading Canadian racehorse trainer.

Mary Mairs Chapot, one of the first women riders on an Olympic jumping team (Tokyo 1964, Mexico 1968), was one of the first Californians to excel in international jumping competition. Her elegant, effective riding with Tomboy, White Lightning, and Anakonda won top events as well as style awards at home and abroad during the 1960s.

Steve Stephens, a top grand prix winner during the early 1970s, has recently returned to the grand prix ranks—at the top. He is also an outstanding course designer, whose credits include all the major North American events and a stint as assistant to Bert de Némethy in designing the highly praised Prix des Nations course for the Los Angeles Olympic Games.

Jim Day

Touch wood, I've never had a terrible fall. I've had lots of them, but nothing really dramatic. I've never hurt myself, never broken anything.

I believe in the old tradition of getting right back on after a fall, as long as you're not severely injured. The quicker you can get on to the next step and forget about the fall, the better off you are.

Jimmy Day, longtime anchorman of the Canadian team, riding his team-gold-medal Olympic mount (in 1968), Canadian Club. Photo: Budd

The things I'm most apt to be apprehensive about are certain obstacles on the cross-country courses in Eventing. There's probably a greater risk of injury during the cross-country because you're usually going at high speed and the fences are solid. You can't be quite as accurate when you're riding a cross-country course as you can when riding a show-jumping course. In show jumping, it's quite unusual for a horse to fall. But in the cross-country of the Three-Day Event, falls are not at all unusual. Because the fences are solid, if a horse makes a bad mistake— down he goes. I fell off one horse twice in the same day at a drop fence on a Three-Day course. It's one of the most insecure fences to ride; you never really feel that you've got the thing under control. When you fall off, you usually get a little mad; if you fall off twice, you're fairly fuming! I think this helps overcome any fear you may have felt.

Half of the secret of keeping your nerve is having confidence in yourself and picking horses you trust to jump difficult fences cleverly and wisely. If I didn't have faith in a horse, I certainly wouldn't ride him around some of the courses we have today.

When you're young, you're a lot braver—or perhaps more foolhardy. Then you get a little more experience, you get a little more sensitive or a little smarter, or perhaps a little more cautious—who knows what? Ten years ago I was doing a lot of things I sure wouldn't do today, riding a lot of horses that I simply wouldn't consider riding now.

Feeling a little apprehensive about riding a certain course or a certain fence is not necessarily a bad thing. If you want to live longer and not get hurt, it's just common sense.

Mary Mairs Chapot

I can't say that I've ever lost my confidence after a fall. Ever since I was a child, a fall has never been made much of. We used to have a little tin can, and every time we fell off, we had to put a quarter in it. That's all falling off meant.

I've been privileged to be mounted on some very fine jumpers, and although I've had falls with all of them, I've never lost confidence in their jumping ability and thus never felt any apprehension about getting back on again.

I think that people who have been brought up in an environment where any little ache or pain is reason for going to bed are going to have a harder time overcoming a fall than those who get knocked around on the football field and come right back. Personally, I've always felt that you have to overcome pain; you've got to be tough. And I imagine that a child just beginning to ride who has a bad experience would be disheartened much faster than a person with more experience, who has seen riders fall off and then get back on.

I had one bad fall a couple of years ago, riding a horse of limited ability; but I never had the opportunity to ride him again, so I can't say what my feelings would have been about heading down to a big fence on him afterward. However, I think that when an experienced rider loses confidence in his horse's ability to jump the obstacles at hand, the harmony between horse and rider is lost, and it's time to break up the partnership. Perhaps it's also time to move the horse down to a lower level of competition.

The situation in which I lost the most confidence was not a fall but a bad round at Tokyo in the Olympic Games. I didn't fall, but I lost confidence in my ability to do it right. I wasn't afraid of being hurt; I was afraid of messing up. What cured me was jumping a lot on the same horse and finding that things would still work out.

What I'm most apprehensive about today is jumping a big fence on a horse I know is overfaced, whether it's a 3-foot fence on a horse that has never jumped before in his life or a 6-foot fence on a 5-foot horse. That sort of thing bothers me. And a wide fence gives me more pause for thought than a high vertical.

When Tomboy was getting old and a bit over the hill, she started to swim through oxers. I got to the point where I felt I had to get everything perfectly right or she'd put her feet in it. In trying to reach the perfect spot, I'd end up going slower and slower to a big wide oxer, and Frank would be saying, "Go on, go on! If anything, go too fast, but don't park at it or you're bound to swim through!"

Mary Mairs Chapot on Anakonda. Photo: Budd

A little nervousness can be a good thing before a big class. It can make you ride a bit above yourself, although in the extreme it can be detrimental. When you're tense, you're apt to get very tight through your shoulders and hands and telegraph your nervousness to your horse. You can do much more on a horse when you're relaxed and sitting quietly. You can see your distances better, and the horse stays relaxed too.

I imagine everyone gets butterflies before an important event. At the Olympic Games, when you sit in that tunnel waiting to go in there, you're all by yourself. You say to yourself, "What am I doing here? Why did I think I could do this?" It's apprehension. But it's not fear of falling down and getting hurt. Perhaps stage fright is the best term for it. Once you're on course, it disappears. I think you rise to the occasion.

That's one of the reasons why Bert de Némethy likes to take the team to Europe. You can get all the grand prix experience you need in this country now, but you don't feel the same pressure that you get when you're competing for your team. It's very different from riding in the Gold Cup, for example, and worrying about the owner getting mad if you mess it up.

I don't think any experienced rider would lose confidence because of a single fall. Over and over again, perhaps! But a beginning rider might. In the case of my own children, they climb right back on and are thrilled to get a whirlpool bath that night. When they're older, perhaps they'll donate a quarter to the "dump can" as I once did.

If they were to fall off over a jump, I'd like to see them try again, but not a repeat performance. So I'd lower or rearrange the jump, if possible. I've seen children in the show ring, still shaky, put back on, aimed at the fence, only to put in a bad one, refuse, even fall off again. I think they'd have been much better off heading for the schooling area and trying something easier.

Steve Stephens

I've never had the problem of losing confidence. That's just something that has never bothered me, and I don't think it bothers anyone else on the grand prix circuit either.

I've had some pretty good falls, but I've always jumped right back on and gone after it again. I've been fortunate in never getting smashed up. I had a really spectacular fall at the Cleveland Grand Prix one year, taking The Spoiler over a liverpool. He did a flip and landed on the

Steve Stephens rides semi-pro in the 1976 American Gold Cup. Photo: Karl Leck

saddle. I got to my feet so fast that I watched him hit the ground and run off. I caught him, climbed back on, and rode the rest of the course.

Right now I'm at the stage where that sort of thing doesn't bother me. I simply don't worry about it. I couldn't compete if I did—not with what they're asking horses to jump today. Ten years ago, we'd never have dreamed of jumping the things you have today in an ordinary Open class, where you see a vertical hanging there at 5 feet 6 inches, and spread fences 6 feet 6 inches and 5 feet square, sometimes even bigger than that. When you start worrying about it going down there to a big fence, you're in trouble. You need a parachute. You're going to get hurt.

I like to see someone who has fallen get back on if they can. If they wait, they'll think more about it and their fear will grow, particularly if they're green at it in the first place. Sometimes, however, it's not a good idea to make a person get right back on if you aren't sure that he's not really hurt. You might cause more damage than would be done by waiting for a while.

As a rider ages, his reflexes tend to slow down and I think that's when he starts to worry. I haven't reached that stage yet, but some of the people I've coached and worked with know that they bruise easily from a fall and are sore the next day. Naturally, that can take some of the spark out of them.

To overcome a real loss of confidence about jumping big fences takes a lot of practice, because the fear is basically there. When you're scared, you're scared, and most of the time you have a reason for being scared. I think that's true of any sport. In a way, a little bit of apprehension is good. It may stop you from doing something foolish.

The other day I was talking to Buddy Brown about the fact that we seem to get ourselves in the position of riding anything. We don't have to, but we find ourselves doing it because we can't say no. Sometimes you feel like saying, "What do I look like, an idiot?" when somebody brings you a horse that doesn't impress you very favorably. But we go ahead and try anyway. And a lot of the time we succeed. If you come riding down to a fence on a horse that maybe doesn't have a lot of heart, and you do something his regular rider wouldn't do, it makes him go on and he finds himself jumping the fence, or at least trying to. Instead of getting refusals and refusing out, he's gone ahead and maybe made it. But if we were really smart, we'd say, "Definitely not!" more often, because we're bound to get hurt one day from somebody bringing us something that is overfaced.

There were a couple of horses on the Florida circuit that wrecked consistently. One rider in particular would land in the middle of about

six fences each trip, and I mean really land in them. John Ammerman
supplies the jumps there at some of the shows, and tears would stream
from his eyes when he'd see this rider come into the ring. This person
just keeps coming down at them. He shouldn't, because he doesn't make
it through any of them, but boy, he sure charges down there. He landed
in every one of them at Ocala—boom, boom, boom. That guy has no
fear!

11

Jumping for the Team

—

Frank Chapot

Of Frank Chapot, member of five U.S. Olympic teams and winner of innumerable international show-jumping events, longtime USET coach Bert de Némethy once said, "Frank is one of the strongest competitors I've ever met. In the most prestigious events—the Prize of Nations, the Olympics—he always came through with everything he had. I always trusted him."

Although no longer riding in international competition, Frank remains a prominent figure on the show-jumping scene. He is a member of the FEI World Cup Committee, former secretary of the AHSA, a member and former chairman of both the AHSA Jumper Rules Committee and the USET Show Jumping Selection Committee, and a director of the National Horse Show, and has served as USET coach and *chef d'équipe* for many important competitions, including the 1984 and 1988 Olympic Games and many World Championships. He also breeds and trains horses at his home barn in Neshantic Station, New Jersey, and is a leading course designer and judge.

How does a rider get to be a member of the Olympic Jumping Team?
Anybody who has to ask how to get on the team probably doesn't belong on it, because he or she is obviously not very aware of the sport or sufficiently interested to keep up with what's going on.

There are always rider-selection trials held prior to the Pan-American

Frank Chapot and Coach Stop, shown on the way to winning the Adirondacks Grand Prix at Lake Placid in 1976. Photo: Barrows

and Olympic games, and anybody qualified in respect to age, amateur status, and citizenship is eligible to take part. But anybody who's had enough experience in the sport to make the team couldn't help but know about the procedure just from being around jumping competitions.

But couldn't there be a rider of Olympic potential tucked away in some remote part of the country?

I wouldn't say so. In any case, you couldn't take that rider from some remote part of the country and have him ride in the Olympic Games the following week. If he's tucked away somewhere, he hasn't had the exposure necessary to compete in international events. Given the right experience, he might eventually make the team. In the same way, there might be someone in the wilds of Africa who could be a baseball superstar, but he wouldn't be ready to play in the World Series this fall.

So you think the best thing for an Olympic aspirant to do is go out and get some mileage?

Yes, get experience. Perfect your skills. If you go only to leaky-roof horse shows, your abilities stay at a low level. If you go to A shows and compete with the best, there's a better chance of developing your ability.

Enhance your chances by getting the best horse you can find. There are now many riders in the United States who are good enough to make the team. If the entire jumping team disappeared in a plane crash, we could replace them with a few phone calls. But not so with our horses. Olympic horses are very hard to find. If someone has one, his chances of making the team are much greater.

What about somebody who doesn't own an Olympic-caliber horse?

In the year following the Olympic Games, screening trials are held throughout the United States. Anyone who's interested can enter. The trials are not competitive; there are no scores, no faults; and you don't need a good horse in order to take part. From these trials there have always been a number of riders selected for further training, about twenty from the last ones. And from these a further selection is made for additional training. Many of our team riders have come out of these trials, my wife being one. Buddy Brown is another.

Where do you look for horses with the potential to become international jumpers?

Personally, I have no specific sources. Olympic-caliber jumpers sell from $100,000 to $250,000. Now, with inflation, there's probably no limit. If there is a good source, everyone would like to find it.

In the past we've found a lot of horses on the racetrack that were too slow or had soundness problems that kept them from racing but didn't interfere with jumping. But that source has dried up to some extent due to the increase in the number of racetracks, especially cheaper tracks. Since almost every horse can win somewhere today, horses cost more than they used to; and when a horse can't win for $1,250 at Pocono Downs, there's not much left of him.

So I take them where I can find them. I figure I'm better off giving more money for somebody's first-year green or preliminary horse than buying a horse off the track at today's prices with no idea of his jumping ability. I'm better off taking one from somebody who has sorted through a hundred horses, even though I have to pay a premium.

I look at the one-day shows; or sometimes I see a horse being schooled before he goes to his first show. You have to spot him before everybody else does. By the time he gets to Devon, it's too late.

Haven't you been successful in breeding some good show horses?

Yes, I've bred some very useful horses and some good jumpers. Just as every Thoroughbred breeder hopes to breed a Kentucky Derby winner, I'd like to breed an Olympic winner. [Editor's note: Frank came very close to his goal when his homebred Gem Twist, ridden by Greg Best (both of whom he'd trained), won the Individual Silver Medal at Seoul in 1988.] Nevertheless, I'm old enough to know that the odds of that fairy tale coming true are not very good. Still, I certainly wouldn't be breeding if I didn't think I could breed horses that are competitive in the show world today.

When you buy a green horse, what is the likelihood that he'll turn out to be an Olympic horse?

One in ten may be capable of competing at the international level. But only one in a thousand will be a potential Olympic horse.

What is the difference between an international jumper and an Olympic horse?

An Olympic horse has to have tremendous scope to jump a great many big, wide fences under very difficult competitive conditions. The Olympic Games are not like an ordinary horse show, where you have a number of competitions spread over a week. There are two Olympic jumping events, the individual and the team. The fences are at maximum height the first time the horse sees them. The courses are very big, very long, very difficult. They demand the best from the best horses in the world. The courses have to be demanding in order to separate them.

There are a lot of very good jumpers that win in this country and win internationally and yet won't make Olympic horses. There are various types of international competitions: for example, speed classes that don't demand the ability to jump high, and puissance classes requiring sheer scope over a limited number of very high fences.

Even Olympic horses don't compete over Olympic courses every day. They couldn't do it and survive.

I think the biggest problem we have now is that many course designers are demanding too much of our horses each time. They're building courses higher and wider, exposing more the horse's scope than the rider's skill. In order to limit the number of clean rounds, they raise

Frank Chapot rides San Lucas at Aachen in 1970. This partnership was practically unbeatable in puissance events at home and abroad. Photo: Courtesy of USET

the fences instead of making distance problems between fences to test the training of the horse or the skill of the rider.

Also, I think we've become accustomed to a jump cup so deep that a horse can go around the course hitting his fences very hard but still go clean because the rails don't come down easily. I'm not saying that the fences should be spindly. They should be solid and inviting. But solidity is overdone when a horse can hit most of the fences on a course and still go clear. That's why I believe it's a good thing that we still have rub classes for our green jumpers. You can get a very good result from a competition without jumping too high or too fast. What ruins green horses quickest is jumping them too high, too soon. And the green horse is at the time of his life when he tends to be most careful, when he wants to jump clean.

When you watch a green horse jump a relatively low fence, what do you look for in evaluating his prospects as a jumper?

A feeling that the horse comes off the ground with some power, that it's not a great effort for him to jump small fences, and that he does it in the correct way: he uses his front legs correctly, has some bascule to his jump, and is careful. He must have the desire not to hit the fences.

But I'll probably see him hit something, and I'll note his reactions. The next time I'd like to see him be more careful. He shouldn't come back unfazed and hit the fence again. On the other hand, it shouldn't shake him up so much as to suggest that he might be a little chicken.

What sort of a course do you like to see him jump?

Not necessarily any course at all. There are only two kinds of fences, verticals and oxers. You have to adjust your fences according to the horse's level of training. I'd buy a horse after seeing him jump 3 feet 6 inches or 4 feet if he impressed me.

Height isn't always meaningful. Any horse that's had any schooling at all can jump 5 feet. Someone might show me a horse jumping 6 feet over a single fence, but he might not be able to handle a 4-foot course. Many people are fooled by seeing a horse jump one big fence.

If you only see a horse jump a few low fences, how can you know he'll be able to handle a course?

It's very hard to tell. By the time you find out enough about a horse to know whether or not he can jump a course, he's already gotten more expensive.

How would you describe your riding style compared to that of other successful jumper riders?

It's hard to judge oneself. If I had to do it all over again, I'd do it differently. Kids today have a great advantage. They have very good instructors teaching them the things that prepare them to be international riders. When I was a child, this wasn't available to civilians. We were represented in international competition by the army. They had the experience, and there was no need for civilians to pursue that type of riding. The first time I went to Europe in 1956, I'd never ridden in a speed class in my life. Now every kid in the Junior Jumper Division does it every weekend.

I guess what I'm trying to do is make excuses for my style being so crude. I don't think I have a very elegant style. Part of it may come from riding a lot of green horses, horses that may stop or run out, and having to ride a bit defensively. This tends to carry over to all the other horses you ride, more than if you only ride nice horses every time.

What do you consider your strong points as a rider?

I'd say that my riding deficiencies are overcome by my competitive spirit.

Is there any type of horse you ride better than any other?

I really don't know. I wouldn't think so. I've ridden all types. San

Lucas was a 17.3-hand Thoroughbred with the ability to jump very high. Good Twist was a small Thoroughbred who excelled in all types of competition, including very fast jump-offs. I've also had success with German types, including Anakonda and Diamant.

Is there any type of horse you don't like to ride?

The type of horse I don't care for is the cold-blooded horse. In many cases he'll let you down when you need him most. The horse with blood can go a little bit on nerve, even when he's tired or sore. Not that every horse needs to be a Thoroughbred, but somewhere in between. You need a horse with some sense but also with the courage to keep going when it's easier to quit.

In the finals of the Men's World Championship, when each of the four finalists had to ride his own horse and then the horses of the other three finalists, how did you use the short time allotted to familiarize yourself with the strange horses?

We were given three minutes with each horse and permitted to jump two fences, a vertical and a spread. The important thing was to find out how the horses reacted when you asked them to go forward or to wait, whether a great deal of strength was required or they'd respond to a light signal. They were all very good horses, four of the best in the world. If it had been four of the worst, it would have been a different contest. But it wasn't all that difficult in that particular situation because anyone with basic riding skills to compete even at a national level could have ridden those horses successfully. They were super horses that would forgive many mistakes.

Do you do anything to prepare yourself psychologically for an important competition?

No, I don't have to get myself up for a big competition, although I don't get into a very competitive frame of mind as often as I used to. It's not as important to me every day as it used to be, but on certain days it's very important.

Anybody at a high level of competition experiences some nervousness. I think their success or failure depends on how they channel their nervous energy, whether they use it to their advantage or whether it ruins their ability. As soon as the bell rings, my anxiety disappears. I'm not aware of being in a stadium with perhaps 100,000 people watching. The problems associated with each horse and the way I've planned to ride the course become second nature, like coming to a red light—you don't have to remind yourself to stop.

How do you plan your strategy before riding a course?

Most competitions are finally won on time. So when you walk the course, you try to figure out where you can make the best time in the jump-off without knocking down jumps, where you can get an edge. How much of a risk can you take at a particular fence? How sharp an angle can you approach from? It all depends on the height and width of the fence and the distance from the fence before. Say you have two fences with a five-stride distance in between. You can often put in only four strides and save time. But if, in doing that, your momentum forces you to make a wider turn after the second fence, it might not be such good strategy after all. You might be better off putting in the fifth stride and starting to turn in the air.

In the jump-off, the odds of winning against time are much greater if you go last rather than first. You know what you've got to beat. You may have to pull out all stops. Or maybe you can play it safer than you would have if you'd gone first. Actually, I tend to go all out even at the beginning of the jump-off, but most people don't.

Frank Chapot no longer appears on the national and international show-jumping scene as a rider but in the role of judge, official, course designer, or (as here) *chef d'équipe* of the U.S. team. Photo: Courtesy of USET

Do you tend to take greater risks than other riders?

No, I don't think I take risks. There's nothing I'd try that Rodney Jenkins, for example, wouldn't try.

Do you recommend any particular schooling method or techniques?

No. Training is a continual learning process. What works for one horse won't necessarily work for another. Anyone who claims to follow a strict schooling method puts himself at a disadvantage, because no single method can solve all horses' problems.

I continue to learn from the people I respect—even from some I don't particularly respect. I'll see someone riding with some gadget that I may not like, but if the horse goes well for him, maybe there's a place for it in my training too.

Horsemen are very inquisitive. They see someone doing something with a horse, and they'll stop and watch. Maybe he knows something I don't know. Wherever you see good horsemen together, you'll notice that they're always watching each other.

12

Riding in the Olympic Games: Ideals and Realities

William Steinkraus

Bill Steinkraus's riding career is one of the legendary success stories of American show jumping: from winning the Medal, Maclay, and Good Hands finals as a child, to an individual gold medal in the 1968 Olympic Games. He was a member of six Olympic teams, including the first civilian one in 1952, and had won practically every major national and international jumping event, sometimes more than once, when he retired from active competition at the end of 1972.

Always an active promoter of American show jumping, he has chaired and long served on the AHSA Jumper Committee; was president for many years and is now chairman of the USET; and is a member of the FEI Jumper Commission and delegate to its General Assembly. As a rated judge, he has officiated at World Championships, Pan-American Games, and World Cup finals, as well as many national and foreign shows. Author of *Riding and Jumping* and editor of numerous horse books, he is a leading television commentator of equestrian events and the "star" of several equestrian video films.

Are Olympic riders especially brave people?
I think courage is equally important for both horse and rider. The Olympic horse will be asked to do things right at the limit of his ability, and to meet this challenge he's got to be brave. Of course, this kind of courage, like courage in warfare, doesn't mean that you aren't scared at

Bill Steinkraus rides Bold Minstrel at Hickstead, England. Photo: Clive Hiles

that moment, that you don't respond to the potential danger of the situation. It simply means that when you get squeezed, you go forward instead of drawing back. A courageous horse, faced with the biggest fence you've ever headed him at, takes a shot at it, and that's the kind of horse you need in the Olympic Games. The kind of horse that says, "Wait a minute, that's too hard," and sucks back is doomed. So is the human athlete who has the same reaction. So I think a certain kind of courage is critically important.

What are the other physical and mental qualities that make an Olympic rider?

Well, you have to be a good rider, of course. And you also have to be a good competitor, which is not necessarily the same thing. Some people never really show their true worth except under the pressure of competition, and other marvelous riders never perform to their best advantage under pressure. Some of the best riders I've known didn't have outstanding competitive temperaments, while others had outstanding competitive temperaments and maybe not much else. But for the Olympics, you'd ideally like to have both.

It's the same for the horse. He has to have good ability and also a good enough temperament to "put it all together" under very difficult conditions. The kind of horse that falls apart whenever the stands are crowded isn't going to be much good in the Olympics, no matter how well he can jump in a small ring out back. In the final analysis, temperament or courage probably makes the difference in the games more often than sheer ability.

Other than that, would you make any distinction in terms of ability between an Olympic rider and a "civilian" rider?

Of course not, because all the Olympic riders started as "civilian" open jumpers and still ride mostly in national shows. The Olympic rider is simply someone who is good under pressure, and there's a lot of pressure in our regular shows too. If you're trying to win the Stake at Madison Square Garden or a big grand prix somewhere, you make the same effort you'd make abroad. In fact, most good competitors in any field learn early in their lives how to concentrate, how to put out a maximum effort. They get a lot of practice at competing under pressure because they accept and respond to pressure, whether it's a local horse show, a Little League baseball game, or whatever.

Maximum is maximum. You can't give any more than your very best. I think that good athletes, good competitors, learn how to use the adrenal stimulation that pressure creates to help achieve these maximums.

Then you think that the best jumper riders could be transplanted with very little notice onto the team?

They could be, have been, and will be again. The standard of courses at home has improved so much that it's not much of a transition anymore, and I can't think of a young rider in recent years who has come onto the team and found it all that different from the riding point of view. Of course, when you're representing your country, hearing the anthem played and all that, perhaps you feel a greater sense of responsibility. But if you have the temperamental quality we were talking about, of being able to produce under pressure, it just helps you to try harder.

Don't some team riders, when showing on their own, fail to follow the schooling methods and principles taught at Gladstone?

That's possible. After all, we have to experiment and find out what works best for us. At Gladstone, Bert de Némethy and Jack Le Goff used to give riders the benefit of their extensive experience and profound knowledge of the classical tradition, but the riders had to learn to apply these things for themselves. The team has never attempted to turn out riders who were little carbon copies of each other; it would be foolish and futile. There are certain ingredients we want them all to have, but they must make their own applications. They often work this out while showing on their own.

A good athlete has to develop his own style. Nobody would expect the hitters on a championship baseball team to all use the same batting stance, or all golfers to use exactly the same grip. Tall men, short men, thin men, thick men, all have to execute the same fundamentals a bit differently in order to get the same results. The fellow with fast reaction time and the fellow with slow reaction time can't develop the same style, even though they apply the same fundamentals and aim for the same average at the end of the year. Each individual must work out what's most effective for him.

You've got to have developed pretty far as a rider to get to Gladstone in the first place. Anyone who makes a squad has a fairly well developed style of his or her own before they get there. Gladstone usually provides a stimulus to their thinking and shows them how to apply what are to them new solutions to their problems. But when you're riding in a big competition, you have to do what comes naturally. There are things I used to do occasionally that I don't consider very stylish, and I wouldn't ride hunters that way. I don't even think they're right, but I found sometimes that I could get more out of the horse by doing them.

What sort of things?

Oh, for example, holding a horse's head leaving the ground. It's not classical, and you certainly wouldn't want to do it over every fence. But certain horses will try harder, will put out more and jump higher when you do that than if you didn't do it, and so you win the class. You can't rely on this as one of the foundations of your technique, and you don't do it at every fence, but you still may do it under pressure.

Many authorities maintain that any intervention by the hand after the horse has left the ground is wrong in principle, because it impedes the bascule and so forth. Generally, this is true. But that doesn't mean that when Rodney Jenkins takes hold of Idle Dice's head leaving the ground and says, "Come on, old boy, give me a couple of inches more," that it doesn't make the difference between winning and losing the class.

As a particular case in point, during the Olympic Games with Mainspring, I rode him much more the way I wanted to ride him in the morning round than I did in the afternoon round, and I started the afternoon round the same way. However, he rubbed the first three or four fences pretty hard, and I just didn't dare go on that way. He was a horse you could stop in the air with your hands, for he was very funny about his mouth. But if I kept hold of his head and used some discretion, he'd jump some fences cleanly that he wouldn't have otherwise. I suspect that if I'd ridden him more "correctly" in the afternoon, more to my taste, I probably would have had a couple of fences down instead of none. But of course I may be wrong! You never know because you can't make an instant replay and try it the other way. In the end, I think that good riders learn to trust their own experience and instincts and to accept the consequences.

Were there certain kinds of horses you rode better than other kinds?

Oh, sure. I think every rider has a type that he prefers and that suits his temperament best. In my case, I preferred a type like Snowbound or Riviera Wonder, a horse with a lot of natural impulsion. This type often has a difficult temperament but usually a lot of courage and a lot of "bottom." And they are capable of responding to very refined aids. Most cold-blooded horses never become that fine.

On the other hand, the cold-blooded temperament sometimes has a great advantage. On a big occasion, with thousands of people in the

Bill Steinkraus on Riviera Wonder, his 1960 Olympic mount, at Aachen, Germany. Photo: Courtesy of William Steinkraus

stands, they're less likely to blow up, because they don't see anything to get excited about. The more highly strung temperament may have wheels whirling at a thousand RPM, and you have to live with it. Snowbound was not a nice parade horse. He was annoyed by having to stand still for anthems, and he didn't like applause. I'd have liked him to have a steadier temperament, but I'd settle for him the way he was. Today's courses increasingly demand the scope, nerve, and gymnastic ability that a Thoroughbred horse specializes in. So the average horse in the games tends to be a Thoroughbred or to have a lot of Thoroughbred blood. The heavier type of cold-blooded horse has pretty much disappeared.

How would you describe your famous jumping style?

I'd like to think of myself as a very economical rider. I believe that in all sporting performances you should seek economy—that is, the maximum result from the minimum effort of the physical mechanisms involved. I'd like to be remembered as a rider who didn't intervene very much but still retained complete control over every situation. I think the best kind of intervention takes place so far back from the fence and so subtly that it's not noticeable. I aim at that because it's the most effective style as well as the most attractive to watch.

But I hasten to add that I don't think any style should be a goal in itself; style is always a by-product of economy and effectiveness. The old phrase "crude but effective" is a contradiction in terms. You can't be both truly effective and also crude, because *truly* effective means that there is no waste motion.

It's true that there have been successful athletes who seemed to win almost in spite of their form, in spite of their technique rather than because of it. On the average, however, the best competitors in sports tend to have sound basics, good fundamentals of form. For example, some people would say that a rider like Joe Green had bad form. Well, Joe may have had some mannerisms that a horsemanship coach would have changed if he were riding for the Maclay Cup. But to my eye he was a marvelous rider because the fundamentals were so solid. I think that's been generally true of riders in the Olympic Games too.

Did you try to cultivate any kind of mental attitude before going into the ring, especially for something like the Olympic Games?

No, I don't think so. The situation cultivates it for you. You don't need to remind yourself that the Olympic Games are important. I like to think that I rode better most of the time when the chips were down than when they weren't, and in that sense, I think I respond to psychological pressure in a positive way. All competitors know what it's like to try too hard and blow things that mean a lot to us.

With Snowbound at the 1968 Olympic Games in Mexico City, Bill was the first American to win the individual gold medal. Photo: Courtesy of William Steinkraus

When you're young, you try to seize the moment too aggressively. It's very easy, for example, to override the last fence in a clear round that's going to make a tremendous amount of difference to you. When you finally see a good stride, you run your horse through it because you want to embrace that good stride—and you blow it. As you get older, you learn that the safest thing to do, if it's the kind of fence that can be overridden, is not to ride it any differently than you would any other fence.

On average, I'd say that a higher proportion of my good performances came at the right place at the right time rather than vice versa; but if there was any "psyching," it wasn't something I did to myself. I think the situation does it to you.

Before an important competition, I liked to have some time for myself, more for technical than psychological preparation. I'd go over the course in my mind in many different ways, think of different situations that might arise, try to anticipate problems that might occur, so that the apparently instantaneous response I might have to make in the ring would be the best one. I'd go high up in the stands to look down on the course, and I'd want to be alone. I never thought I was a good improviser. I preferred being able to refer back, while riding the course, to solutions I'd already worked out for every possibility, even improbable ones, rather than trust myself to come up with the right answer on the spur of the moment.

Is Gladstone still as important as it was when you were captain of the team? Hasn't it served its purpose? Don't most top riders now have their own coaches and go their separate ways?

There have certainly been a lot of changes since the USET first set up its Gladstone operation, and I think we should remain open to change as conditions and circumstances change. However, I think that a totally decentralized training system is a luxury only the very strongest horse countries can afford. In practice, it can be very wasteful of material, and I might point out that a number of countries that have more horses and riders to choose from than we do have trouble beating us. In fact, a lot of foreign team officials speak enviously of our system.

In any case, I'm not sure we have too many alternatives. No country has succeeded in having centralized dressage training without a military establishment; on the other hand, most countries have centralized Three-Day training because few individuals can afford to produce privately adequate training facilities, even when they have the skills. The jumping team falls somewhere in between. I hope the USET is flexible enough to change when we can strengthen ourselves by doing so.

Yes, many team riders train largely on their own now. If they can do things outside Gladstone to help their riding, it's going to help the team and I'm all for it. But I can't imagine totally abandoning some kind of a permanent training center for a long time to come.

Do you think there's any prospect of our national sports priorities changing in respect to horse activities in general?

Very definitely. We're becoming a stronger, more sophisticated horse nation all the time. There are over eight million horses in the United States, we're told, and that means more and more people who are sympathetic to horses and familiar with them. Moreover, we're starting to get more attention from television, which was a major factor in developing big audiences for show jumping and eventing abroad. If audiences for horse sports grow as fast as participation is growing, then our national priorities are bound to change and we'll become very, very competitive. The U.S. Olympic Committee has long thought of equestrian sport as an offbeat, minor activity, and they may have been right at one time. But now we're beginning to get some development funds from them, and they're finally recognizing the increasing extent of interest in equestrian sports in America.

We're an important horse country, and we still have vast untapped resources. Today we're stronger than we've ever been in international competition. The civilian horse-show community is more oriented our way than it's ever been; the Pony Club is developing prospective international riders, and the Jumper Division at horse shows is developing first-class Olympic material in both horses and riders. The future of horse sports in the United States has never looked brighter.

America's gold-medal team at the 1984 Olympics receives congratulations from then–president of the International Equestrian Federation Prince Philip. Photo: Courtesy of USET

Original Publication Dates of
Selections Edited for This Book

Part I

First Lesson for a Young Horse: Longeing (January 1983)
Training on the Flat in Five Easy Lessons (July 1980)
Schooling on the Flat at Gladstone: Why and How (October 1977; April 1978)
When to End a Training Session (October 1975)
How to Get Your Horse to Accept the Bit (January 1980)
Putting a Horse in a Frame: What Does It Mean and How Do You Do It?
(January 1977; January 1980)
How to Teach Your Horse to Halt (November 1982)
Retraining a Retired Racehorse (August 1982)

Part II

The Best Seat for Hunter Equitation (June 1982)
Jumping Clinic (November 1987)
Training Winning Riders (March 1984)
The Jimmy Williams Method (September 1975)
Handling Show-Ring Nerves (March 1982)
Winning the Medal Finals (May–June 1985)

Part III

Horse Shopping (July 1987)
Progressive Education for Hunters and Jumpers (September 1985)

Conversation with a Conformation Hunter Expert (June 1974)
Selecting, Breaking, and Training a Show Hunter (February 1977)
How to Develop Proper Head Carriage (October 1986; March 1983)
Planning the Career of a Show Hunter (July 1982)

Part IV

Packing for the Horse Show (July 1978)
Setting Up Your Horse-Show Stall (August 1984)
Winning Horse-Show Strategy (August 1979)
Horse-of-the-Year Specialist (July 1973)
Warming Up a Hunter (September 1981)
Riding Hunter Courses (January 1984; April 1984)
What the Hunter Judge Likes (May 1975)
Judging Jumper Style (January 1980)
Winning Strategy for a So-so Mover (August 1983)
Performance Faults That Lower Your Score (March 1981)
How to Keep a Show Horse Sharp During the Entire Season (May 1975)

Part V

Jumper Talent Scouts (May 1976)
What I Look for and Look Out for in Selecting and Training Jumpers (July 1976)
A Professional View of Buying and Training Show Jumpers (October 1975)
Using Cavalletti to Teach Your Horse to Jump or to Jump Better (September 1972)
Seeing the Distance (August 1974)
Teaching Your Horse to Jump Grand Prix Obstacles (May 1984)
From Equitation to Open Jumpers (June 1979)
From Pony Club to Grand Prix (February 1974; March 1974)
Training an Olympic Jumper (August 1976)
What My Horses Have Taught Me (March 1986; April 1986)

Part VI

Year-by-Year Goals (January 1983)
Warming Up a Jumper (September 1981)
Grand Prix Glossary (March 1982)
Analyzing Grand Prix Jumper Courses (April 1976)
Jumping Grand Prix Fences (May 1975)

To the Top with Fred (August 1987)

Handling a Champion Problem Horse: Abdullah (August 1985)

Riding a Timed Jump-Off (February 1984)

Jumping Safely at Speed (February 1973)

How Do You Keep Your Nerve in a Hazardous Sport? (May 1977)

Jumping for the Team (October 1974)

Riding in the Olympic Games: Ideals and Realities (April 1973; May 1973)